COMMUNICATION TOMORROW

COMMUNICATION TOMORROW

New Audiences, New Technologies, New Media

E. W. Brody

PRAEGER

New York
Westport, Connecticut
London

Library of Congress Cataloging-in-Publication Data

Brody, E. W.
    Communication tomorrow : new audiences, new technologies, new
media / E.W. Brody.
        p.   cm.
    Includes bibliographical references.
    ISBN 0-275-93280-X (alk. paper). — ISBN 0-275-93281-8 (pbk. :
alk. paper)
    1. Mass media.   I. Title.
    P90.B74   1990
    302.23—dc20   89-16175

Library of Congress Catalog Card Number: 89-16175
ISBN: 0-275-93280-X
        0-275-93281-8 (pbk.)

First published in 1990

Praeger Publishers, One Madison Avenue, New York, NY 10010
A division of Greenwood Press, Inc.

Printed in the United States of America

The paper used in this book complies with the
Permanent Paper Standard issued by the National
Information Standards Organization (Z39.48-1984).

10 9 8 7 6 5 4 3 2 1

For Sandy

Contents

x Contents

Preface

The twenty-first century will arrive slightly more than ten years hence at just after midnight on January 1, 2000. By that date, it now appears, the Age of Information also will have arrived in the United States and throughout the postindustrial world. The so-called wired grid will be in place. Not only will computers be talking to computers, but humans will be communicating with computers and one another through an interconnected network of telephone, electronic mail and cable television systems. Information flowing through that network, moreover, will be readily entered in spoken and written as well as keyed form, and the system will be able to respond to inquiries in any of those formats.

How accurate is this forecast? Making predictions is dangerous, as others have said, "especially when one starts dealing with the future." To describe this book, or the statement above, as predictions or projections, nevertheless would be gross overstatement. All of the technology necessary to create the grid is in place. The last few connections are in the process of being made as this is written. All of the facts already have been published or broadcast, although not at one time or in one place.

This book, in a sense, is a demonstration of the power of the Age of Information. The bulk of the raw information in the following pages was assembled in a computer using an information management program called Agenda. Produced by Lotus, the program enables authors to manipulate electronic files in much the same manner that Lotus 1-2-3 manipulates numbers.

Much of the content of the following pages, in addition, is a synthesis of information so new that little of it has earlier appeared in book form. As lists of additional readings at the close of several chapters indicate, a great deal of the information has been gathered over a period of almost two years from the pages of *The New York Times*, *The Wall Street Journal*, *Business Week*, *Industry Week*, and other periodicals. To those who read regularly and extensively on business and mass communication, as a result, neither the information that follows nor the conclusions drawn will be surprising. The early onset of the Age of Information, as anticipated here, may be another matter.

The research techniques leading to these conclusions are neither new nor unique. They are the same techniques used by John Naisbitt and others who monitor events and trends by tracking the content of the mass media. In this case, media content has been supplemented by information from a host of other sources, many of them in the communication disciplines and in the academic world.

Those who seek theoretical constructs in works such as this will find the work of Richard E. Petty and John T. Cacioppo especially enlightening. Their elaborate likelihood model of persuasion suggests that persuasive communication is most effective where supported by peripheral cues. They do not differentiate between mediated and other forms of communication.

The bulk of the content of this book focuses on mediated communication because that form at present is of primary concern to the disciplines addressed here: advertising, marketing, public relations, and sales promotion. Members of these professions depend on mass media to convey their messages. Mass media are deteriorating in delivery efficiency, however, and the disciplines involved necessarily will be forced to seek alternative communication techniques. Some already have expanded into some forms of interpersonal communication, but further expansion will be necessary, with behavioral and environmental communication offering the greatest potential.

As an academic, I have been privileged to help develop curricula at Memphis State University that equip students to cope with change in the communication disciplines. As a public relations practitioner, I wonder whether a majority of contemporary professionals in this or other communication disciplines are adequately sensitive to the changes going on around them. Too many, I fear, are so caught up in the issues of day to day practice as to preclude adequate attention to their futures. Only time will tell whether this indeed is the case.

Many of the few practitioners sensitive to contemporary communication trends are to be found in the Technology Section of the Public Relations Society of America. Their support in the development of this book is most appreciated.

I also am especially indebted to colleagues in the Department of Journalism in Memphis State University's College of Communication and Fine Arts. Journalism Chairman Dan L. Lattimore and Dean Richard R. Ranta created an atmosphere that encourages projects of this sort and others in the college and university have been equally encouraging. Professor Art Terry's insights into the development of computer technology and electronic imaging techniques have been especially helpful. Professor Ron Spielberger's comments concerning trends in advertising and sales promotion also contributed significantly to this project.

Much of the credit for any merit found in this work belongs to all of these individuals. The weaknesses are mine alone.

1 Communication Today

Historians who one day analyze the evolution of commercial or business communication through the closing decades of the twentieth century will find that the focus of the process had returned to its early origins: reality. Quality and value in products or services by the year 2000 will have replaced media and messages as primary components of communication.

The focus of advertising, marketing, public relations, and sales promotion, in other words, will have shifted from persuasion to reality. Practitioners will have become primarily concerned with seeing that products and services are worthy of consumer support. Communication will become a secondary function oriented toward informing rather than persuading.

Retrospectively, the transformation in commercial communication will appear to have been inevitable. The process was predated by accelerating change in many areas fundamental to societal development. Several factors involved were especially significant to commercial communication. Educational levels improved across society. Research and experiment produced new knowledge at accelerating rates, spawning academic disciplines that in turn gave birth to new technologies. The new technologies, in turn, made knowledge and information almost universally available.

Universal access to information confounded mass communication traditionalists. Public relations, advertising, sales promotion and related disciplines long had been committed to imagery rather than substance. Reality, from the traditional perspective, was what audiences perceived rather than what really existed. Commercial communicators were viewed, and viewed themselves, as manipulators of perception rather than molders of reality.

The practicality of the traditionalist approach to communication thus was being destroyed by social and technological change. Rapid and inexpensive access to knowledge and information progressively is undermining ability to create credible images that contradict reality. Communicators instead are being forced to develop and establish communication techniques consistent with reality.

These changes are occurring in an era in which mass communication is becoming progressively more difficult. Two parallel processes are responsible. One was identified by futurist Alvin Toffler as "demassification," a process through which once homogeneous societies splinter into special interest groups. The second is audience fragmentation, which occurs as entrepreneurs apply emerging technologies to produce new communication channels. Numbers of available communication channels already have grown to a point at which the words "mass media" are contradictory.

Demassification and audience fragmentation have produced three monumental problems for communicators. First, audiences are becoming less trusting and more skeptical. They are more and more predisposed by education and experience to test rather than readily accept new concepts, services, or products. Second, audiences are growing more difficult to reach with mediated messages. Target group members increasingly have less time available and commit their time more selectively to still-growing numbers of information delivery channels. Third, and most important, the pace of change continues to accelerate.

Communicator survival and prosperity through the twenty-first century and beyond will be governed by ability to cope with these problems. Three factors will contribute to that ability: understanding of the past, knowledge of the present, and, as a result, ability to anticipate the future.

The past, present, and future of society are most readily understood in terms of life cycles. The cycles are most obvious among humans but govern other living systems as well. Because they govern the destinies of humans, life cycles also are evident in the organizations humans create.

THREE ERAS

While humans and their organizations progress cyclically, societies have evolved along a continuum from nomadic to post-industrial or informational. The bulk of the continuum has been shaped by three developmental stages or eras: agricultural, industrial, and informational. The stages are equally significant for two reasons. First, each continues to predominate in some nations. Second, each persists while the world's national economies are fast becoming an integrated global economy. The globalization process is less than complete, but every nation ultimately will become an integral part of a global economic system.

Nations, with one exception, thus develop in patterns akin to those of organizations. Nations differ from organizations in that they develop through sequential rather than cyclical phases. Organizations evolve in phases similar to those of human development, again with one exception. Organizations differ from individuals in that their "lives" are of indefinite duration. Organizations can be regularly "reborn" through orderly management transitions. Nations, organizations and individuals all are subject, however, to three cultural transitions: From nomadic to agricultural, from agricultural to industrial, and from industrial to postindustrial.

The Agricultural Revolution

The term transitions is used here in the spirit of conservatism. Each of the three has been referred to at one time or another as a revolution. "Revolution" may be too strong a word to apply to the changes that occurred in agriculture. Revolution implies suddenness, but changes in agriculture have occurred suddenly only in a relative sense. The transformation of societies around the world from nomadic to "landlocked" or agricultural occurred with the invention of the deep plow. Only with this device, and with the application of metalworking skills to farm implements, were former nomads able to develop the agricultural practices that encouraged their remaining in one place.

The agricultural revolution thus was triggered by the invention of a mechanical device. The device was perhaps only marginally more revolutionary than what followed, especially in terms of suddenness. The deep plow nevertheless is noteworthy in its role as a trigger mechanism, since each of the revolutions that followed can be traced to a mechanical device.

Most former nomads applied the deep plow to intensive agriculture close to fortifications established by more warlike tribes. The mutual dependency of the groups led to development of towns and cities. These communities also provided a favorable environment for the second revolution.

The Industrial Revolution

The deep plow's role in the age of agriculture was assumed by the steam engine in the industrial era. The steam engine, an invention seldom adequately recognized in contemporary society, triggered the industrial revolution. While limited in concept and rudimentary in design, the steam engine became the driving force of the industrial age.

The first steam engines were designed for a single application: to remove water from mines. Neither inventors nor users recognized that they were dealing with a "metatechnology," a concept that literally would change the world. While designed to drive pumps, steam engines could be harnessed to almost any mechanical device, stationary or moving.

The steam engine became a tireless extension of man's muscular/skeletal system. As such, the engine was soon harnessed to almost every stationary device that earlier required consistent use of manual energy. Pulleys, gears, and clutches were added to extend the range of steam power applications. Then the engine was put on a wheeled platform as a transportation device. Alternative fuels, up to and including nuclear, were developed to further enhance efficiency. At bottom, however, was the steam engine. The steam engine was more than a good invention; more than a great invention. The steam engine spawned a new era in human development, the industrial age.

The Information Revolution

The transistor now is proving itself as much a metatechnology as the steam engine. Miniaturization and durability, in comparison to vacuum tubes, first were perceived to be the transistor's primary advantages. With transistors, room-size computers were made radically smaller and considerably more reliable. What first were perceived to be the transistor's major benefits, however, soon proved to be less significant than anticipated.

Computer technology advanced at an accelerating pace with the advent of the transistor. Improved speed, capacity, and breadth of applications quickly were found to equal size and reliability as transistor attributes. Transistors first were linked together to conduct current through semiconducting solid materials, usually silicones, creating chips. Then, transistors were grouped together to create microprocessors, the equivalent of central processing units for small computers.

Microprocessors applied in satellite communication spawned instantaneous worldwide communication systems. Satellite communication systems gave birth to new eras in publishing and broadcasting. Newspapers applied satellite communication systems to publish simultaneously in multiple plants across a nation or around the world. Television stations used satellites to free themselves from dependence on networks and telephone-based transmission systems.

In an even more innovative application, microprocessors were applied to data storage to spawn a new information industry. Computer data bases already number in the tens of thousands and are proliferating at almost geometric rates. In addition, microprocessors have been applied in personal computers, in telephones, in timepieces, in automobiles, in household appliances, and in thousands of other commercial and industrial uses.

Those who pause to contemplate the late 1900s can only conclude that the technological developments of the past twenty-five years have surpassed those of the previous twenty-five hundred; that humanity is caught up in a new age and a new era. The age of information has begun, and, in communication, the era of the integrated grid is dawning. Electronically, humanity has progressed from the wired era (1845-1900) through the wireless era (1901-1970) and now stands at the threshold of what might be termed the era of the integrated grid.

Integrated grid, or wired grid, refers to the communication infrastructure now taking shape in postindustrial societies, a network that ultimately will cover the developed world. The term encompasses satellites overhead as well as microwave and fiber optic networks on earth. Linked to ever more powerful supercomputers, they form the first components of what ultimately will become a global information utility.

The steam engine and microprocessor thus differ in only one way. Where the steam engine created an extension of the human musculature and skeleton, the microprocessor serves as an extension of the human brain. It permits manipulation of more information more rapidly and more efficiently. Still more important, while practical limits exist to mankind's need for physical strength, human capacity to benefit from improved mental ability is infinite.

Revolution and More

The speed with which the age of information will bring tangible benefits to different nations will be a major variable during the remainder of the twentieth century and beyond. The information revolution is occurring concurrently with major economic and geopolitical changes. Each can enhance or detract from the impact of the other. Variation in rates of change among nations and organizations will compound the challenges communicators will face in the years ahead.

Technological, economic, and geopolitical changes are pervasive. Now almost global in scope, they reverberate through every level of society. Technologies and trends that influence worldwide development progressively involve nations, states, cities, neighborhoods, families and individuals. Success in communication requires the ability to identify developments at the macro level in order to deal with them effectively at the micro level. An understanding of changes engulfing hemispheres, continents and nations, in other words, is prerequisite to communicating successfully with their residents in states, cities and neighborhoods.

The impact of macro level changes often can be successfully anticipated at the micro level. Decline in the public stature of large corporations during the 1980s, for example, should have been easily anticipated. Employment by large corporations had been considered by workers to be nearly permanent. Lifelong service to the corporation, it was assumed, would be rewarded by comfortable retirement. Results of economic globalization required that the "contract" be broken. Survival in many cases was at stake as domestic corporations were confronted by unprecedented international competition. Survival required that some jobs be eliminated, that others be exported, that still others be subcontracted.

The computer, for better or worse, enables corporate managements to successfully defend themselves from overseas competition, but only at the expense of domestic workers. Computers rendered industrial age organizations with multiple echelons of information handlers obsolete. Senior executives no longer needed layer upon layer of managers and supervisors who existed only to gather and summarize data.

Technology thus produced a benefit and exacted a price, demonstrating again (a) that progress generates as many problems as it solves and (b) that technology is not value-neutral and applicable to produce good or bad. The good and bad outcomes are inseparable and occur simultaneously. Because they are inseparable, however, outcomes should be relatively predictable.

In the industrial downsizing of the 1980s, for example, accompanying economic dislocations predictably traumatized communities, plants and families as well as corporations. The scars remain. No organization's stakeholders groups are without memories of the eras of corporate downsizing and merger mania. Lost jobs and profits, dislocated careers and families; repossessed homes and automobiles, all left scars. Scars remain because the wounds ran deep. They are found in the form of skepticism, cynicism, and outright distrust. And the scars will contribute to communication problems for decades if not generations.

CHALLENGES IN COMMUNICATION

The corporate experience of the 1980s suggests that once reliable norms are reliable no more, that the assumptions that support traditional communication programming deserve careful reexamination. Communicators traditionally have assumed that

1. they are dealing with traditional audiences
2. the audiences are little influenced by emerging technologies and
3. the audiences are attuned to the same media that have attracted them in the past.

In fact, all of these elements are in a state of flux. None are what they were a few years ago, and few are apt to stabilize in the near future.

Audiences, technologies, and media are changing at an accelerating pace. The changes involved are being driven by the information revolution in the same manner that the steam engine generated the forces that drove society through the industrial revolution.

New Audiences

Today's audiences differ demographically and socioeconomically as well as psychologically from those of earlier decades. The occupational traumas of the 1980s are only a part of the societal changes responsible. Single parent households continue to increase in number. Cohabitation has become more or less socially acceptable. By the end of the 1980s, the traditional nuclear family already had become atypical in the United States.

Economically driven change also has been pervasive, especially as it involves females. Women are working in record numbers and in more economically rewarding positions than ever before. The aging of the work force also is contributing to socioeconomic change. Few teenagers who want to work are without jobs, and able-bodied retirees are returning to the work force in growing numbers.

Demographic data suggest the latter trends will continue through the first decade of the twenty-first century. Numbers of eighteen-to-twenty-four-year-olds will not increase significantly before 2010. Improving longevity and health among those once considered elderly will help meet the nation's need for workers, but the nature of the work force also will continue to change. Improvement in average educational levels will continue, as will the needs and interests of the work force.

Changing occupational, economic, and family circumstances have produced change in behavioral patterns. Changed behavior patterns limit communicators' access to audiences and alter audience responsiveness to mass mediated messages. Some audiences have become more accessible and responsive, while for others the reverse is true. Working females tend to be less accessible than their nonworking counterparts. Women usually are inaccessible to mass media during working hours and tend to have less time for the media during nonworking hours. The children of households with two working parents are another matter. Latchkey children, as they have been called, tend to spend more time with the mass media, especially television, and to have more disposable income than peers in traditional households. Marketers report parental tendencies toward larger allowances, presumably granted to compensate for reduced personal attention, has created a new class of younger consumers.

New Technologies

Changing audience characteristics nevertheless are but one of the complexities with which communicators must contend. Contemporary technologies contribute equally to productivity and to communication problems. Foremost among the technologies are those built on or around the microprocessor. These technologies range from new media at one extreme to mechanical devices at the other.

Some mechanical devices permit users to exercise unprecedented control over mature media. Other devices enable entrepreneurs to compete in industries once so capital intensive as to effectively bar newcomers.

New Channels. Among the new media are electronic data bases and a host of communication devices built around satellite technology. Data bases are nothing more than massive information warehouses accessible to anyone with a microcomputer, modem (modulator-demodulator), and a telephone line. Numbers of data bases increased from three hundred to more than four thousand between 1979 and 1987. Experts in the field then estimated that new data bases were being introduced at a rate of about one thousand annually.

Data bases increase the speed and reduce the cost of research. Researchers can use home or office computers to gain immediate access to more information than is contained in typical college and university libraries. Experienced users, in addition, often can obtain needed information at costs comparable to those they would incur in driving to a library.

Satellite technology has proven equally productive in moving information across the nation and around the world. The technology is applied in many forms but is most evident in the international content of television news. Banks use the same satellite systems to transfer funds. Multinational corporations link satellites to computers to create organizational information systems accessible at any hour, anywhere in the world. Some, as in the case of Federal Express, have used satellites to conduct worldwide employee videoconferences. Satellites and teleconferences, however, originally created a slighter impact on society than did mechanical devices such as the videocassette recorder.

Mechanical Devices. The videocassette recorder, or VCR, arguably has done more than any other technological device to change the world of mass communication. Seemingly simple in concept, the

VCR has generated more frustration for electronic communicators than any device since the on-off switch.

Pragmatically, the VCR transfers control of television from network programmers to viewers. Programs recorded automatically while viewers are otherwise occupied can be watched at their convenience. Periods once exclusively the domain of the evening news can be rededicated by viewers to "The Edge of Night." Even worse, the VCR's fast forward control, or "zapper" as it has come to be known in advertising circles, enables viewers to bypass commercials.

Comparable disruption in established communication channels eventually may be created by microcomputers. Microcomputers came into common use in the early 1980s. Only in the waning years of the decade, however, did microcomputer technology mature to a point at which users could compete in the world of publishing. Today, a newcomer to publishing with ten thousand dollars readily can launch a small weekly newspaper. Comparable efforts a few short years ago would have required ten times the investment.

New Media

New technology has been no less disruptive among established media than among information consumers. Changes in technology have been accompanied by two sets of changes among the mass media. One set has been evolutionary; the other, innovative. The first set involves continuing adaptive change among mature media struggling to remain economically viable in competitive circumstances. The second set involves the emergence of new communication channels based on one or more technological developments.

Evolutionary change has occurred in every area of mass communication. Change among print media has encompassed daily and weekly newspapers as well as magazines and books. In broadcast, television has changed more rapidly than radio, but success formulas are no more readily developed in the latter area than in the former.

Although spurred onward by technology in some sectors, evolutionary change among mass media has been as evident in content as in mechanical terms. Content has changed in keeping with the interests of media audiences, while technological change has been more oriented to media economics.

The demassification process forecast by Alvin Toffler has been the driving force behind extensive media content changes. Editors and program directors have been forced by competitive factors to make changes to maintain circulation or audience levels. Content changes in most cases have been designed to appeal to more narrowly defined audience segments. Only rarely has the reverse has been true. Both circumstances have occurred, however, among print as well as broadcast media.

Print Media. Evolutionary change in the print sector has assumed different forms among different media. One trend, occurring primarily in magazines, involves increasing specialization. General interest magazines such as *Look, Colliers, Pageant*, and the like no longer exist. A host of publications has supplanted them, each of the newcomers specializing in subjects such as computers, desktop publishing, and data base management.

Among newspapers, in contrast, general interest and specialized publications have flourished but in different ways. Growth in newspapers has occurred among two types of publications. Most prominent among them, but fewer in number, are national newspapers, such as *USA Today, The New York Times*, and *The Wall Street Journal*. More numerous but less obvious are many specialized weeklies, including business publications that have appeared in most large cities.

Only the metropolitan dailies that once dominated among newspapers have been in decline. While fewer in number, the survivors appear to have regained relative economic stability after several decades of mergers and closings. Some suggest that the surviving dailies, like community weeklies, have capitalized on the specialization trend by focusing their efforts on local news.

Electronic Media. While the pace of change among the print media may be slowing, the electronic sector remains relatively volatile. Increases in numbers of outlets appears to be producing greater competition among individual media.

Radio remains a healthy but relatively slowly growing medium. In television, cable systems and local stations are moving collectively toward stronger positions in relation to the networks. Cable companies have gained strength through greater market penetration. Local stations have become stronger by applying new technologies to newsgathering, reducing their dependency on the networks. Only the networks have suffered.

Both print and broadcast media have applied the latest in technological processes, primarily in the interest of economy. Both use computers and satellites extensively, for example, although change in the appearance of their products does not reflect the extent of the changes involved.

Innovative Media. New technologies have been adopted more rapidly among companies and individuals than across industries. The early adopters, in addition, often have been organizations in which communication is secondary to other functions. For example, 3M applied computer technology to establish an internal data base system long before many of today's commercial computer data bases were established. Federal Express Corporation, in like manner, early applied satellite-based telecommunication systems in worldwide employee communication programming.

Technology-based innovation has been more commonplace among entrepreneurs using less costly hardware. As prices of microcomputers and microcomputer peripherals have declined, for example, tens of thousands of organizations have become involved in desktop publishing. Many, if not most, writers use computers rather than typewriters. When writing is complete, increasing numbers use page composition programs to bypass commercial typesetting services.

Efforts to apply technology in revolutionary fashion to create new or radically changed communication channels have been limited and results have been mixed. There have been no striking successes and several major failures. In some cases, the economic jury is still out. Early videotext ventures such as the Qube system in Columbus, Ohio, and a Knight-Ridder effort in Dade County, Florida, ultimately were abandoned. Computer utilities such as CompuServe and The Source have yet to become major profit generators. Sears, Roebuck and IBM nevertheless are preparing have launched a new videotext venture.

The cumulative impact of change in audiences, technologies, and media nevertheless creates unprecedented challenges to professionals in the communication disciplines. Every new medium that survives necessarily captures a segment of the total media audience at predecessors' expense. Resulting audience fragmentation contributes to communicators' problems.

THE COMMUNICATION CHALLENGE

The primary challenge to communicators arises out of a simple concept. Time is a finite, inflexible, and irreplaceable commodity. Time exists in limited volume for every individual and can be used only once. In a sense, time is more precious than money. Money lost or wasted often can be replaced. Lost time is gone forever.

The nature of time is the same from the standpoints of individuals and of organizations. The media compete for attention and individuals commit time to one or another of them in keeping with personal preferences. Because individuals' supplies of time are finite (and for one other reason), what one medium gains, another inevitably loses.

The other reason arguably is less important but remains significant. Like time, demand for information is limited among individuals and organizations. Informational needs satisfied through one medium seldom are addressed through another. Those who satisfy their desires for information about current events by reading newspapers become less attentive to television, and vice versa. Those who systematically search computer data bases for information on specific topics are less likely to seek similar information from other media.

Competition among the media for audience time, like competition for dollars in the commodities markets, is a zero sum game. Commodity speculators' winnings come from the pockets of less successful investors. Each medium's audience gains, in like manner, occur at the expense of other media. The competition may be among media within a given category, as in network television's ratings races, or across categories, as in the case of newspapers versus magazines. The results are the same and they imply difficulties for those engaged in mass communication.

Developmental Patterns

The magnitude and complexity of communication problems become clear as one examines the mass media and developmental patterns within media groups. Growth in numbers and fragmentation in audiences is almost universal, although patterns vary with type of medium. Media compete within and across categories. Seemingly straightforward comparisons therefore can be misleading to the uninitiated.

Numbers of newspapers and newspaper readership, for example, at first glance appear to be growing in the United States. There are more newspapers than ever before and their owners, especially the publicly owned corporations among them, are more profitable than ever. Newspapers nevertheless are in relative decline as mass media. The audience once concentrated in metropolitan daily newspapers has fragmented. National dailies and urban business newspapers compete with traditional dailies and weeklies for that portion of the total audience more disposed toward print than electronic information sources.

A similar transition from generalized to specialized publications has long since changed the face of the magazine industry. *Life*, *Look*, the *Saturday Evening Post, Colliers*, and a host of other once prosperous magazines have been replaced by hundreds of special interest publications dealing with almost every conceivable vocational or avocational topic. *Life* and other older publications reborn for sentimentalists have attracted only small audiences.

The specialization trend in magazines shows no sign of abating. A typical year in the late 1980s saw more than three hundred new titles added to the list of published magazines. Net annual increases concealed relatively high attrition rates, but publishers continue to search out new niches to serve. Niches are subject areas in which magazines' contents are sufficiently attractive to gain and hold the interest of audience segments. Interest levels must be sufficient to permanently capture time and attention presumably committed earlier to other media. Audiences also must be sufficiently affluent to attract advertisers.

Electronic Media

Change among electronic media has been as extensive as in the print sector. Television has been a growing industry although network audiences have been declining. Networks' losses have been offset by gains among cable systems and local stations. Direct broadcast satellite systems, local low power stations, and competing cable systems may produce further changes in audience distribution in the years ahead. Economically sound videotext systems ultimately may add to the competitive mix as well.

Impending change in television will be market driven only in part. Technology will play a role in several ways. Telephone companies intent on sharing the economic rewards of the information age are already experimenting with information services. Further change will develop as cable systems make the transition from copper wire to fiber optic transmission systems. Most first generation cable systems were wired with copper, which has a useful life of about ten years. Replacing copper with nondeteriorating fiber optic cable will require major capital investments. Replacement often will become necessary as original franchise agreements expire, opening the door to competitors.

Only in radio does there appear to be some semblance of stability among groups of communication channels traditionally considered to be mass media. Numbers of stations have been relatively constant in most markets for years. Audience use of the medium suggests little variation other than as a function of community size and demographics.

Most competition in radio revolves around programming although change in technologies may intrude as well. Persistent programming or content changes usually are symptomatic of station managements' ongoing search for greater audience shares. Such changes will continue regardless of external factors. Additional change will occur, however, with increased technological sophistication.

Technical changes can be expected in artistry and economics in television as well as radio. New technology will continue to produce improved sound quality, always highly prized among broadcasters. Technological advances also will permit development of sophisticated automation in radio broadcasting. Over time, and especially in an era of diminishing human resources, automation can produce disproportionate economic benefits for early adopters. Television audiences conceivably may grow with the advent of high definition pictures. Better picture definition will add nothing to the informational value of programming, however, and low power stations ultimately may prove more potent as generators of audience change.

THE NEW MEDIA

Change among traditional mass media encompasses only a small part of the change occurring in the communication industry. No discussion of change in communication is complete without attention to new media that have developed in three forms. The first group consists of channels that are products of human ingenuity rather than of new technology. The second group may or may not use new technology. The channels involved are extensions of preexisting technologies into new application areas, perhaps with incidental assistance from new technologies. The third set of channels consists of new communication devices or techniques founded in new technologies.

The three categories specified above to some extent are artificial. Boundaries between them are inexact. Arguments readily could be made that any member of one group would be equally at home in another. Groupings are helpful, however, in examining differences among components of a large set of innovative approaches to mass communication.

Components of the group based in ingenuity rather than technology often are perceived as inconsequential because they lack the novelty of "high tech." Nothing could be further from the truth. Any medium that survives the test of capitalist economics is consequential. Ingenuity-based media are no less significant than any other in their contributions to audience fragmentation.

Innovative Media

The new media groups are most readily examined in light of the amounts of new technology they involve. At the bottom of the scale are many apparently minor but economically significant communication channels. They include systems that deliver messages in new locations or in different ways to established locations.

These innovative media include such devices as broadcast systems in tunnels otherwise shielded from the intrusion of electronic messages. The objective: supplant broadcast stations to which motorists are tuned as they enter tunnels and exploit temporarily captive audiences. The same principle is involved in supermarket systems where video screens are being installed on grocery carts. As carts approach product displays, transmitters in the displays trigger mechanisms causing messages to appear on the screen.

Innovation of the same sort is occurring in other areas. Municipalities, for example, are renting space above and below parking meters to entrepreneurs for resale as miniature billboard space. Miniature billboards also are appearing on supermarket shopping carts and elsewhere. Advertising displays have appeared in public restrooms, where posters are mounted inside cubicle doors or on walls above urinals.

The ingenuity group also includes extensions of Alexander Graham Bell's old technology applied to telemarketing. First, computers were used to compile call lists and record results. Then the computers were programmed to dial the calls. Finally, recorders, computers, and telephones were programmed together to make calls, "converse" through taped messages, and record orders or other information.

Extended Media

Computers also have played a role in extending the usefulness of preexisting communication technologies, especially in producing print and electronic messages. Computers and other devices, many involving videotape, have been used to extend the applicability of media technology.

The term extend refers to enhanced ability among individuals or small organizations to accomplish what once could be achieved only by those with substantial, if not massive, resources. Printing of the sort required for newspapers, magazines, and books once required investments far greater than those necessary today. Similarly costly barriers stood between prospective users and videotape production.

The barriers collapsed under the impact of the microprocessor. Relatively low-cost microcomputers can be used to set type for printed materials. Microprocessors also spawned a new generation of video cameras less costly and more productive than their predecessors. The result is reductions in print and electronic production costs, adding radically to organizations' ability to communicate.

Enhanced communication ability is most evident in programs directed toward employees, shareholders, dealers, and other relatively small groups. Audience size and relative economy go hand in hand in mass communication. Technological advances enable organizations to economically apply sophisticated techniques in dealing with smaller and smaller audiences.

The same technologies assist entrepreneurial individuals in establishing small businesses in printing and audiovisual production. Resulting impacts on mass communication may at first appear insignificant. Closer inspection shows, however, that competition among production organizations inevitably produces lower costs and message proliferation. These circumstances add to the flood of messages that inundates every individual and renders communicators' tasks more difficult.

Really New Media

The proliferation problem is further compounded by what might be called the "really new" media. These are channels of communication based on new technologies, virtually all involving one or more computers. Some of the new media are pure computer applications, as in electronic data bases, on-line shopping services, automated telemarketing systems, and desktop publishing. Others involve combinations of new media and old, as with cellular telephones and broadcast shopping services.

Computers or microprocessors in either case are central to the functions involved. As the heart of the computer and in other applications, the microprocessor already has supplanted the steam engine as society's driving technology. Information users benefit at the expense of distributors in almost every application.

Information has become more accessible, more manageable, and less costly. To the extent that knowledge is power, the microprocessor, especially as the heart of the computer, has empowered the individual at the expense of the organization. Vendor organizations and organizations to which information users belong both have become progressively disadvantaged. Both must compete more strongly to retain patronage.

Direct Applications

Computers or microprocessors thus are a logical beginning point for discussion of the new media. Computers applied directly to enhance human capability deal almost exclusively in information. Computers increase ability to gain access to information, to store information, and to manipulate information, enabling individuals to accomplish in minutes what once took days.

Computers make the content of huge libraries available to anyone, anywhere, at any time, and at negligible cost. Information once accessible only through days or weeks of effort or at great expense can be obtained in minutes without physical access to the source. Much of the information in this book was obtained by computer, from libraries, databases, and on-line information services.

Once gathered, information is readily and inexpensively stored in electronic form. Mass storage devices for microcomputers have grown consistently in capacity while declining in cost. Before delivery to the publisher, this book was stored in a microcomputer that contained eighty megabytes of memory. The "manuscript" required little more than one megabyte. Storage devices then available could be purchased at a cost of about ten dollars per megabyte.

The book's content was developed through three computer applications. The first application was an information management program that permits information to be entered at random and then reorganized in almost any manner. The second was a word processing system. Although designed primarily for writing, many word processing systems quickly perform such otherwise tedious tasks as assembling indexes. The third application was a desktop publishing program through which the manuscript was made ready for printing without using traditional typesetting and composition processes.

Collectively, productivity enhancements created by the computer reduced the time required in creation of the book to about 20 percent of what would otherwise have been necessary.

Indirect Applications

Indirect computer or microprocessor applications, while less evident to users, are no less pervasive. Home shopping services developed and offered via television, for example, are extensive users of computers. Cellular telephone systems could not function without computers. Neither could facsimile machines.

None of these, of course, are "pure" computer applications. Each involves additional technologies. Television-based home shopping services involve satellites, telephones, and computers, as well as television. Cellular telephones and facsimile systems both use telephone as well as computer technology.

Audiovisual devices being field tested in supermarkets similarly involve computers in addition to traditional audiovisual technologies. So do many telemarketing systems. Newer, more sophisticated computers can select and dial telephone numbers, deliver messages, and take orders without benefit of human intervention. In a variation on this technology, computers also have been linked to facsimile systems to transmit automatically during hours when telephone rates are lowest, redialing numbers as often as necessary to get messages through.

THE FUTURE OF MASS COMMUNICATION

What does it all mean? What does the future hold? What will be the status of mass communication at the turn of the century?

Making predictions can be a very risky business, it's been said, especially when one starts dealing with the future. Enough of the future already is in sight, however, to suggest relatively precise answers to these questions.

The meaning is simple. Societies are moving rapidly into the age of information, an era in which individuals will be informationally empowered at the expense of organizations. More educated populations will be better equipped to challenge any effort to mislead them. Most members of society will apply a broader range of informational resources in decision making. Synthesis and transmission of messages, as a result, will decline in importance among organizations.

While the meaning of "all this" is relatively clear, however, the future remains hazy. The future is produced by response to the present. The manner in which communicators will respond to the present is far from clear. Behaviors of information distributors and consumers, the mass media and their audiences, are predictable. More media will distribute more information to progressively smaller audiences. The responses of those who fashion and transmit messages, the professional communicators, is another matter.

Producers of products and services will continue to demand results of the communication disciplines. Advertising, marketing, public relations, and sales promotion departments and consultancies will be held accountable for the results of their efforts. Measurable behavioral response among organizations' stakeholders will become the sole measure of communicator success.

Consumers of products and services concurrently will become less responsive to the siren song of today's communicator. Fewer and fewer will be tuned in to what no longer can be called "mass" media. Those who read or listen will be more and more skeptical of message content. Mediated communication, in other words, will become progressively less influential in consumer decision making.

The status of mass communication in the year 2000 and beyond will be governed by communicators' perceptions of, and responses to, contemporary conditions. How can the behaviors of progressively better informed and more skeptical stakeholders be influenced? What kinds of messages will be most convincing? What media will most productively deliver those messages?

Answers to these questions are most readily found by examining the several ways in which organizations communicate. Four sets of channels are involved: environmental, behavioral, interpersonal and mediated. Organizational commitments to stakeholders, in other words, are reflected in

1. environments to which they expose their stakeholders,
2. behaviors of organizational personnel,
3. statements of organizational personnel, and
4. mediated messages that are accurately received, assimilated and believed.

Each of these factors makes a variable contribution to stakeholders' perceptions of any organization. The variation involved is a function of channel credibility. Messages transmitted interpersonally generally are more credible than the mediated variety. Behavior always is more persuasive than words, and environments usually are more convincing than behaviors. From the standpoints of customers, for example, environments that merchants create and the behaviors of merchants' personnel make the strongest of quality statements. These statements are stronger than any verbal assurances employees may provide. Mediated messages are still lower on any valid credibility scale.

The relative weakness of mediated messages and the deteriorating efficiency of the mass media raise substantive questions as to the future of the mass communication disciplines. Can advertising, public relations, marketing, and sales promotion meet emerging performance standards? Can members of these disciplines induce measurable behavioral response among organizational stakeholders by applying traditional disciplinary tools? Or must disciplinary change accompany societal and technological change if the disciplines are to survive?

Contemporary realities suggest that disciplinary change is essential. The mass communication disciplines are oriented toward persuasion rather than reality. Other than in entertainment and athletics, however, the age of hucksterism is gone. No amount of persuasion will long protect an exploitative organization. Reality will prevail and stakeholders will respond accordingly.

Success in communication, then, requires consistency in messages regardless of origin. Environmental, behavioral, interpersonal, and mediated messages must be mutually supportive. Inconsistency destroys credibility. Perhaps more important from communicators' standpoints, deterioration in credibility produces reduced response levels.

The status and stature of disciplines now committed primarily to persuasive communication will, at the turn of the century, be determined by the scope or operational limits of the disciplines involved. Ability to orchestrate messages, to establish consistency among message sources, will be vital to survival as well as success.

Communicators will have to choose between conforming messages to reality or reality to messages. Only the second of the two options can preserve the communication disciplines as they now exist. Their futures rest in creating realities adequate to support messages that organizations want to send in order to obtain the support on which survival depends.

Conforming realities to messages implies creating and then communicating attractive realities to consumers. The process requires more than communication skills. Consumer preferences must be known at the outset. Continuing communication with all stakeholders becomes essential. All the knowledge and skills of the communication disciplines is necessary to success.

Conforming messages to realities is another matter. Such an approach assumes a producer knows best approach to the market-place, an approach predestined to failure in an increasingly competitive world.

IN SUMMARY

Driven by new technologies, new media, and new audiences, the primary focus of commercial communication is shifting from perception to reality. Rather than merely attempting to persuade consumers of the value of a product, service, or organization, communicators more and more are reshaping realities to merit support.

Driven primarily by the transistor as applied in computers and elsewhere, new technologies are joining with educational processes to create better informed and more skeptical audiences. The computer, as a metatechnology and an extension of the human brain, has proved to be an especially potent force in creating the age of information.

The onset of the information age creates challenges to long-prevalent assumptions underlying communication efforts. No longer can communicators assume they are dealing with traditional audiences little influenced by emerging technologies and attuned to the mass media. Contemporary audiences differ demographically, socioeconomically and psychologically from those of earlier decades.

They are strongly oriented to innovative information sources created by the new technologies, and they are far less attentive to the mass media of decades past.

Increases in numbers of media, new and old, print and electronic, have created mounting competition for the limited time available to individuals for information acquisition. Each medium that gains an audience of sufficient size to be commercially viable succeeds at the expense of predecessors, further fragmenting the message marketplace.

The relative weakness of mediated messages and the deteriorating efficiency of the mass media require that communicators reassess the primary thrust of their disciplines; that they reorient their activities to deal primarily in creating salutary realities rather than in persuasion.

2 The Information Society

Communication succeeds only where communicators overcome barriers erected by new technologies, new media and new audiences. Together these factors are creating—or are being created by—what has been called an information society.

Information or postindustrial societies are successors to industrial societies. Industrial societies supplanted agricultural societies, which in turn were spawned by nomadic societies.

The United States and other emerging information societies are caught up in what Peter Drucker described as an era of discontinuity, a period neither wholly industrial nor truly informational in character. Technologies, media, and audiences in these conditions may in part may be products of discontinuity. In the alternative, they may be producing discontinuity. Social scientists will argue the difference for years. Communicators immediately must deal with the results, however, regardless of their origin.

Each of the primary factors—technologies, media, and audiences—can be most readily examined in the context of the characteristics of information societies. An information society is a nation, region, or city in which knowledge and information have value and are sources of value. The two concepts are different. Information has value where it is saleable. Information is a source of value where it is applied to enhance the commercial worth of products and services.

As in agricultural and industrial societies, information societies have tools and products. The tools of information societies are the computing and telecommunication technologies that permit data to be easily and economically transmitted, stored, and manipulated. The products are new knowledge in any of a number of forms.

The words new knowledge are broadly applied. New is a relative word in the world of information and knowledge. It refers to data or knowledge previously unknown or inaccessible as well as to literally new information. Both varieties are significant in that the former often produces the latter. Ability to quickly and inexpensively assemble and analyze masses of data enhances researcher capacity to generate new information. Understanding information societies for these reasons requires insight into their tools, products, and environments.

COMPONENTS OF INFORMATION SOCIETIES

Tools, products, and environments are most readily understood in light of six themes that regularly recur in a growing body of literature dedicated to describing the emerging information society. The presence of these themes points to a growing consensus among academics and futurists as to the characteristics of that society. They include the following, as Rutgers' Jorge R. Schement specified:

1. Information exchanged as an economic commodity. While information has been bought and sold since the dawn of history, only in recent years has it become a commodity in its own right, competing with manufactured goods and agricultural commodities in commercial marketplaces.

2. A large information work force. Producing, recycling and maintaining information become the primary functions of a significant segment of the work force in a broad range of occupations.

3. Enhanced interconnectedness among information technologies and institutions. Improved information flows and often more homogeneous industries result. In finance, for example, differences among banks, brokerage houses, and other institutions are slowly disappearing.

4. Special status for scientific knowledge. While valued for its own sake in academia, scientific knowledge also is pursued and applied as a commercial resource.

5. Social environments that increasingly become creatures of the mass media. Proliferating communication channels and messages have become major interpreters and shapers of reality.

6. Information technology diffused through society. Mechanical devices enable individuals to store, transmit, and manipulate information.

Most researchers and futurists attribute these trends to one of two developmental processes. One group views the developments specified above as evidence of a clear break with the past, what Peter Drucker called a discontinuity. They see the United States today as an emerging post-industrial or information society in the process of supplanting the industrial age. The second group sees the same trends as evidence of a new developmental phase in the industrial era oriented toward information rather than manufactured products. Schement takes the latter view, declaring:

If there are new social forces whose existence has prompted the growth of informational activities, then there is indeed a basis for proposing that the information society is post-industrial. On the other hand, the continuing influence of the determinants of industrial society on the pattern of information uses would indicate a strong connection between industrial and the informational society.

Schement's concept is not without merit. The issue he raises deserves careful examination, which doubtless will be forthcoming within the academic community. Professional communicators, however, must deal equally with the products of technological and social forces regardless of their origins. Tools, products, and environments all are pertinent from the communication perspective, whether produced by new technology or by changing social forces.

Information Environments

Information environments have been defined by many authors over the past decade and more. Among the more prominent are Daniel Bell, Fritz Machlup, Drucker, and Marc Porat. Bell advanced a theory of postindustrialism from which most of today's concepts of the age of information have been drawn. The postindustrial world, he suggests, is one in which the following occur:

1. Economies shift from goods-producing to service-producing with growth concentrated in communication, health, education, research, and government, as recently has been the case in the United States.
2. Professional and technical workers increase in numbers and influence, as have scientists and engineers in the U.S. for the past decade and more.
3. Societies become organized around knowledge, and organiza tions are dependent on research and development activities most involving applied information technologies.
4. Organizations focus their efforts on tracking and managing technological change, including second- and third-order consequences as well as primary effects.
5. Intellectual technology is systematically applied to challenge or synthesize nature to improve the human condition, as in medical or biological research.

Bell suggests that intellectual technology—the microprocessor as embodied in the computer—is the driving force behind the age of information. Machlup, Drucker, and Porat focus on social changes they anticipate with the onset of the information society. All predict radical change in the nature of work and in distribution of workers. These authors' forecasts vary quantitatively only with differing definitions of the term knowledge worker.

Information societies usually are defined as nations in which work forces consist primarily of information workers—men and women engaged in producing, processing, and distributing information or information technology. Information, according to Everett M. Rogers, is "patterned matter-energy that affects the probabilities available to an individual making a decision." Information differs from other economic resources in several ways. As an intangible that can be expressed in physical or electronic form, information tends to be undervalued. Information's abstract form can make it appear relatively unimportant where the reverse usually is true. Information, in the mid-1980s, had become the primary commodity of the United States. Information work then was estimated to encompass 55 percent of the nation's total work force, to account for 67 percent of all labor costs, and to consume 70 percent of all work hours.

Porat sorted organizations of which the information sector is composed into five primary categories, as follows:

1. research and development organizations
2. information services or providers of information
3. the mass media, regulated and unregulated
4. those producing the tools of information technology at industrial and consumer levels
5. those selling the products of information technology at the retail level

A brief examination of some of the types of organizations that would fall within Porat's categories quickly provides substantial insight into the magnitude of the information sector. Research and development organizations, for example, necessarily would include all of the nation's postsecondary educational institutions, most of governmental agencies at all levels, and a host of foundations, institutes, and similar organizations dedicated to generating information on a limitless number of topics.

Information services and providers would range from the nation's 14,000 libraries and 3,000 commercial data bases to the 165,000 membership organizations and more than 3,000 noncommercial research organizations that populate the United States. The mass media category would include more than 96,000 publishers, 11,00 0 commercial broadcasters, and almost 30,000 advertising firms.

Those producing the tools of technology include manufacturers and assemblers of products from radio and television receivers to computer hardware and software, photography equipment and supplies, and electronic devices of all kinds. Those selling the products of information technology are even more diverse. They presumably range from retailers selling books, videotapes and the like to information entrepreneurs such as those offering directories of all kinds.

A review of data compiled by Dun and Bradstreet as to numbers of business establishments within each of the Standard Industrial

Classification (SIC) categories established by the federal government indicates that some 3.6 million firms in the United States are involved in one or more of the five areas Porat specified. While any effort to estimate numbers of employees or owners would be futile, they necessarily constitute a large percentage of the nation's population.

Information Products

The products of the information society are as diverse as the organizations that function in information environments. Product diversity is a function of the fact that neither information nor information products can be considered end products in the usual sense. Both breed subsequent generations of "products," and reproduction rates appear to be growing with succeeding generations.

Most information products fall into one of two categories: information and the packaging and delivery systems through which information is introduced into the marketplace. Information must be accessible and applicable in order to have value. Access requires what those in the computer industry have labeled "user-friendly" delivery systems. Traditional systems consisted of print or electronic packaging—books or newspapers, videotape or audio tape. New technologies have spawned computer-based systems that store words and images in electronic form, in ASCII files or as bit mapped graphics.

An ever-increasing percentage of human knowledge is stored in electronic form. It is not unreasonable to anticipate that the world's knowledge one day will be contained in databases despite the fact that computers are creating new knowledge at an unprecedented rate. The knowledge explosion is a result of systems that enable researchers to quickly gather, organize and analyze unprecedented volumes of information. What once required months or years now can be accomplished in minutes or hours. Research results also become available almost immediately to others, speeding the production of still further knowledge.

The same sort of process influences information organizing and delivery systems. Computers have grown in capacity and sophistication at an accelerating rate. More advanced computers already are being applied in the design of successor generations. Rudimentary expert systems outstrip human capabilities in such areas as medical diagnoses. Information products, moreover, extend beyond computers and their contents. New technologies are blended with old, and old technologies are applied in new ways to extend and amplify knowledge processes.

Computers, for example, are critical to systems that permit facsimile transmission of documents via cellular telephone to moving vehicles. Fiber optic cables are compounding the capabilities of telephone and other communication systems. The outcomes of innovative applications of existing technologies often are more productive than conceived of by their early developers. Each application, moreover, is as likely as not to lead to still further innovation.

Emerging Applications

No matter how pervasive the communication revolution now appears, the future promises more change than has occurred in the past. Consider these developing trends and their long-term potential:

- Technicians are becoming artists, and vice versa. Computer graphics has emerged as a challenging and rewarding art form. At the same time, computer technology is starting to replace film in cameras. "Prints" soon will be shown on television screens. "Photos" already are being made, transmitted and reproduced in newspapers and magazines without benefit of the photographic process. The cost of the technologies involved soon will decline to a point at which they will be within reach of home computer users.

- Fast-disappearing regulatory constraints are making broadcast technology available to almost anyone. While commercial network television remains regulated, Federal Communication Commission policies for direct broadcast satellites are all but nonexistent.

- Communication and computerization have almost become one, especially in the hands of IBM and the American Telephone and Telegraph Company (AT&T). Both are now in the information business, processing as well as transmitting information. Meanwhile, AT&T's offspring, the "Baby Bells," are preparing to compete with cable companies in offering television and other services via telephone lines.

• Time and space are disappearing as barriers to communication. From real-time speeches and rocket launches to shopping services, networks and cable systems are creating a global village whose residents have immediate and instantaneous access to information. Within that village, organizations are using the same technologies to destroy internal temporal and spatial barriers.

• Consumers are taking active control of electronic infrastructures, seeking out the information they want and need rather than passively accepting or discarding that which vendors elect to transmit. Interactive television, videotext, and data bases are among the fastest-growing information sources, and their growth rates are accelerating rather than declining.

• Individual channels of communication more and more serve multiple roles. Computers, for example, receive, store, and transmit information. Network and cable television content, live or on tape, readily can be transmitted by satellite, delivered by cable or microwave, and shown on television.

EVOLUTIONARY PATTERNS

The immediate future and the recent past of the information revolution can best be understood in historical context. The most insightful perspectives include those provided by the history and patterns of technological development. Both are important.

The historical perspective suggests that technologies, despite their development to date, still may be in their infancy. The new technologies appear destined to become for the age of information what printing was to the industrial age, what writing was to the agricultural age, and what language was to the nomadic era. Some 370 centuries have elapsed since the probable birth of language in the Cro-Magnon era. Most of what today are called the new technologies have developed over the past five decades. The 50 years in question cover a fraction of 1 percent of the 37,000 years that have passed since the invention of language.

Developmental patterns are less impressive but no less important than historical perspectives in examining the new technologies. The existing and potential status of each technology is readily understood where the technology is examined in terms of its individual development as well as its historical context. Some technologies are in their infancy while others border on obsolescence. Knowledge of technological life cycles thus fosters understanding of the present and the future.

Historical Context

Analyses that begin with examinations of historical perspectives are most rewarding, especially where they focus on the 37,000 years that have passed since the arrival of homo sapiens and the invention of language. The first component of mass communication as we know it arguably did not appear until 300 centuries later, when the Sumerians developed writing in 4000 B.C. The word "arguably" is appropriate in that some in advertising doubtless would attempt to trace their antecedents to cave painting, which first appeared about 18,000 years earlier, in 22,000 B.C.

More important, however, is the fact that writing has been with us for only 60 of Homo sapiens' 370 centuries. We have had an alphabet for only 30 centuries, while printing has existed for little more than a millenium, for fewer than 550 years. Nothing that today might be remotely identified with a "new" communication technology has been in evidence for more than 100 years.

The 1900s one day may be described as humanity's century of technology. In the alternative, depending on developments yet to come, the twentieth century may be seen as only the beginning of a far more advanced civilization. Homo sapiens nevertheless has made considerable progress since the turn of the century.

Contemporary communication technology can somewhat arbitrarily be said to have been born in 1900 with the first transmission of speech via radio waves. The telephone then was almost twenty-five years old and the telegraph had been invented in 1835, but wireless transmission of speech was prerequisite to radio and television.

The years after 1900 were marked with one technological landmark after another:

1912 - DeForest's discovery of amplifying qualities of the
       vacuum tube
1920 - Establishment of regularly scheduled radio stations
1927 - Television demonstration by AT&T
1941 - First commercial television broadcast
1942 - Creation of first electronic computer

1946 - Invention of ENIAC, the first mainframe computer, with 18,000 vacuum tubes
1947 - Invention of transistor at Bell Laboratories
1949 - Invention of first stored program computer
1951 - Introduction of color television
1956 - Invention of videotape
1957 - Launching of first earth satellite by Soviets
1958 - Introduction of stereophonic recordings
1961 - Arrival of push button telephones
1962 - Launch of Telstar satellite
1968 - Introduction of portable video recorder
1969 - NASA's first manned space flight guided by a computer 3,000 times smaller than ENIAC
1971 - Invention of microprocessor
1975 - Perfection of fiber optic signal transmission
     - HBO's transmission by satellite to cable systems
1976 - First use of teletext in Great Britain
1977 - Launch of first interactive cable television system 1978 - Marketing of first microcomputer
1979 - First use of videotext by British Post Office
1980 - Drop in Home computer prices below five hundred dollar level
1981 - Space shuttle Columbia mission
1982 - Successful multiple satellite launch

The latter years of the century were no less prolific from a technological standpoint, but significant developments were more broadly distributed across the technologies. Home and small business computers proliferated at unprecedented rates. So did software necessary to drive them. Desktop publishing was born, for example, complete with optical scanners and a host of other peripherals. Cellular telephones came into vogue, as did facsimile transmission.

In the latter cases, as in many others, value added innovators quickly were attracted by the new technologies. What was first introduced in free standing and somewhat cumbersome and costly form changed rather quickly as the technologies progressed through life cycles akin go those experienced by humans and organizations.

Technological Life Cycles

The life cycle model progresses from birth to death through an almost-limitless number of identifiable stages. Most cycle descriptors—the terms attached to specific stages—include growth, maturity, and decline. Any specific stage or phase can be subdivided, however, to constitute several others. Growth, for example, might encompass both adolescence and early adulthood.

The same sort of variation and greater complexities arise in product life cycles. Viewed simplistically, product cycles begin with discovery and end with obsolescence. The real world is more complex. Metatechnologies are long lived and may approach immortality. The deep plow and steam engine (see chapter 3) continue to exist although in forms different from those in which they were created. The transistor promises to be with us at least as long. Technologies, as opposed to metatechnologies, have shorter life spans, but few disappear in their entirety.

With these caveats in mind, the stages or phases of product life cycles deserve examination. The seven-stage "life-cycle of a technology generation" elaborated by University of Montreal economics professor Kimon Valaskakis is typical. Valaskakis' stages include the following:

1. Discovery, featuring "the discovery either of a scientific principle or law of nature or a natural resource [for example, electricity]."

2. Invention, or the application of the scientific principle or law to a specific purpose, leading to the invention of a particular machine [for example, the microprocessor].

3. Innovation, involving "commercial use and marketing of the particular invention [for example, incorporation of a microprocessor in a pocket calculator]."

4. National dissemination, during which "the technology spreads throughout the land."

5. International dissemination, involving "the international marketing of the innovation."

6. Decline, "due to the rise of alternate technologies."

7. Obsolescence, in which new technology replaces the old.

The Valaskakis model, parenthetical examples by the author notwithstanding, is applicable here only in part. Most in communication technology believe their products' life cycles begin with invention. A strong argument could be made, in addition, that while some contemporary technology may be in decline, no significant communication technology has disappeared. The developmental track of contemporary technology instead appears to resemble a spiral continuum more than a cycle with clearly defined beginnings and ends.

The Technology Spiral
Consider, for example, today's telephone system. Predecessor long distance signaling systems can be traced to prehistoric drums or plumes of smoke, although the telegraph Samuel Morse introduced in 1835 is a more logical point of analytical departure.

A great deal has transpired since 1825. David Hughes linked Morse's electronic technology to printing processes dating from the thirteenth century and in 1855 produced the printing telegraph. The transatlantic cable was completed eleven years later and telephone appeared in 1876.

A steady stream of incremental changes occurred over the next one hundred years before practical fiber optic signal transmission was achieved in 1975. Today, fiber optic cables are replacing copper wire, compounding carrying capacities and paving the way for further innovation.

The many steps involved in the evolution of the telephone system were not atypical of technological progress. Similar evolutionary patterns can be traced in other areas. In addition, none of the technologies that eventually contributed to contemporary telephone systems developed in a vacuum. Each was linked to others during its developmental cycle.

Parallel Patterns. Developmental patterns essentially similar to those that occurred with the telephone are most readily seen in printing and photography. Books first were printed in China in 600 A.D., some eight hundred years before Gutenberg's Bible. It was not until the nineteenth century, however, that the process began to evolve at a relatively rapid pace.

First, in 1819, David Napier invented the flat bed press. A dozen years later, the press was linked to a steam engine. By 1936, printing and photographic processes had evolved to a point at which *Life* magazine could be successfully launched, in the process integrating the two technologies.

Photographs on metal plates had existed since 1827, but film processes and far better printing presses than those that existed in the 1820s were necessary to produce a pictorial magazine. The film process essential to magazines such as *Life* also led to development of Auguste and Louis Lumiere's motion picture camera, which in turn spawned another industry.

Progressive technologies. The linkage of photography and printing was but one of many successful technological marriages. The bulk of them postdated the identification of radio waves in 1888, an event from which the evolution of the broadcast industry can be traced.

Guglielmo Marconi introduced radio telegraphy in 1895. In 1900 speech was transmitted over radio waves. Twenty-seven years later, television was first demonstrated by the American Telephone and Telegraph Company. Many of the principles of photography were incorporated into television, which subsequently was transmitted via cable and satellite as well as through traditional broadcast channels. With the advent of fibre optic systems, radio and television as well as data transmissions will be handled over the same lines that transmit telephone calls.

Photography, or what used to be photography, today continues to change in ways that could not have been conceived of just a few years ago. The changes are offspring of a marriage with computer technology. Computers are being used to manipulate photographs and to replace the photographic process.

The manipulation involves loading photographic images via optical scanners into computers, where they can be edited, altered, and ultimately combined into word-and-picture images for use in printed products. The photographic process is being supplanted with the incorporation of microprocessors into cameras. Miniature computers first were used in photography to read light levels, to adjust lens openings, and, at least theoretically, to produce better negatives. By the mid-1980s, however, functional "cameras" were being constructed of microprocessors and lenses. No film was necessary. Images were stored in electronic rather than photographic form.

The images little resembled what early photographers had captured on metal plates. Neither did the processes through which the images were reproduced. Images captured by microprocessors can be displayed on computer screens or printed on paper. They also can be transmitted by computer, satellite, or telephone to distant points such as newspaper offices or television studios. At newspapers, images can be edited by computer and transferred directly to press plates for printing.

Sorting Labels. What technologies were used in the process described above? Printing certainly was involved, although only to create the product ultimately sold on newsstands. No longer was it necessary to use film processes to create photos. What once was called telephone or radio technology was used in image transmission, although the systems little resembled their predecessors. Computer technology was used in photography and in transmitting and in recreating electronic images. Photography remained part of the process only in that the camera had a lens and resembled its 35 mm. forebears.

Technologies also are often combined in the course of entrepreneurial pursuit of value-added products. Attributes of multiple technologies in these circumstances are combined to extend product (as opposed to technology) life cycles.

Consider, for example, the combination of radio, telephone, facsimile, and, on occasion, television systems with that old offspring of the steam engine, the automobile. Cars now can be equipped with all of these devices and futurists look to a day when motor vehicles may be controlled in whole or part by wire networks rather than by drivers.

Another recent example of combined technologies involved facsimile equipment. First designed exclusively to transmit messages on paper (combining printing and telephone transmission technologies), facsimile machines soon became available with telephones, answering machines, and copiers built in.

Technologies also were combined to create portable televisions incorporating radios and tape recorders, console televisions that answer the door and the telephone, binoculars equipped with sound recording equipment, and an almost limitless number of other products. Finally, new technologies are being applied in innovative services designed to meet individual and business needs. Typical of these in the late 1980s were satellite-based paging systems that enabled business people to be contacted by their offices anywhere within the United States, even when airborne.

Developmental Directions

Three developmental trends, including continuing entrepreneurial innovation, can be expected to characterize communication technology for the near future. The other trends potentially are more significant. Proliferating computers, fiber optic cable, and associated equipment first are apt to come together to create communication networks of unprecedented scope and capabilities. Those networks then are likely to be used in ways that only in part can be envisioned today.

The late 1980s, for example, saw the beginning of an amalgamation of electronic mail systems in a pattern apparently paralleling that earlier followed by the nation's several telephone companies. The result ultimately may be a global electronic mail distribution network supplanting large segments of existing postal systems.

Other similar developments logically would follow as the age of information comes to maturity through an extensive set of interactive media. The era of interactive communication began with the University of Pennsylvania's ENIAC computer, which used eighteen thousand vacuum tubes. Only now, however, is interactive communication coming into its own, primarily in six forms:

1. Microcomputers, especially small, stand-alone units capable of a broad range of software-driven functions and amenable to use in networks and for communication purposes.

2. Teleconferencing in any of several forms. Those based on computer, telephone and television systems are most often used.

3. Teletext or interactive information services that enable users to call up frames of information transmitted as part of television signals onto television screens.

4. Videotext services that, like teletext, are interactive but that call up information from central computers rather than from broadcast signals.

5. Interactive cable television, which provides for transmission of text and graphic frames as well as video pictures on request to television sets through cable systems.

6. Satellite-based communication via telephone and/or television.

In general terms, the new media share two characteristics. They are interactive and further the process of demassification described in chapter 1. Many also share a high level of what Rogers described as "asynchronicity." He used the term to refer to the extent to which simultaneous use by message senders and receivers is necessary to communication processes involved. Computer bulletin board systems, for example, are highly asynchronous while teleconferencing is low on the asynchronicity scale.

Classifying Media

The arrival of the interactive media signaled the start of the age of information. Many have yet to realize the potential of these media. Some, especially in the videotext, teletext, and interactive cable categories, have been less than successful in pilot applications.

More important from the perspective of communicators, however, is the fact that few of the interactive media yet play a significant role in contemporary information delivery. Only computer-based systems have become everyday information tools. The so-called information explosion largely is a product of two other types of media. One might be called hybrid technologies, involving amalgamations of old and new devices to create new information delivery systems. The other consists of little more than innovative applications of long-existing devices.

Among the new systems based on amalgamated technologies, for example, are nationally circulated newspapers such as *USA Today* and the *Wall Street Journal*. Each day's editions are published simultaneously in multiple plants across the country from images transmitted by satellite. Innovative devices range from mini-billboards on shopping carts, parking meters and the doors of lavatory stalls to audiovisual technology applied in supermarket displays.

Collectively, these and other similar information delivery systems contribute significantly to mounting difficulties experienced by communicators in dealing with contemporary audiences. Audiences, technologies, and media are discussed in greater detail in subsequent chapters.

SOCIAL IMPLICATIONS

Where does all of this take us? How will the age of information influence society? Who will be the winners and the losers?

The answers to these and a great many other questions are beyond human ability to predict. Some, such as the University of California's Herbert I. Schiller, anticipate disaster in several forms. Others, such as Daniel Bell, are more sanguine. Most authors' concerns focus on three areas specified by Michigan State University's Benjamin J. Bates:

1. The impact of information trends on patterns and levels in employment. The computer has been envisioned on the one hand as a potential destroyer of jobs and on the other as a creator of more leisure and greater productivity. The computer also has been seen by some as a potential contributor to deterioration in quality of work life.
2. Access to information utilities, the storage, retrieval and transmission systems created through the integration of computers and telecommunication networks. The issues involved relate to the information that goes into such systems and who has access to them and to the issues of privacy, equity and censorship.
3. The political implications of the information society. Some envision increased democratization and reduced authoritarianism developing as a product of the interactive capabilities of the new technologies. Others are concerned over the potential of sophisticated information systems for surveillance, censorship, and the emergence of a totalitarian regime rather than for a more participatory democracy.

Extended discussion of such issues would be inappropriate here. Further development of the information society may produce the worst or the best of the several outcomes or something in between. The impact of the outcomes, whatever they may be, will be influenced for better or for worse by then-prevailing social circumstances. And communicators will have to deal with the results regardless of their size, shape, or the speed with which they develop.

IN SUMMARY

More and more residents of the world's developed nations today live in what can best be described as postindustrial or information societies, societies in which knowledge and information have value and are sources of value. Knowledge and information, in other words, are the tools and products of the age of information.

The tools, products, and environments of societies are most readily understood in light of six themes applied by authors in describing the information society, as described by Rutgers' Jorge R. Schement:

1. The exchange of information as an economic commodity.
2. Large information work forces.
3. Increasing interconnectedness among information technologies and institutions.
4. Special status for scientific knowledge.
5. Social environments shaped by the mass media.
6. Information technology diffused through society.

The information-intensive societies prevalent in the postindustrial world, according to futurist Daniel Bell, share several characteristics. Their economies shift from manufacturing to service sectors, with growth concentrated in communication, education, research, and government. Their professional and technical workers grow in number and influence. They organize around knowledge, and organizations become dependent on research and development. The primary focus of organizations shifts to managing change, and intellectual technology is systematically applied to improve the human condition.

Information societies produce a broad range of products. Neither information nor information products can be considered end product in the usual sense, however, in that both breed their own successors. Most products can be categorized as information or information delivery systems. Information utilities or databases and microcomputers are typical of the two categories.

The development of information societies is most readily understood by examining them in terms of their historical and technological development. History suggests that the technologies may be in their infancy, that the future holds more change than the recent past. The new technologies in large part have emerged during the latter half of the twentieth century, which represents a very small fraction of humankind's history. Color television, satellites, microprocessors, teletext, fiber optics, microcomputers, and videotext all have been products of the past forty years.

The technology life cycle, if indeed it exists, is more complex. Researchers suggest that technologies, like individuals and organizations, progress through predictable stages. Specifically, they suggest that technologies progress from discovery through invention, innovation, national and international dissemination, decline, and obsolescence. Close examination of recent developments, however, suggests that the evolution of technology is more a spiral than a cycle, that technologies tend to build on one another.

Technological development for the remainder of this century and much of the next will be characterized by three distinct trends. Most noticeable among them from the perspective of the layman will be continuing entrepreneurial activity in application of new technologies and in innovation using existing technologies. Most important among the development trends, however, will be the coming together of computers, fiber optic cable, and associated equipment to create networks of unprecedented scope and capabilities. The so-called integrated grid, in other words, will be coming to life, first in postindustrial societies and later around the world. The new networks then are likely to be used in ways that are difficult to envision today. A global electronic mail system, for example, will be not only technologically possible but highly desirable.

The social implications of these trends are another matter. No consensus has been reached among futurists or others as to the potential impact of emerging technologies over time. It appears safe to assume, however, that no technology will be without its unforeseen consequences and that some of those consequences will spawn the social problems of tomorrow.

ADDITIONAL READING

Bates, Benjamin J. "Evolving to an Information Society: Issues and Problems" In *The Information Society: Economic, Social and*

Structural Issues, edited by Jerry L. Salvaggio. Hillsdale, N.J.: Erlbaum, 1989.

Bell, Daniel. *The Coming of Post-Industrial Society.* New York: Basic Books, 1976.

Drucker, Peter. *The Age of Discontinuity.* New York: Harper and Row, 1969.

Hudson, Heather E., and Louis Leung. "The Growth of the Information Sector." In *Measuring the Information Society,* edited by Frederick Williams. Newbury Park, Calif.: Sage, 1988.

Machlup, Fritz. *The Production and Distribution of Knowledge in the United States.* Princeton, N.J.: Princeton University Press, 1962.

Porat, Marc. *The Information Economy: Definition and Measurement.* Special Publication 77-12, U.S. Department of Commerce, Office of Telecommunications, Washington, D.C.: U.S. Government Printing Office, 1977.

Rice, Ronald E., et. al. *The New Media: Communication, Research, and Technology.* Beverly Hills, Calif.: Sage, 1984.

Rogers, Everett M. *Communication Technology: The New Media in Society.* New York: Free Press, 1986.

Schement, Jorge R. "The Origins of the Information Society in the United States: Competing Vision." In *The Information Society: Economic, Social and Structural Issues,* edited by Jerry L. Salvaggio. Hillsdale, N.J.: Erlbaum, 1989.

Schiller, Herbert I. "Information for What Kind of Society." In *The Information Society: Economic, Social and Structural Issues,* edited by Jerry L. Salvaggio. Hillsdale, N.J.: Erlbaum, 1989.

Valaskakis, Kimon, "Leapfrog Strategy in the Information Age." In *Communication and the Future: Prospects, Promises and Problems,* edited by Howard F. Didsbury. Bethesda, MD: World Future Society, 1982.

Williams, Frederick. *The Communications Revolution.* Beverly Hills, Calif.: Sage, 1982.

_____, ed. *Measuring the Information Society.* Newbury Park, Calif.: Sage, 1988.

3 Media in Society

The most successful of communicators in the age of information will be those who are better equipped informationally than their contemporaries. Success will require insight into the nature of mass communication, media economics, and the evolution of communication systems. Each must be understood in historical context and as currently defined. Knowledge of historic and contemporary definitions is necessary because the concepts that underlie words can change.

The term *mass communication*, for example, is less precise than appears to be the case. *Communication* refers to the transfer of ideas, but *mass* is another matter. How many of anything must be assembled to create a mass? Until a mass exists, one must assume, mass communication can not occur, but mass never has been satisfactorily defined.

Mass media and *mass medium* are no more amenable to precise definition. Attempts toward definition are rendered doubly difficult because *media* and *medium* can be applied with equal accuracy to classes of communication channels or to components of those classes. For example, radio is a medium. Radio and television are media. In like manner, a radio station is a medium. Two radio stations are media. But while radio and television are mass media,can the word *mass* be applied to individual stations? Are their audiences large enough to be considered mass media? Confusion readily can arise in either case as a result of radical variation in audience sizes within and across classes.

Contemporary media economics compounds the size issue. Revenues in more and more cases are a function of audience quality rather than of mere numbers. Quality in media audiences is a function of the extent to which an audience is valued by a prospective advertiser. Media dealing in small audiences therefore can be highly profitable, while some with larger audiences can be economic cripples. Specialized magazines such as *Yachting* can prosper with circulations measured in thousands while newspapers such as New York's *Daily News* have collapsed with circulations of a million or more.

Economic factors rule supreme in most cases regardless of the age of the media. Success and failure know no categorical boundaries. Both occur among new media as readily as among their older competitors. Considerable insight and discrimination often are necessary, however, in attempting to differentiate between old and new. Definitions of these words, as in the cases above, often are misleading.

TERMINOLOGY DEFINED

Mastering new or more precise sets of definitions is part of a continuing process of adjusting to change that society requires of communicators. That ability, in turn, can be acquired only by understanding mass communication systems, their components, and the processes through which systemic changes occur. Changes have occurred and continue to occur in mass communication systems and subsystems.

Changes continue because complex societies spawn complex mass communication systems. Systemic change usually is slow, paralleling the evolutionary development of parent societies. System components—the media or channels of mass communication—therefore may appear unchanging while substantial change is in progress.

Systems theory is a useful lens for viewing the many components of the mass communication system, itself a subsystem of society. Mass communication systems, like the societies with which they are associated, are composed of multiple subsystems. Primary among these are the print and electronic media. Each category itself can be viewed as a system composed of multiple parts, in these cases, the individual media. The primary parts or subsystems of the print system are the newspaper and magazine groups. In the electronic sector, the primary subsystems are radio and television. Each subsystem—newspaper, magazine, radio, television, and the like—consists of multiple channels of communication.

Mass Communication

Channels of communication are the basic components of mass communication systems, often referred to as mass media. The meanings of the terms *mass communication* and *mass media*, however, are less precise than they appear. Most assume that mass communication occurs where mass media are used; that mass media necessarily produce mass communication. The assumptions are based on broader definitions of mass communication and mass media than many would accept.

Scholars identify mass communication as one of four types of communication. The others, all involving in-person exchanges between individuals or between individuals and groups, are interpersonal, small group and large group communication. Mass communication, in contrast, involves transmitting messages through impersonal channels of communication or mass media.

Mass communication thus is characterized primarily by the presence of at least one mass medium. In addition, mass communication messages, message sources, and audiences differ from those involved in the several forms of interpersonal communication.

Messages and Sources

Messages in mass communication are transient, public and rapidly transmitted. *Transient* refers to what might be called the "here today, gone tomorrow" nature of mass media content. The immediacy of the broadcast media, in fact, renders the words *today* and *tomorrow* inappropriate. The lifetime of broadcast messages usually is measured in seconds other than where recorded for repetitive use.

Mass media messages are public in that they are addressed to any and all recipients. Messages are designed to assure that their content is intelligible to all recipients. The best efforts of the media toward broad audience appeal do not always succeed, however, and broad in recent years has become a relative term. Many media, especially in the magazine sector, are oriented toward smaller, carefully circumscribed audiences. Automotive, computer and similar magazines are examples of narrowly focused publications.

Mass media messages are rapid in that they are designed, within media categories, for relatively fast delivery. Competition to be first, and thereby to attract larger audiences, is endemic among all media categories.

Where mediated messages are designed for transmission with maximum speed, interpersonal communication often involves more time in transmission, as with letters or memoranda. Interpersonal messages also are usually conveyed more privately and more personally between and among individuals who know, or at minimum, know of one another. Mass media messages, in comparison, usually are impersonal, originating with organizations or institutions rather than individuals.

Audience Characteristics

Similar differences exist between typical audiences in mass and interpersonal communication. Audiences in interpersonal communication usually are small and known to communicators. Interpersonal audiences consist most often of members of formal or informal groups in social, business, political, academic, or similar settings. Virtually the opposite circumstances prevail in mass communication, where audiences usually are large, anonymous, and heterogeneous. While their sizes vary, mass media audiences must be large in relative if not absolute terms. Media that attract the largest numbers of readers, viewers or listeners conforming to advertisers' target profiles are most likely to be selected by those advertisers.

The nature of the mass media also renders their audiences anonymous. Each audience member knows he or she is not alone but is unaware of the identity of other audience members. Finally, mass media audiences generally are heterogeneous. They are composed of people of all sorts brought together by their interest in the types of information or entertainment that media offer. Consider a definition of audience heterogeneity advanced by Kathleen Jamieson and Karlyn Campbell:

> [T]he mass audience is *heterogeneous*; it is made up of all sorts of people. The mass audience is so varied because nearly everyone has access to the media—you can read or watch or listen whether you are old or young, rich or poor, educated or uneducated, in a city or on a farm.

Assessing Variables

All of the audience, message, and source characteristics specified above must be present to meet traditional definitions of mass communication. Where any are missing or radically changed, the form of communication involved is not "mass communication," or is it? Some generally accepted characteristics of mass communication, as traditionally defined, are coming into question. Message sources continue to be organizational or institutional and impersonal. Messages continue to be rapidly and publicly transmitted. Audiences, however, are changing.

Affluent democratic societies in one sense grant access to the media to virtually everyone. Any individual *can* gain access to any of the channels of mass communication. The bulk of what once were mass media, however, are read, watched or listened to by smaller and smaller audiences. In each case, style, content, format, technology, or some combination of these factors discourages attention from the bulk of the population.

Mass. These circumstances suggest that the terms *mass media* and *mass medium*, if not *mass communication*, today are applied rather loosely if not promiscuously. Mass communication necessarily requires one or more mass media. Television, radio, newspapers, and magazines are mass media. Individual components of those media groups, however, are another matter. If mass media must command large, heterogeneous audiences, the issue becomes a matter of how large and how heterogeneous?

Since most individuals watch television, and since television programming as a whole attracts a relatively homogeneous audience, television can be categorized as a mass medium. But is one network a mass medium? And what of one station? Some networks meet the homogeneous audience test while others do not, and larger percentages of stations than networks probably would fail the test of audience homogeneity.

One network, in the early days of television, might have been characterized as a mass medium. CBS, NBC and ABC then shared the total audience more or less equally on most occasions. One third or 33.3 percent of all viewers might have been successfully defined as a mass. Today's typical viewer has some two dozen stations at his or her disposal. The major networks' audience shares have declined to almost 20 percent, at best a much smaller mass.

The same circumstances exist in radio and among magazines and newspapers. Each group may be a mass medium engaged in mass communication, but group members or components are becoming progressively more specialized, more audience specific. The content of individual media is oriented to appeal to ever smaller populations, populations their owners hope will be attractive to advertisers.

Specialization. In creating ever more narrowly focused media to serve the progressively more specialized interests of smaller audience groups, media organizations compound the issue of mass. Their efforts produce not only more specialized media but more media. Logic suggests that the potential of individual media to attract audiences and convey messages inevitably declines as numbers of media increase.

Population growth rates in the United States have been declining and some demographers expect declining growth rates to turn into a decline in total population by the turn of the century. If time dedicated to information gathering is relatively inflexible within the population, reallocation of time is a zero sum affair. What one medium gains, another must lose. Media first survive and then prosper by capturing sufficient user attention to warrant advertiser support. Advertisers select media for the same reasons that makes those media attractive to other communicators: audiences. Those attempting to sell products or services use a simple process in selecting advertising media. Audiences of choice are those that encompass the greatest numbers of prospective buyers or users of those products or services.

Media selection on the part of advertisers or their agencies also must be considered a zero sum affair from an economic standpoint. Rarely will an advertiser increase a budget to add a new medium. Dollars instead are reallocated within budgets in a process that almost inevitably spreads them more thinly over a greater number of media.

Survival. Competition for audiences is a fact of media life. Competition flourishes across and within media and types of media. Magazines compete with newspapers and with other magazines. The few remaining magazines oriented toward mass audiences fight off continuing assaults from armies of special interest publications. Within special interest groups, professional and vocational publications battle the recreational and avocational for reader attention. And within each of the latter four categories, individual magazines struggle for survival against direct competitors—usually at least one and occasionally several of them.

Mass Versus Class

Where generic groups are appropriately termed mass media, then, their component parts more logically are categorized for the most part as class media. Even "McPaper," as *USA Today* has been called, is designed for and marketed to an audience much narrower than the total population. The product is unlikely to satisfy the tastes of *Wall Street Journal* or *New York Times* readers, and vice versa.

The same conditions prevail in other media groups. Magazines are a mass medium but individual magazines, to a greater extent than in other media categories, are designed to capture precisely defined audiences. With rare exceptions, magazines are audience, vocation, or avocation specific. Some are gender or race specific. Others are age or life style specific. And each is marketed to readers and advertisers on the basis of specificity.

Television and radio follow parallel paths, although perhaps with less intensity. The major television networks compete only with independent stations in the broadcast sector, but different circumstances prevail in cable television markets. Cable systems carry the networks and, in most cities, several dozen specialized video channels. Channel content specialties range from news and sports to popular music, religion, and motion pictures. Radio stations are most readily categorized by the volume of talk, as opposed to music, and the types of music that they broadcast. While most radio content formats are accessible in most markets, little content-specific competition exists within markets. Only rarely will markets have more than one country, hard rock or classical music station.

The conditions described above suggest that while the mass media label may remain solidly affixed in most cases, contemporary media are better viewed within a typology proposed by Jamieson and Campbell. They suggested that media be categorized by scope and audience, by ownership or affiliation, and by technology, structure and function. They suggested that there are national media, specialized media, and elite media, and that components of the major news carrier groups—television, radio, newspapers, and magazines—can be sorted out accordingly.

Despite the power and wealth of concentrated mass media owner ship, few media are national in scope. Instead, most outlets aim at specialized audiences based on location, age, sex, income, education, ethnic background or other variables important in determining a person's interests. The mass media speak with varied voices to varied audiences.

Even the national media orient their content, however, in keeping with the demographic and sociographic characteristics of predetermined audiences. These conditions encourage entrepreneurs to develop more and more media. While the United States thus continues to be served by mass media—television, radio, newspapers, magazines, and books—the mass medium, in the form of individual publications or broadcasters commanding large audiences, no longer exists.

Continuing Fragmentation

The process producing the appearance of more and more mass communication with fewer and fewer mass media is apt to accelerate in the years ahead. Well-established media development patterns suggest that the trend toward specialization will continue. Technological advances inevitably will speed the proliferation of communication channels, commercial and organizational.

Mass media, like individuals, organizations, and societies, develop over time. Development proceeds, moreover, through a series of phases long ago identified by media scholars. New or emerging media usually are first used by a small elite, as most recently has been the case with computer data bases. Elitism usually is produced more by economic factors or variation in adoption or adaptation rates among prospective users than by developer design.

Variation in adoption rates can occur for any of several reasons. Computer phobia, for example, has played a role in the relatively slow rate at which data base use has developed. Cost was a factor in the speed at which television was adopted and plays a role in the computer area as well. Less-than-universal literacy dampens sales potential for books.

As early barriers subside, the new media become mass media before entering a third developmental phase. The third stage of the process is specialization or segmentation, in which technologies and/or techniques perfected in commercial communication channels are applied to the benefit of specialized audiences. Newspaper, magazine, and television applications have become quite common, for example, within organizations of all kinds. Specialized newspapers, magazines, and television channels also serve an increasing number of special interest audiences. Cable television systems offer channels dealing exclusively with news, weather, sports, religion, and shopping, to name only a few. Magazines and newspapers address virtually every vocation and avocation known to humanity.

MASS MEDIA ECONOMICS

The fragmentation process that persists among channels of mass communication is a product of media economics. Stripped of journalists' rhetorical references to the public good, the mass media are judged by those who support them on their ability to "deliver" specific audiences. The process requires that media organizations develop content that induces consistent readership, listening, or viewing. The audiences involved then are rented to advertisers.

The content development process places the media universally in the business of information or entertainment or both. Some appear to specialize in one or the other, but appearances usually are deceiving. Even where products appear wholly entertainment oriented, as with television outlets specializing in motion pictures, media are informational to the extent that advertising is information. Advertising is what media are paid to convey. Equally important, as evidenced by shopping channels on television and "shoppers" competing with newspapers, advertising content is perceived by consumers at least in part as informational.

To say that all media are in the information or entertainment businesses also is to say that almost all are for-profit organizations. The for-profit nature of the media too often is neglected by lay people and academics alike. Both groups tend to expect too much from organizations that essentially are creatures of the free enterprise system, that live or die based on their ability to produce results for advertisers and thereby generate profits for their owners.

Information and Entertainment

Producing results requires attracting audiences to meet advertisers' criteria by creating attractive mixtures of information and entertainment. The process has produced mixed results across and within media groups. Entertainment to the exclusion of information and information to the exclusion of entertainment both exist in broadcasting. Radio has news/talk as well as all-music stations, while television's offerings range from Cable News Network to movie channels. Print media are more news oriented. Significant numbers of the controlled-circulation "shoppers" have appeared in recent years, however, together with magazine-like publications dealing in real estate and automotive advertising.

The value of individual media as channels of mass communication varies with their content formats and with their credibility. Potential for variation requires that communicators consider two questions in making media selections: to what extent are individual media dedicated to informing as opposed to entertaining their audiences, and to what extent are individual media perceived as credible by those who read, watch or listen to them?

Responses to these questions, in individual circumstances, may or may not provide adequate information to those seeking to estimate potential media effectiveness under any given conditions. The information versus entertainment question is more readily answered, but answers may or may not be indicative of potential for results. Relative credibility, especially within competing media, usually is more easily measured.

Information content. The entertainment versus information issue is more complex than it appears. Before beginning to examine media in terms of information and entertainment content, basic terminology must be clarified. *Information*, as discussed here, is defined to include advertising as well as news. Professional journalists might take an opposing view, but those who read, listen to, or watch the media generally consider advertising content as information. Only infrequently, as in the case of some beverage commercials, do advertising messages more closely resemble entertainment. Viewers and listeners even then treat message content more as information than entertainment. For analytical purposes, therefore, advertising must be categorized as part of the informational content of the mass media.

Classifying advertising as information does not, however, render the basic information versus entertainment issue more easily managed. Percentages of media content dedicated to information are significant only in relation to the sizes and interests of audiences involved. One edition of *The New York Times* contains far more information, with or without advertising, than is provided in all major network news broadcasts of the same date. *The Times's* circulation is measured in the hundreds of thousands, however, while networks count audiences in millions.

Volume of information as a percentage of total content presumably might be an indicator of potential media influence levels. Volume tends to be a misleading indicator, however, especially where comparisons are attempted across media groups. The informational content of network television, for example, is small in relative and absolute terms in comparison with that of the print media. Within the ranks of television news outlets, however, major networks are more or less at the midpoint of a range of viewer information options. At the extremes are the all-news programming offered by Cable News Network and the all-entertainment approach of independent broadcasters. Ranges of the same breadth exist within most media categories. Few daily newspapers can do more than pretend to compete with *The New York Times* in national news content. Many dailies' national news content readily can be contained in a few columns as opposed to dozens of pages.

Audience Factors. Is the television network, then, a better channel of communication than the *Times?* Audience size, unfortunately, is no better indicator of efficiency or effectiveness than volume of informational content. The relative value potential of individual media as communication channels can be estimated only in the context of specific communication problems and the groups or stakeholders involved. The variables with which communicators must deal, in other words, are three: media audiences, media content, and communication objectives. Successful efforts convey the bulk of communicators' messages to most members of specified stakeholder groups.

Returning to the network versus *New York Times* analytical framework addressed earlier, television news would be a superior medium in dealing with a consumer product recall resulting from tampering or other health hazards. Newscasts would rapidly bring messages to the attention of more members of the target group. Information intended to influence decision makers in a national debate over toxic waste or acid rain, however, would be better placed in the *Times*, which probably numbers more "influentials" among its readership than any other newspaper. Influentials constitute minute percentages of television audiences, even in cities such as New York and Washington, D.C.

Messages and Credibility

The *Times* is a superior communication medium, however, for yet another reason that can be expressed in one word: credibility.

Credibility is essential to successful communication. Communication succeeds, in fact, in keeping with the credibility of sources and media. A *Times* report identifying an authoritative source probably would rank 9.99 on a 10-point credibility scale.   Variation in credibility is a concern to communicators regardless of the media groups with which they deal, especially in light of intergenerational differences in information-gathering patterns. Print media tend to be perceived as more authoritative among older groups in part because the latter grew up during what might be called the golden age of newspapers and mass circulation magazines. Group members are predisposed to rely on such media as information sources. As communicators move downward on the audience age scale, electronic media tend to grow in use and credibility.

A sort of synergy among audiences, media, and messages also tends to exert a strong influence over media credibility. Credibility is greatest where audience members are predisposed toward the type of medium involved and the message is suitable to the medium. Given the demographic characteristics of the audience, unusually high numbers of *New York Times* readers, for example, probably are coin collectors. The newspaper regularly publishes a column on numismatics, as the field is called, but numismatists and hobbyists alike are far more influenced by what they read in *Coin World*, the leading specialty publication in the field.

Source credibility, the factor at work in the above example, has been demonstrated to be one of the strongest contributors to message strength. Much of the research supporting this point has dealt with individuals rather than mass media, but the principle applies to communication channels. Credibility varies within and across media groups. Some newspapers and magazines are perceived as more credible than others, just as some television commentators are granted greater credibility by their viewers.

Message content also relates to source credibility, but in a manner too easily neglected by communicators. Media considered most expert in given subjects lend greater credibility to content information in those areas than to other information. Credibility is compounded where message content and media reputations coincide, and potential for salutary results presumably improves as well.

Consider, for example, three of the nation's leading, and competing, newspapers: *The New York Times*, *The Wall Street Journal*, and the *Christian Science Monitor*. The *Times* is an acknowledged leader in reporting on socioeconomic trends. The *Journal* is recognized as the nation's leading business newspapers, while the *Monitor* is generally considered preeminent in reporting foreign affairs. Message credibility therefore varies by subject matter within these publications. Some of the information communicators seek to convey may be of almost uniform media appeal, but potential productivity of messages varies among media.

Appropriateness of media to messages, moreover, involves more than credibility. Where communicators design messages and select media carefully, messages also are most attractive to gatekeepers, and to audiences those gatekeepers are attempting to attract and retain.

These concepts are not new. The principles involved are increasing in importance, however, as media proliferate and audiences fragment. With mass medium increasingly a contradiction in terms, communicators find it progressively more important to select media with extreme precision.

OLD, NEW, AND RENEWED MEDIA

Communicators' efforts toward precision are not always successful. Failure, in whole or in part, can result from any number of factors. One of them, however, has become increasingly troublesome. With intensifying audience fragmentation has come a marked tendency among communicators and their employers or clients toward anything that is new, different, or "high tech."

None of these factors create any assurance of success. Too often, in fact, the reverse may be true. Abandoning tried and true communication techniques for the superficially appealing can be disastrous, especially where those involved may be unaware of the nature of the media involved. The latter circumstances often occur because of a growing level of confusion created by labeling. Labeling is a process through which negative factors are concealed with attractive labels, as was the case in sea food markets until government regulators stepped in to protect an overly credible public.

Confusion in the mass media world arises over several factors. Mass media functions are more complex than they appear, especially where the terms new technologies and new media are applicable. Difficulties develop as often through misuse of words, however, as through complexity in communication processes or terminology. These circumstances suggest a preliminary sorting-out process on the part of those who would understand contemporary conditions and potential future developments.

Within each of the primary media groups, the sorting out must address at least three areas of potential confusion. First, there is the matter of new technologies and new media. The terms are not interchangeable despite contemporary tendencies in that direction. Second, there is the word *new* in and of itself; it has too long been used with misleading abandon in the context of mass communication. Finally, there is the terminology of mass communication, which has also been applied with less than optimal precision.

Media Groups

The media with which communicators are involved can readily be sorted into three categories: new, not-so-new, and traditional. The new, which will be discussed in detail in a later chapter, are so new as to require little attention here. Media in this category all are interactive. They include computer-based communication systems as well as teletext, videotext, and conferencing systems. The not-so-new media are another matter. These are innovative devices often based on established technologies that contribute to burgeoning numbers of messages individuals are called upon to sort through every day. Finally, there are the old or established or traditional media that are struggling to maintain their audiences in the face of increasing competition for individual attention.

Technologies Versus Media

The terms *new technologies* and *new media* have been overused and generally misunderstood in much of the world of communication. New technologies and new media are not the same. New technologies may enhance the value of existing media and stimulate the development of new media. In and of themselves, and regardless of their value, technologies are merely technologies, bodies of knowledge and skill that enhance the capabilities of mass media only to the extent that they are productively applied.

The microprocessor, to illustrate, is a product of semiconductor technology—in relative terms, a new technology. In and of themselves, neither the semiconductor nor the microprocessor has made a direct contribution to mass communication or the mass media. Without the microprocessor, however, few media would exist in the forms in which they exist today. The microprocessor put computers within reach of individuals as well as businesses. The microprocessor made today's satellite transmission systems possible. The microprocessor is at the heart of today's media and tomorrow's. But the microprocessor, while relatively new, is not a communication medium—mass or otherwise.

Old and New

Confusion over "new" media is at least as pervasive as the tendency to confuse new media with new technologies. Many apparently new media involve nothing more than new applications of existing technologies. Others involve innovative use of long-established, nontechnical devices. Regardless of label, each becomes a new channel of communication compounding professionals' media selection problems. Every surviving medium attracts an audience and advertisers sufficient to meet operating costs, presumably at the expense of preexisting media.

Continuing change among traditional mass media complicate efforts to sort out developments in the field. The sorting out process is necessary, however, to understand contemporary developments and future media potential. Change among traditional media is a logical point of beginning because, pragmatically, there are no old media. Long-established print and broadcast media have not stagnated over the past several decades. All have been early adopters of new technologies. Adoption rates have varied within and across media categories, however, and in some cases have produced substantial change in adopting organizations.

Public perceptions of new media encompass a host of devices and techniques that are neither new nor media. Electronic equipment is especially susceptible to the new media label, although the term is applied with equal abandon elsewhere.

In the equipment sector, electronic mail systems, cellular telephones, phone mail, facsimile machines, and a host of other devices of relatively recent vintage often are labeled "new" media. While used to a greater or lesser extent as communication channels, these contrivances are not new media. At best, they are artifacts of interpersonal communication.

A host of innovative advertising techniques also have been erroneously referred to over the years as new media. They range from miniature billboards in restroom stalls to low power radio stations operating in tunnels impervious to conventional radio signals. While perhaps qualifying for the mass media label, devices such as these are not new. Although perceived as young by many, cable television is a new medium only to recent subscribers. Other than in rare circumstances, this newest generally available mass medium also lacks the single essential characteristic found in all new media: interactivity.

The new media are interactive media. Cable systems can be made interactive, but few have been designed to function in this manner. In addition, and perhaps more important, the few interactive systems to date have been economic failures. Interactive systems catering to general audiences have been abandoned or operationally curtailed in Dade County, Florida and Columbus, Ohio and computer-based in-home banking systems elsewhere have attracted too few customers to achieve economic success.

What of the "old" media? They only appear to be old. Publishers, broadcasters, and their products superficially have changed little in recent years. Products especially appear to be no different from those of several decades ago, but appearances are misleading. Few organizations that produce today's news resemble the news organizations that existed at midcentury. Production processes have undergone radical change, as have organizational personnel structures.

In publishing, hot-metal production processes have been replaced by lithography. Computers have supplanted typewriters in newsrooms and in composition processes. The same changes have occurred in magazine production and threaten to revolutionize book publishing. Content orientation in the print media has been subjected to change of comparable magnitude. Traditional metropolitan newspapers in part have been supplanted by "national" newspapers and in part have reoriented their own content to specialize in local news. General interest magazines largely have been replaced by publications oriented to narrow interest groups.

Broadcasting has experienced similar changes. Satellite delivery systems have revolutionized broadcast news operations among once-dominant networks and at local stations. The same systems enabled television entrepreneur Ted Turner to launch the Cable News Network — two channels that broadcast news in digested and extended form 24 hours a day, 365 days a year.

New Media

Extensive use of new technologies does not, however, make new media of old. *New* today implies interaction between media and users. Interactivity is a characteristic of an emerging generation of communication channels that are expected to grow rapidly through the early years of the twenty-first century. Some interactive systems, especially those involving computer technology, already are in place and are attracting increasing patronage among "techies" and early adopters. Others remain to become available to many if not most prospective users.

Interactive as well as other media are most readily understood by those prepared to differentiate between and among terms common in mass communication: *medium*, *message*, and *content*. The words are simple. Their meanings are somewhat more complex.

Medium. A medium in mass communication is a channel through which messages can be transmitted to specific groups. The word can be applied, however, in ways that can be confusing, especially in view of the fact that the plural is *media* rather than *mediums*.

As discussed earlier, television is a mass medium. Individual networks and stations also are popularly if imprecisely referred to as mass media, and the same principal applies in other communication industries. Radio is a medium, and so are radio networks and stations. Magazines are a medium, and so are individual publications.

Message and content. The word *message*, although apparently simple, is more complex. Broadcasts, articles, commercials, and advertisements often are inaccurately characterized as messages. Each of these elements is a container rather than a message. Messages consist of information contained in broadcasts or articles, advertisements or news releases.

These concepts are crucial in advertising, public relations, sales promotion, and marketing, where results are measured in behavioral response rather than in messages delivered. The very word *delivered*, in fact, is open to question. Is the message delivered when the morning newspaper arrives, when it is retrieved from the front porch, when it is read, when the article or advertisement is seen and comprehended, or when the message is acted upon?

Not-So-New Media

Message delivery is the primary variable involved in what might be described as not-so-new media. Even in this area, however, one finds no little change in progress. Advertising especially is more and more pervasive, appearing even in places where it is not perceived as advertising. The work of public relations and sales promotion professionals is equally ubiquitous.

Each member of each of these groups is fighting for audience attention in the midst of an increasingly competitive media marketplace. As the old and not-so-new media are joined by the new, the competition will become fiercer still.

Perhaps most important, development of new technologies and new mass media cannot be safely presumed to be over or ending. The advent of artificial intelligence, although less than a metatechnology, will produce radical change in the manner in which knowledge and information are accumulated and disseminated in information societies.

IN SUMMARY

Working knowledge of the nature of mass communication, the principles of media economics, and the evolution of communication systems will be essential to communicators in the age of information. The principles underlying these concepts and the terminology that attaches to the subjects involved are critical to communication success.

The meanings of *mass communication* and *mass media*, for example, are open to interpretation. While the meaning of *communication* is relatively well established, *media* can encompass a number of new and not-so-new media as well as those traditionally labeled mass media. The word *mass* is another matter. While categories of media such as television and radio may indeed be mass media, networks and individual stations may be another matter. At issue here is the definition of *mass*: How large a group constitutes a mass?

Mass communication messages differ from interpersonal messages in that they are transient, public, and rapidly transmitted. Mass media audiences traditionally have been characterized as large, anonymous, and heterogeneous, while interpersonal audiences tend to be smaller, known, and interest oriented.

Audience size in mass communication remains large. Anonymity persists, although some may be lost as the new, interactive media become more prevalent. Heterogeneity, however, already has been reduced and continues to deteriorate as more and more media become oriented to specialized audiences.

The tendency toward media specialization is a creature of media economics. Mass media organizations survive or expire on the basis of their ability to attract audiences that can be profitably rented to advertisers. Any audience with potential for commercial value thus is fair game for a media entrepreneur. All use entertainment and information, alone or in combination, to attract audiences. Audience quality rather than quantity governs media ability to command large profits through advertising. Quality is a function of media credibility as well as the nature of the audience. Audience size tends to be a secondary concern other than as a percentage of the advertiser's targeted market.

In a sense, almost all media are new media. Long-existing media have been radically changed in recent years through the application of new technologies. Media content also has changed in keeping with competitive and other factors. The term *new media* is applied accurately only to the emerging interactive media although a number of "not-so-new" media also exist. The latter category consists primarily of innovative applications of preexisting communication techniques to enhance message delivery.

ADDITIONAL READING

Howitt, Dennis. *The Mass Media and Social Problems*. 4th ed. New York: Pergamon, 1986.

Jamieson, Kathleen H., and Karlyn K. Campbell. *The Interplay of Influence: Mass Media and Their Publics in News, Advertising, Politics*. 2nd ed. New York: Wadsworth, 1988.

Selnow, Gary W., and William D. Crano. *Planning, Implementing and Evaluating Targeted Communication Programs: A Manual for Business Communicators*. New York: Quorum, 1987.

4 New Audiences

Audiences that communicators seek to influence today bear little resemblance to those of yesterday. Differences of similar or greater magnitude will develop between today's audiences and tomorrow's. Demographically, by lifestyle, and in terms of need and desire for information, audiences are continually changing. Variables at work in each of these categories directly or indirectly influence the productivity of the communication process. As such, they demand continuing attention of every communicator.

Demographic data describe distributions of populations by age, geography, educational level, economic status, and so on. Today's U.S. population is older and better educated than ever before. The center of population gravity is moving from north and east to south and west. The nation's middle class is in numerical decline, while the poor and rich increase in number.

Psychographic data describe populations' thought patterns; their predispositions to respond or react to stimuli in one way or another. In the United States, the population has become progressively less trusting and more skeptical. Relative consistency of thought on major social issues has been supplanted by special interest orientations. Institutions and organizations once accepted as good by definition are viewed with suspicion or distrust. Where most individuals once were concerned primarily with the welfare of the nation, narrower issues such as conservation, birth control or animal rights often dominate their thinking now.

Lifestyle refers to behavioral patterns as defined by the nonoccupational activities with which individuals occupy their time. Cultural, recreational, and avocational activities all are among what might be called lifestyle behaviors. The word *lifestyle* and an underlying valuative system emerged from the work of the late Arnold Mitchell and his colleagues at the Stanford Research Institute, now SRI International. Results of their efforts were published in 1983 in a seminal work titled *The Nine American Lifestyles: Where We Are and Where We Are Going* (New York: Macmillan). The values and lifestyles (VALS) research of the Mitchell team spawned a mini-industry that develops and sells demographic and lifestyle information to marketers, advertisers, and others.

CHANGING PATTERNS

Communicator need for lifestyle and other information about audiences has been growing at an unprecedented rate for two reasons. First, media have been multiplying in number and type. Second, content of many newer media is oriented to consumer lifestyles and to informational interests arising out of those lifestyles. Changes in lifestyles and among the media have been accompanied by change in patterns of information acquisition among individuals and across groups. Sensitivity and response to such changes is vital to those who would communicate effectively and productively with special interest groups.

Responses must be oriented to media of choice in an era characterized by continuing change among information users' media selection patterns. Newspapers once were the nation's primary source of information. They have been supplanted or supplemented by television, magazines, and a host of new media, many catering to the specific interests of population subgroups. Typical consumers select from some two dozen television channels and perhaps half that number of radio stations. Almost 12,000 magazines are published in the United States, and their number is increasing at a rate of 300 to 350 annually. While metropolitan daily newspapers have declined in number and readership, national, suburban, and specialized newspapers are multiplying. Catalogs and other direct mail advertising, billboards and bus signs, and point-of-purchase messages add to the din created by message senders clamoring for attention. Increasing numbers of communicators are using proliferating media to send an ever-growing flow of messages to recipients whose information absorption capacity is substantially unchanged.

All terms used here are applied in their broadest senses. *Communicator*, for example, refers to members of every discipline involved; to those in sales promotion and marketing as well as in advertising, public relations, and organizational communication. *Communication* refers to that process in its entirety and in all of its forms, to the synthesis, delivery, receipt, and assimilation of messages as well as recipient response; to interpersonal, behavioral, and environmental as well as mediated communication. *Demographics*, *psychographics*, and *informational needs*, are used here in similar breadth. In each case, the words refer to all factors pertinent to or influencing communication processes.

The collective influence of these factors in the communication process cannot be overestimated. Demographics, psychographics and the information acquisition patterns they produce govern levels of success communicators achieve in any given circumstances. Success requires eliciting predetermined responses from selected audiences by transmitting given messages through specified channels. Those who employ communicators will accept nothing less. These conditions require that communicators become demographers and psychographics, that they master the arts of audience and media analysis or otherwise gain sufficient insight to meet performance specifications.

DEMOGRAPHIC PATTERNS

Experienced communicators acquire, by the nature of their work, a feel for or insight into the demographic characteristics of the groups with which they attempt to communicate. Instinctive or intuitive approaches to communication based on these insights served communicators well in a simpler world. The efficacy of professional instinct and intuition deteriorated, however, with increasing demographic and social complexity. From the 1970s forward, as the "integrated grid", started taking shape, communicators became increasingly dependent on hard data—quantitative and qualitative analyses of audiences as well as media.

The most dependable basic information about populations and population subgroups is found in the mass of data gathered primarily at ten-year intervals by the Bureau of the Census. The bureau, a component of the U.S. Department of Commerce, makes basic information available in printed or electronic form for every postal zone in the nation. Included in the basic data is information concerning the primary variables with which communicators are concerned: age, educational level, income level, household composition, and occupational type.

Age Factors

Age is perhaps the strongest determinant of interests and behavioral patterns. Individual responses to messages or other stimuli are governed by personal perspectives. Individuals' views of the world are shaped by their experiences and circumstances. Experiences and circumstances, in turn, are more directly governed by age than by any other factor. Educational and income levels, factors often combined in the term *social class*, play lesser roles, as will be discussed later. Age is the primary determinant of information need and becomes especially important where populations are less than evenly distributed across age categories.

The latter circumstances now prevail—and will continue to prevail for several decades—in the United States. The nation has been through a "boom-bust", birthrate cycle now reflected in the population's age distribution. The boom-bust cycle, in fact, is producing what has been called "the greying of America,", now occurring as the post-World War II baby-boom generation approaches retirement age.

The Baby Bust. The same cycle also produced a baby bust generation now starting to enter the work force. The result is a growing shortage of entry-level workers that will continue through the remainder of this century and the early years of the next. First evidence of resulting problems developed during the mid-1980s when a shortage of teenaged babysitters developed in affluent sections of the nation. By the end of the decade, worker shortages had reached near-crisis proportions in the fast food industry. Organizations that hire large numbers of graduating seniors on the nation's campuses were feeling the pinch as well. No relief is in sight for employers before the turn of the century, when a small baby-boom "echo,", detected in the primary grades in the 1980s, will start entering the labor force.

The intervening years will be traumatic for individuals and organizations alike. Individuals—depending primarily on their ages—will gain or lose through variation in the size of the labor force. The gains and losses, however, will not be one-sided.

Labor Markets. The baby bust, for example, inevitably will produce a seller's market in labor. Jobs will be chasing workers where workers once chased jobs. Labor intensive organizations will find worker recruiting and retention to be their most pressing problem. Wages and benefits will improve as a result. Working conditions or perquisites will improve even more. The improvements involved, however, will not come without a price.

As the entry level labor force declines in numbers, retirees will be increasing numerically. The same age distribution that creates unprecedented job opportunities will also strain the nation's Social Security system. The trend producing the strain, moreover, will place unprecedented political power in the hands of the elderly, discouraging any effort to reduce benefits. The result could be intergenerational economic and/or political conflict of substantial proportions.

Educational Levels

Change in population educational levels can be expected to produce similar but less stressful social consequences. The United States is becoming a better educated society at an accelerating rate. Between 1978 and 1988, for example, those with baccalaureate degrees increased by 10 percent. Almost 30 percent of the national population has been graduated from a four-year college or university. At the close of World War II, in comparison, fewer than 5 percent had achieved this educational level.

The trend toward more education is continuing, Bureau of the Census data indicate, but in a different manner from what earlier was the case. Enrollments in baccalaureate degree programs have remained relatively constant in recent years. Change has occurred in at least one and possibly two areas. Graduate school enrollments are moving sharply upward, and undergraduate enrollments early appeared to be holding their own despite the impact of the baby bust on postsecondary education.

Reasons for Growth. Most academicians attribute the increase in graduate school enrollment to two factors. The first is increasing competition among baccalaureate degree holders for declining numbers of supervisory and managerial positions. Commercial and industrial downsizing during the 1970s and 1980s reduced numbers of positions open to younger baby boomers. Graduate degrees, in these circumstances, create competitive advantage.

The second factor driving graduate school enrollments higher is the declining durability of knowledge. Some in education, using a term taken from nuclear physics, estimate the half life of knowledge at five years and suggest that traditional degree systems be replaced by a process appropriately called lifelong learning.

Application of the half-life concept to knowledge rather than to radioactive materials may be open to question. There is no doubt, however, that bodies of knowledge in every academic discipline are growing at exponential rates. Since most of the research scientists who ever lived are alive and working today, that pattern will continue.

Differences in Graduates. Growth in knowledge will continue to drive graduate school enrollments, and increases in graduate education will produce change in populations with which communicators are concerned. The primary change is small but significant. Where too many undergraduate educational programs are designed to pour knowledge into students' heads, master's level curricula are another matter. Rather than the "read and regurgitate", approach to learning, graduate programs are designed to induce skepticism and challenge. Students are required to synthesize information, reach their own conclusions, and support those conclusions through secondary or primary research.

Most who hold master's degrees for these reasons differ from those who have completed only undergraduate programs. More important from the communicator's perspective, differences in educational backgrounds induce different reactions to messages. Those who have completed master's theses, for example, are more prone to critically examine data presented—or not presented—in support of advertising claims. Graduate education thus contributes to skepticism of media and mediated messages.

Income Levels

Generally optimistic media reports concerning income levels in the United States during the late 1980s concealed several discouraging trends. First, most data were expressed as household rather than individual incomes. While the former improved to some extent, the latter were deteriorating. Second, the data often were given in arithmetic means and concealed a growing maldistribution of income across population subgroups.

Less obvious but also discouraging from the wage earner viewpoint was a trend toward simplified, bare-bones organizational structures. Economic conditions in the late 1970s and early 1980s produced massive restructuring in many commercial and industrial organizations. Entire echelons of management were stripped away to create "lean and mean", organizations. While more profitable, lean organizations involve shorter management ladders offering fewer opportunities for individual economic progress.

The resulting reduction in potential for upward mobility among wage earners will add to worker frustration through the remainder of the century. Census data suggest career ladders will become unclogged only as frustrated baby boomers retire, abandoning upper and middle rungs to the baby bust generation.

Concealed Distress. Clogged career ladders over time may be least significant among the factors specified above. The trend toward multiple wage earner families is most disturbing. Several significant elements are involved. Perhaps most important in the context of other societal trends is an inevitable decline in parenting time that can only contribute to juvenile problems. Time dedicated to children is reduced in almost direct proportion to increases in income producing effort.

Another element may be equally threatening over the longer term. Relatively high household income levels produced through the combined efforts of multiple wage earners conceals family economic problems from those who deal with social statistics. Household income is a primary indicator of family economic health. Data involved can be misleading, however, where considered without regard to numbers of wage earners involved. Potential for variation in wage earner numbers also should signal caution over any tendency to equate economic health to psychological health. Multiple incomes help families cope with declines in earning power among heads of households. The additional income is produced, however, only at a nonmonetary price most often paid in increased stress.

Income Distribution. Efforts to generalize concerning income levels are equally risky. Incomes in general have been rising. Americans were earning more during the late 1980s than earlier was the case. Closer examination showed, however, that arithmetic means concealed disturbing changes in income distribution patterns.

Data published by the Bureau of the Census in 1988 showed incomes had moved upward only among the upper 20 percent of the population in earnings. There were more wealthy individuals in the country than ever before, the data showed. There also were more impoverished people, while the middle class was declining in numbers. Income flows were shifting to benefit the wealthy at the expense of the poor and the middle class. The results in part were seen in a marked increase in homelessness, especially among the working poor. While members of the political establishment argued through the late 1980s over whether the problem was real or perceived, more and more families appeared to be joining the homeless—and hopeless—population.

Increases in homelessness may appear to be of little business consequence to communicators. The homeless are not consumers in a marketing sense. They exercise little direct influence over organizations or their stakeholders. Superficially, the homeless appear deserving of little professional attention from communicators.

Assumptions developed along the lines defined above are dangerous, however, in an era characterized by continuing governmental efforts toward "cost shifting.", Faced with developing social problems, governments often respond by calling on corporations for "greater social responsibility.", The term threatens to become a code word signaling governmental unwillingness to assume responsibility. What appears to be primarily a social problem and secondarily a governmental problem comes home to roost, as a result, on the doorsteps of nongovernmental organizations.

Other elements promising problems for organizations include burgeoning numbers of rights groups throughout the nation and the world, mounting worker demand for more control over the work place, and the emergence of new values among workers. The origins of the special interest groups can be traced to the political and social activism of earlier years. Racial minorities in the 1960s, women in the 1970s, and homosexuals in the 1980s have established precedents now followed by those advocating animal rights, parental rights, fetal rights, and any number of other causes.

Composition of Households

Unlike declining income levels, neither the cost shifting efforts of government nor the ongoing battles of special interest groups and their adversaries can be characterized as good or bad. These trends instead are symptomatic of social soul searching that apparently will continue into the twenty-first century. The primary issues are simply stated: What are society's obligations to citizens? How shall these obligations be met? Who will pay?

A set of secondary questions, less pressing but equally disturbing and pervasive, also call for attention: What should be society's definition of the word family? What should be society's obligation to the family? Perhaps most vocally expressed of late, what should be the obligations of individual family members to society and each other?

An Era of Change. Continuing change in composition of households complicates the questions and intensifies the need for early response. Economic and social stresses have produced radical change in the social fabric over the past several decades. The so-called nuclear family—breadwinner, spouse and offspring—no longer predominates in the United States. Single parent households are more common. "Significant others", supplant spouses with increasing frequency.

Development of these conditions has been accompanied by an increasing public preoccupation with family-related problems of all kinds. The rights of parents and children, from conception to burial, are debated in the media and in the courts. Debate persists over artificial insemination, surrogate parenting, parental leave, and a host of related topics.

Organizational Concerns. Some of the issues superficially appear more individual than organizational in their orientation. Pragmatically, these issues defy neat compartmentalization. If children's rights are radically redefined, what might redefinition imply as to their legal interests in parental assets? Some courts already have ruled that worker interests in pension or profit sharing funds, for example, are open to adjudication.

Perhaps more potentially troublesome, can requirements organizations establish for workers be interpreted as influencing workers' behaviors as parents? In other words, can an employer's requirement that a parent travel extensively be deemed to have contributed to parental failure to meet obligations to offspring?

Such questions today may appear farfetched. Tomorrow may be another matter. Those who doubt need only consider the extent to which courts have become involved in other matters once considered beyond their purview. Rights of all kinds continue to be re-examined and redefined. Each redefinition exacts a price, and organizations almost inevitably are among the payers rather than the payees. Redefinition invariably influences one or more and perhaps all of every organization's stakeholder groups. Organizations and their communicators neglect these facts at their peril.

Occupational Types

Like the several factors considered above, individuals' occupations are contributors to rather than establishers of demographic profiles. Demographic profiles are defined by sets of interrelated characteristics. Statistically, the word *correlation* is applicable here. Correlation refers to the extent to which individual characteristics tend to coexist. Causality is not assumed to be present. Relationships instead are said to exist between, for example, income level and occupation.

Similar relationships exist between education and income levels, between education and social status, and between income and occupation, to name but a few. Differences arise, however, where occupational typologies are addressed. Occupational identification, to a greater extent than almost any other demographic factor, is an indicator of psychographic predispositions.

Higher education equips students for occupational settings and, in the process, creates the attitudes, predispositions or mental sets they carry with them through their lives. Occupational categories also relate to income levels, neighborhoods, and the life styles individuals tend to follow. Each factor is related to the others, although the linkages involved are not cause and effect relationships. Most members of the leading professions, for example, become relatively affluent and economically conservative. Many if not most are politically conservative as well. The majority live in relatively expensive homes in more prestigious sections of their communities.

Professional Predispositions. As members of occupational groups, individuals tend to behave in predictable ways. They are psychologically predisposed, by education and training, toward specific behaviors. In the course of their educations, they adopt the mores and folkways of the groups they plan to join and, subsequently, behave accordingly. Among what normally are accepted as demographic characteristics, occupation is most strongly predisposing from a psychological standpoint, especially where professionals are involved.

Occupational predispositions are strongest in the professions. Consciously or unconsciously, to a greater or lesser extent, professions use education as an indoctrination process, as a rite of passage into the professional world. Members of any profession, or any academic discipline, for these reasons tend to think and behave in similar ways. Mentalities or mental sets popularly ascribed to physicians, attorneys, or accountants are not purely caricatures. Members of the professions are predisposed by training to think and behave in specific ways.

Physicians, for example, deal with death and dying on a daily basis. Psychologically, they must maintain an emotional detachment from patients to preserve their own mental health. This detachment often is perceived by nonphysicians as a "God complex," yet is no different from the predisposition of psychologists to microscopically examine every behavior for evidence of underlying motivation.

A hidden alchemy in architectural education, in similar fashion, renders all who complete the process de facto experts in all matters aesthetic. It makes no difference whether a painting, an example of typography, or an article of furniture is involved; most architects consider themselves qualified critics if not recognized authorities.

Affinity Groups. Characteristics such as these result in something less than universal admiration for members of most professions. Many members of the communication disciplines have experienced difficulties, for example, in dealing with members of the healing arts and the design professions. The difficulties are not significant here. It is important, however, that communicators understand the underlying phenomena. They prevail, to a greater or lesser extent, in virtually every membership or affinity group.

The latter term, used to describe relationships weaker than membership, is most often used in the financial sector, where insurance policies and credit cards can be made available to group members. Holders of a particular bank's credit cards or an insurance company's policies, for example, constitute affinity groups and can be made eligible for other products or services on this basis. Among financial institutions, affinity groups may be presumed to be in some ways superior to those randomly constituted. Group characteristics are seen as engendering behaviors making members more responsible than the population as a whole and, therefore, better financial risks. Affinity in this manner is expected to produce greater uniformity in behavioral patterns than otherwise would exist. The results, if not the causes, are more readily categorized as psychographic than demographic in nature.

Psychographic Factors. Psychographic patterns in the communication disciplines are similar to economic patterns in business. Considerable substance supports both sets of concepts. Efforts to link substance to day-to-day problems is no easier in communication, however, than in economics.

While demographics involve such finite descriptors as age, sex, and occupation, psychographics deal with individual and audience psychological profiles and behaviors expected to arise out of those profiles. Use of psychographic analyses of audiences in communication has been overshadowed, however, by the rapid development of lifestyles research.

Values and Lifestyles

What we know today as lifestyle data originated with research launched in the late 1970s by Arnold Mitchell and Marie Spengler at SRI International's predecessor organization, the Stanford Research Institute. The Stanford Values and Lifestyles project, dubbed VALS, was funded by more than seventy corporate sponsors with more than $2 million.

The driving force behind the VALS project was Mitchell's thesis that individual values and lifestyles were central to personal development, civic action, and consumer behavior on the part of individuals. By understanding values and lifestyles, he hypothesized, one could explain how and why societies change and why people act and consume in predetermined patterns.

Mitchell may or may not have conceived of the extent to which his values and lifestyles concept would influence mass communication in the United States. Coupled with computers, Mitchell's concepts have created a mini-industry dedicated to providing values and lifestyle data to marketers, advertisers, public relations practitioners, and any others who may be interested in consumer behavior.

Basic Concepts

The VALS concept focused on and revolved around Mitchell's concept that " we are what we believe, what we dream and what we value. For the most part we try to mold our lives to make our beliefs and dreams come true.",

If values are our primary motivators and lifestyles are the embodiment of beliefs and dreams, Mitchell theorized, then by understanding the ways in which these elements are formed and acted upon we can understand human behavior. Beginning with these premises, he and his colleagues set out to create a comprehensive typology of lifestyles, the VALS typology. Extensive research led them to postulate a set of four comprehensive groups subdivided into nine lifestyles, each with a distinctive set of values, drives, beliefs, needs, and viewpoints:

Need-Driven Groups
  Survivor lifestyle
  Sustained lifestyle
Outer-Directed Groups
  Belonger lifestyle
  Emulator lifestyle
  Achiever lifestyle
Inner-Directed Groups
  I-Am-Me lifestyle
  Experiential lifestyle
  Societally Conscious lifestyle
Combined Outer- and Inner-Directed Group
  Integrated lifestyle

To these lifestyles, the VALS approach attached a typology of human attributes and qualities ranging from psychological immaturity to full psychological maturity, each amenable to identification with a specific lifestyle. Presented as a pattern of growth, the typology suggests that individuals change as they progress through nine developmental stages. Their central concerns at each stage are as follows:

Stage 1. Survival—just to make it from day to day is enough.
Stage 2. Sustaining and solidifying gains made from the survivor stage and, if possible, extending them.
Stage 3. Belonging, being accepted by others, fitting into a closed, sharply defined, social network.
Stage 4. Breaking free of the local network to make it as an individual within the major system, emulating leaders of the system.
Stage 5. Achievement, success, leadership, and power in the major system.
Stage 6. Breaking free of outer-directed patterns and discovering the inner self.
Stage 7. Living intensely, vividly, and experientially so as to widen and deepen the inner experience.
Stage 8. Focusing on societal issues, especially those affecting the less material qualities of life.

Stage 9. Melding outer and inner perspectives so as to combine
the best of the two into higher-order views.

Mitchell and his colleagues envisioned alternative developmental
paths for individuals in a sort of double hierarchy. Individuals can
arrive at the integrated level through outer-directed or inner-
directed courses, they postulate, by moving from belonger through
(a) emulator and achiever or (b) I-am-me, experiential, and socially-
conscious.

The Mitchell team's concepts were drawn in part from an
understanding of human behavior, in part from developmental
psychology, and in part from arrays of demographic features. The
latter element is critical from communicators' viewpoints in that
it renders the resulting system amenable to examination in the
context of demographic data.

Value-Added Products

Concepts developed at the Stanford Research Institute have been
refined and strengthened at SRI International, which has become
a leading supplier of VALS and other information to marketers and
other communicators. SRI today, however, is but one of many
organizations dedicated to enhancing communicator ability to
successfully convey information, to achieve measurable results.

Collectively, these organizations are but one small part of a
burgeoning information industry. They are noteworthy here for
their ability to provide data valuable to communicators and because
that data is not uniformly valuable. Vendors' products vary in
content and application, and communicators must recognize the
differences involved.

In general terms, information vendors to the communication
industry fall into one of two categories. The first consists of SRI
and that organization's emulators. Lifestyle information is their
primary product. Others offer a broad range of kindred products.
They range from syntheses of census and economic data to mapping
services and include several based on preexisting bodies of information or knowledge.

Lifestyle Products. Among SRI's strongest challengers in the
lifestyle sector is Claritas, an organization that has become known
for its PRIZM system and for the colorful names it has attached to
lifestyle groups. PRIZM, or Potential Rating Index by ZIP Markets,
examines the more than 35,000 ZIP zones in the United States in

forty regional clusters. Some one thousand characteristics are examined on the premise that homogeneous neighborhoods form because individuals are attracted by those of like socioeconomic status. Claritas descriptors for neighborhoods include such labels as "Money and Brains," "Shotguns and Pickups," " Bunker's Neighbors", and "Blueblood Estates."

Other organizations may use more or less colorful descriptors, extended or compacted topologies, or otherwise vary from the SRI or Claritas approaches. CACI Market Analysis' ACORN system, for example, divides the nation into 260,000 neighborhoods through analyses of forty-nine socioeconomic and life-style characteristics. Resulting data may or may not be significantly more beneficial than those of the firm's competitors. Comparative evaluations can be made only in the context of individual circumstances.

Other Products. Some informational services, however, offer readily identifiable advantages in terms of format or content. Format here refers to the manner in which information is conveyed to users. Once delivered primarily in written or printed reports, demographic and life-style information today can be obtained in electronic form as well.

One of the leading innovators in formatting has been National Decision Systems of Encinatas, California, which pioneered in making data available for use with the most sophisticated computer technologies. Others, including a host of software vendors offering products designed to turn raw data into graphic form, were not far behind.

Content pioneers have included innovators and adapters. Innovators such as Woods and Poole Economics of Washington, D.C., blended demographic and economic data to enable users to better forecast commercial and industrial trends. Adapters such as Arbitron, a firm best known for its television program ratings, created ScanAmerica, a system that lets users evaluate television programs based on their ability to deliver specific audience segments.

Even the venerable Standard Rate and Data Service (SRDS) has come into the demographics/lifestyle market with "The Lifestyle Marketplanner,", a product of SRDS and National Demographics and Lifestyles (NDL) of Denver. The Marketplanner provides demographic information from the nation's top one hundred markets with data on fifty of the most popular lifestyle activities.

Data within the Marketplanner is presented in three parts. Section 1 consists of market profiles consisting of demographic and lifestyle activity analyses of adult populations. Section 2 presents lifestyle profiles based on the fifty activities and Section 3 offers segment profiles dealing with twenty-six demographically defined market subgroups.

INFORMATIONAL PATTERNS

SRDS and NDL offer little in the Marketplanner that provides insight into media usage patterns in the United States. That information is readily available, however, from a host of sources, including Standard Rate. SRDS publishes many directories that provide audience, cost, and mechanical data on the mass media for advertisers and others. A number of other directories commonly used in advertising, marketing and public relations provide similar information. So do several publishing and broadcasting industry directories.

The content of these publications provide exhaustive detail concerning consumer use of the mass media. As a group, the media today enjoy unprecedented economic support. Americans are buying more newspapers, magazines, and books, and are watching more television news programming, listening to more radio news, and obtaining more information through every other channel—new and old—than ever before in the history of the nation.

Two other factors cry out, however, for communicator attention. First, usage patterns are not consistent in communication industry groups. Growth rates vary radically across groups, and individual components of each group may be highly successful or terminally ill. Second, and more important, there is no evidence to support a hypothesis suggesting total time devoted to information gathering by residents of the United States is increasing. Contemporary proliferation among types of communication channels and their components instead implies that some must be losing rather than gaining in audience size.

Growth Rates
Newspaper circulation in the overall appears to be increasing. Gains are being experienced among business newspapers, national newspapers, and, to a lesser extent, suburban newspapers. Many

others are suffering. Every major component of the communication industry rightfully can claim increases in audience size. Even daily newspaper circulation is rising despite a continuing decline in numbers of metropolitan dailies. Losses involved are being more than offset by circulation increases among nationally circulated daily newspapers such as *The New York Times*, *The Wall Street Journal*, and *USA Today*.

A similar pattern appears among magazines. They are increasing in number at a rate of more than three hundred annually. Virtually all of the newcomers are highly specialized publications, however, with circulations to match. Few startups early acquire large readerships, and those in leadership positions often are in all-out wars against hordes of presumptuous competitors.

Patterns in electronic communication are much the same. Growth in radio and television appears to be doing little more than keep pace with the national population despite considerable change within these groups, especially in television. Cable systems and independent stations continue to erode network audiences.

Usage Patterns

Audience fragmentation, given the foregoing, probably was proceeding during the late 1980s at a relatively slow pace. Whether this would continue to be the case was another matter. Several then-anticipated events indicated that existing media could suddenly find their audience bases under serious attack once more.

First, the data base industry appeared poised for growth. Sears, Roebuck and Company and others were preparing to introduce Prodigy, an on-line system designed to convey information and advertising in a split screen format to computer users.

Second, the "Baby Bells,", as they are called, were preparing to initiate "gateway services", through which their customers could use telephone lines to gain access to information and other services. Were telephone companies to begin offering hardware—either microcomputers or "dumb terminals"—on rental bases, this market could experience runaway growth.

Third, the nation's cable television systems were on the brink of what might be termed a second generation revolution. The systems for the most part were installed a decade ago using copper wire, a material with a useful life of about ten years in that application. Replacement cost, especially where nondeteriorating fiber optic cable is used, will be considerable.

It is not inconceivable to speculate, for two reasons, that telephone companies could supplant cable systems, opening a new era in communication. First, the telephone companies already are in the process of replacing copper with fiber optic material. They can serve cable customers at little additional cost, thus gaining a tremendous economic advantage over nontelephone cable operators. Second, telephone companies have the "deep pockets", necessary to introduce computer terminals in the same manner that telephones once came into use in the United States—at extremely low rental rates.

There is every reason to believe, given all of the foregoing, that audience fragmentation will continue, at minimum, at prevailing rates. At best or worst, depending on one's viewpoint, fragmentation suddenly could accelerate to a rate beyond anything society has experienced.

IN SUMMARY

The most pervasive challenge facing communicators today is continuing change in audience demographic and psychographic characteristics. Demographic characteristics include factors such as age, educational and income levels, and geographic distribution. Psychographic characteristics are the cultural or lifestyle factors that influence the manner in which individuals behave.

Extent and rate of change in areas such as these has forced communicators to rely more and more on hard quantitative and qualitative data about audiences. The instinctive and intuitive analyses on which most communicators once depended have become progressively less reliable.

The most dependable basic data available to communicators is generated by the decennial population surveys of the United States undertaken by the U.S. Commerce Department's Bureau of the Census. Census data describe the ages and circumstances of individuals involved, characteristics which in turn shape their views of the world and create behavioral predispositions.

Age, educational and income levels, occupational categories and other factors that govern the nature of populations and their subgroups are available for the asking in Census Bureau reports. Also included is information concerning the composition of households and related factors that accurately reflect levels of social stress. Increases in single-parent and multiple wage earner households, for example, suggest increasingly stressful economic and social circumstances.

Educational levels, which have steadily increased in the United States, in like manner are indicators of the mind sets of individuals involved. Tendencies toward unquestioning credibility on the part of consumers, for example, decline as educational levels increase.

Information concerning audience values and life styles is equally enlightening. Most such data is based on or modeled after that first generated by Arnold Mitchell and his colleagues at the Stanford Research Institute, now SRI International. They postulated a set of four lifestyle groups subdivided into nine lifestyles, each with a distinctive set of values.

Sets of human attributes and qualities ranging from psychological immaturity to full maturity was attached to the lifestyles in what has come to be known as the VALS (values and life styles) typology. VALS data in recent years has been integrated with basic economic and other information by entrepreneurial organizations to create a diverse set of value added products for researchers in the communication disciplines.

Even the venerable Standard Rate and Data Service has become involved in delivering lifestyle data through a Marketplanner that provides insight into media usage patterns.

The Marketplanner, together with a directory of Hispanic media and other devices, is designed to help communicators cope with audience fragmentation problems in a progressively more diverse society. Diversity produces opportunities for media entrepreneurs, which in turn produce new communication channels, which in turn produce more audience fragmentation. The continuing process promises to become progressively more challenging through the remainder of the twentieth century.

ADDITIONAL READING

Murray, Alan, "American Consumers Fear It's Downhill From Here,", *The Wall Street Journal*, Centennial Edition, May 1989.

5 The New Technologies

Residents of the United States, awash with cellular telephones, facsimile machines, and microcomputers, tend to believe that the new technologies have arrived. Those that remain to be fully developed, according to popular mythology, are of the more exotic sort, those that will develop around or through superconductivity or genetic engineering.

The truth, as often is the case, bears little resemblance to popular opinion. Superconductivity and genetic engineering are indeed in their infancy, but so, too, are the new communication technologies. While the computer has produced radical change in communication, much of the promise of the new technologies, especially in the form of a true global network, remains to be realized.

The sort of interactive network or integrated grid envisioned by futurists, linking every building in every nation on earth, will be decades if not centuries in its development. Development already is in progress in the United States and around the world, however, on many technology-based communication channels. Most channels have been experimentally applied, but few residents of any nation have experienced the world of communication as it soon will exist.

Progress toward the global network will be slow. Postindustrial societies in North America, Europe, and Asia will move ahead rapidly, however, and the new communication technologies will be in place in the United States by the turn of the century. Among them, in addition to the ubiquitous microcomputer, will be teleconferencing, teletext, videotext, interactive cable system, and satellite communication systems. All exist in infant forms that will change radically in the ensuing twenty years. And all of them, as they mature, can be expected to bleed away a portion of the time information consumers spend with existing communication channels.

NEW COMMUNICATION TECHNOLOGIES

Differentiating between new and existing channels of communication is no easy task. Many seemingly new channels are nothing more than innovative applications of older devices, as in the case of minibillboards on grocery store shopping carts or advertising signs on parking meters. Still others involve entrepreneurial efforts to gain economic advantage by applying new technologies to existing bodies of information. The Dow Jones News Retrieval Service, a computer database, is representative of the latter group. Beyond the innovations and adaptations, however, are a set of truly new media.

The new channels of communication are most easily identified through one attribute. They occupy an area between the established mass media, which are without any element of interactivity, and face-to-face interpersonal communication, which affords total interactivity. The new media or communication channels provide for machine assisted interpersonal communication.

The new channels share a set of characteristics specified by Everett M. Rogers (see figure 5.1) and one other he failed to mention: all of them are information intensive. This characteristic is significant in terms of the potential of new media to supplant the old in the affection of information consumers. More important from the perspective of commercial communicators, variation in information intensiveness is important in evaluating the communication potential of the media involved.

Mass Media

Media or communication channels under discussion here—new and existing—are far from uniform in information content either within or across categories. Information, including advertising, and entertainment are blended to a greater or lesser extent in all media categories. While professional journalists might disagree, advertising is information from the consumer's viewpoint and often is among the more sought after components of the media content. The latter circumstance tends to be more prevalent among newspapers and

Figure 5.1. Main Characteristics of Interpersonal, Interactive and Mass Media Communication Channels. From Everett M. Rogers, *Communication Technology: The New Media in Society*, New York: The Free Press, 1986, reprinted with permission.

Characteristics of Communication Channels	Face-to-Face Interpersonal Communication	Interactive (Machine-Assisted Interpersonal) Communication	Mass Media
1. Message flow	One-to-few	Many-to-many	One-to-many
2. Source knowledge of the audience	Source has knowledge of the receiver as a single individual	Source may have a great deal of knowledge of the other participants in an interactive system	Source is a media organization with little knowledge of the receivers
3. Segmentation	High (de-massified)	High (de-massified)	Low, the same message is transmitted to everyone (massified)
4. Degree of interactivity	High	High	Low
5. Feedback	Plentiful and immediate	Somewhat limited; may be either immediate or delayed	Highly limited and delayed
6. Asynchronicity (ability to preserve the message)	Low	High for most types of the new media	Low, but high for some media, such as books and newspapers
7. Socio-emotional versus task-related content	High in socio-emotional content	Low in socio-emotional content	Low in socio-emotional content
8. Nonverbal band	Lots of nonverbal communication	Some new media provide nonverbal communication	Visual mass media provide much nonverbal band; audio mass media do not
9. Control of the communication flow	Potential for equal control by the participants	Potential for equal control by the participants	Little control by the receivers of the mass media
10. Privacy afforded	Low	Usually low	High

magazines than elsewhere but exists in all of the mass, as opposed to interactive, media.

Components of the print sector among the mass media historically have been more information intensive than their electronic counterparts. While individual volumes may or may not be informationally oriented, books as a group are the equal of any print medium in information intensiveness. While fiction works usually attract more attention from critics, nonfiction titles are more numerous and sell in greater numbers. Newspapers and magazines, given their entertainment components, are generally comparable to books in information intensiveness.

Among the electronic mass media, the reverse generally has been true. Radio and television, with few exceptions, are strongly entertainment oriented. News content during an individual broadcaster's typical day, in other words, ranges from negligible to nil. Network television outlets typically dedicate less than two hours daily to news programming of all kinds. Cable television channels, in contrast, may consist entirely of information, advertising, or entertainment. Most cable channels are committed to entertainment, as are most radio stations. Few radio stations maintain new operations beyond the "rip-and- read" variety, in which announcers read wire service dispatches from in-studio teleprinters.

Interactive Media

The interactive media stand in strong contrast to the mass media in information content. Whether used by individuals or corporations, their content is almost wholly informational. Again, as with the mass media, information is defined here to include advertising.

Limiting definitions of content to applications specified below is necessary due to the presence of the microcomputer. Most microcomputers were early used for word processing, database management, statistical analysis, and other tasks that are in no way interactive. Given appropriate software packages and modems, however, microcomputers can be as efficient as any interactive communication tool.

Communicators should not be misled, however, as to the efficiency induced by computers. Computers at best are marginally applicable as mass communication devices. They can be used to address messages to groups of people, but the groups involved almost universally would have to be characterized as special interest groups. Computers' selectivity, however, on the other hand, make them amenable to application as interactive media.

Other characteristics of the interactive group that differentiate them from the mass media are worthy of brief review before group components are examined individually. The interactive media are "many to many" as opposed to "one to many" communication channels. At the same time, however, they are capable of precise audience segmentation. Interactivity levels are high, although feedback may be delayed, as in the case of computer-based communication. Finally, the new media can be structured to permit equal control by participants in the communication process.

MICROCOMPUTERS IN COMMUNICATION

The diverse functions of which microcomputers are capable can obscure the significance of their role in communication. The microcomputer, to reiterate a point made earlier, is a dumb machine designed to store and sort binary data. Specific instructions in the form of software are necessary to activate the hardware for any specific application. Peripheral hardware in some cases may be necessary as well.

All of the common functions of microcomputers are software based. Word processing requires software. So do database management and statistical analysis. Desktop publishing usually requires several programs. Using microcomputers in communication also may require more than one program depending on the nature and complexity of functions to be undertaken.

Microcomputer-based communication functions usually fall into one or more of several basic categories: computer conferencing, electronic mail, and data base research. The functions vary in terms of the speed and privacy with which information is exchanged. All of these functions require a communication software package as well as one peripheral device to be attached to the computer—a modulator-demodulator or modem. Most who use microcomputers for research also use word processing packages, while those who make extensive use of electronic mail may use one of several specialized communication programs as well.

Computer Conferencing

Participation in computer conferencing requires only a modem and appropriate software in addition to a microcomputer. The latter elements create a link between users' microcomputers through proprietary or public networking facilities.

Computer conferences are most readily compared with telephone conference calls. The two modes of communication differ in two respects. Computer conferencing primarily is a visual medium, while the telephone is an aural medium. Appropriately equipped computers, however, automatically and instantaneously can provide complete transcripts of conferences for which they are used. Participants trigger the transcript mechanism at will by invoking a keyboard code. Codes vary with software but usually are entered by striking a single key. Turning off the transcription mechanism usually is accomplished by striking the key a second time.

Recording Mechanism. When transcription instructions are entered, microcomputers record all messages that appear on the computer screen on hard or floppy disks for later recall. Message appearance differs from one system to another and in keeping with conferencing protocols in use. All protocols, however, provide for microcomputers to display the names of those originating individual messages. Symbols are used to indicate whether messages continue from one line to the next or end with a given line. For users of the CompuServe Information System (CIS), for example, lines in a continuing message end with a hyphen while conclusions of messages are marked with asterisks. Asterisks serve as signals to second parties in two-party conversations, or to moderators of multi-party discussions. Second parties respond. Moderators may respond or call on other participants to "speak."

CIS conferencing protocol requires individuals to identify themselves. Full names or "handles" consisting of initials, nicknames or full names may be used and appear at the beginning of each line that a sender originates. Most participants use nicknames or first names only to conserve line space because communication software requires that enter carriage returns be entered at the end of each line. The CIS system also enables conference participants to call up lists of all involved in any conference, together with their membership numbers, at any time.

Other than ease of transcription, on-line conferences, as they are called, offer one major advantage: low cost. CompuServe rates at this writing are six dollars an hour or ten cents per minute for on-line time. In most areas, these charges include any long-distance fees, because CIS provides local telephone numbers in most communities. Telephone conference call charges almost universally would be significantly higher.

Other Attributes. Another characteristic of computer conferencing may be considered an asset or a liability, depending on individual perspectives. Economy of verbiage is encouraged in that only one participant can "talk" at a time. Since "speakers'" names are shown on each line entered, others involved readily can identify the speaker at any time. Potential for subsequent confusion over who said what, as readily can arise in telephone conferences, thus is eliminated. Potential for brilliant repartee also is limited, however, by the one-at-a-time characteristic and by the relatively slow speed at which thoughts can be converted to on-screen characters. Quick ripostes are discouraged by the medium and by chairpersons usually designated to maintain order during conferences. Those who wish to "speak" so indicate their desires by entering question marks and usually are recognized in order of request by the chair. A dash at the end of a line "holds the floor" for each speaker until he or she yields by placing an asterisk at the end of the last message line.

The same or similar protocols are applied where computer communication systems are used in corporate or proprietary settings. Organizations such as 3M and Hewlett-Packard, for example, maintain extensive computer communication resources for internal use.

Electronic Mail

CompuServe offers three message services of varying formality and privacy for members. They include electronic mail or E-Mail, forum bulletin boards, and "CB channels," so named after the once-popular citizens band radio channels. Electronic mail is wholly confidential, accessible only to sender and receiver. Bulletin board messages can be sent on a confidential basis but respondents may answer without tagging messages to maintain confidentiality, without revealing what the sender had wanted to remain confidential. CB channels are wholly public.

Electronic mail and bulletin boards offer three advantages to users. They are economical, fast, and accurate vehicles for communication. Economy of use is attributable in part to the relatively low cost of services such as CompuServe and in part to the ingenuity incorporated into many communication software packages. Speed, in comparison to that of the U.S. Postal Service or even an overnight service, is superior. Most who use electronic mail extensively check for messages at least daily, a process resulting in turnaround times of twenty-four hours or less.

Accuracy is an often overlooked attribute of the service that contributes disproportionately to the efficiency of electronic mail. Users directly control the content of messages sent to intended recipients. No receptionists or secretaries intervene. Reluctance to leave messages largely is eliminated as a result, and information flows more smoothly than where third parties may inadvertently produce distortion.

One other contingent attribute also adds to the attractiveness of electronic mail and other computer-based messaging systems. As in the case of computer conferencing, complete transcriptions of "conversations" are readily made and maintained. While records of telephone conversations are subject to potential inaccuracy on the part of note-takers or to the vagaries of human memory, accurate transcripts of electronic mail and other computer exchanges are easily maintained.

Data Base Research

Ability to automatically create complete files of results also is a major hidden benefit in using computers for data base research. Recording mechanisms used in conferencing and messaging systems are equally applicable in research applications. The greatest advantages in using microcomputers for data base research, however, rest in their removal of economic and physical barriers between researchers and the information they seek.

Cost barriers may exist in time or dollar form. Economic limits put restrictions on the assistance that researchers can afford. Skilled research librarians are well compensated. Students and academic researchers often find themselves handicapped as a result.

Endurance is a different matter. The word refers to the researchers' physical ability to spend hours poring through libraries and taking notes. Researchers using traditional information-gathering methods have always found it necessary to be selective in dealing with information more for physical than for economic reasons.

Barriers Fall. Cost and time barriers quickly fall away, however, where microcomputers can be used. Small investments in learning computer search strategies and in database access fees open up worlds of information that are easily accessed and copied. Microcomputer ability to store information probably is the most attractive attribute of the device from a research standpoint, and this ability has been growing with each passing year. One megabyte of read only memory (ROM)—enough to store the content of this book—declined in cost from about five hundred dollars in 1985 to little more than five dollars in 1990.

Low cost enables users to configure microcomputers with twenty to eighty megabytes of memory where ten megabytes once was the standard. Researchers therefore find themselves able to retrieve the equivalent of twenty to eighty bound books in the course of a search. Since ROM content can be transferred to floppy disks, the process can be repeated as often as necessary or appropriate to the subject matter. In a matter of hours, the content of a small library can be brought into a researcher's home or office by telephone line and microcomputer.

There remains, unfortunately, one negative factor in the information access picture that might best be expressed as "once you've got it, how do you use it?" Raw information is all but valueless. It must be filtered, organized, analyzed and assimilated in order to be of practical value.

Managing Information. The information analysis problem, until the late 1980s, could be solved only by reverting to traditional methods. Researchers were forced to physically manipulate oceans of downloaded material, sorting, filing, and discarding in much the same manner scholars have used for centuries. In more recent years, developers have started to attack the information management problem with a host of software packages, most of them applying what might be called the index card principle.

Software developers apparently proceeded on the assumption that they needed only to create electronic index cards and provide "filing cabinets" in which to organize them. The result was a generation of information organizers patterned after long-used data base management packages. Lotus Development Corporation, which has dominated the data processing market with Lotus 1-2-3, introduced a package called Agenda for information management. Agenda uses a sort of card-and-file approach. Descriptions of information to be filed are entered on the equivalent of index cards, while the information itself is stored in "file folders" linked to the index cards. Users can organize large amounts of information in a manner that permits easy access and rapid retrieval through a project outline as simple or complex as circumstances require.

Automated Searching. Another form of software used in data base research evolved from traditional communication software. The latter variety of software created electronic bridges between microcomputers and the mainframes that house databases, enabling users to search mainframe files and download information. The new variety of software automates the use of databases and computer utilities such as CompuServe, especially the latter.

One of the more useful of the automation programs is called TAPCIS, as in "tap CIS" or "tap CompuServe Information Service." Written by Howard Benner, the program enters CompuServe on command, retrieves messages or user-specified information, and logs off at a speed far more rapid than any human could manage. Responses to messages received and files ready for uploading are transmitted by reversing the process. TAPCIS logs onto CompuServe, uploads messages and other materials, and signs off, again at flank speed. Other program features enable users to construct and maintain indexes of CompuServe library files in personal computers and to retrieve information of specific interest as needed.

The TAPCIS program can be used only with CompuServe. Similar programs doubtless will become available, however, for use with other computer utilities as well as with data bases. The market for automatic search programs for larger and more popular databases such as Dialog and Nexis presumably would be considerable.

Progressively more sophisticated computer programs, steadily declining memory costs and an ever-broadening range of equipment options make it possible for researchers to handle projects of almost any size by microcomputer with relative ease. External as well as additional internal disk drives, for example, can be installed in or linked to microcomputers as circumstances dictate. Tape backup systems can be used to store inactive files. The author's system over a period of five years grew from an IBM system equipped with an Intel 8088 central processing unit and a ten megabyte hard drive to a Zenith Z-386 equipped with an Intel 80386 CPU and twin eighty megabyte hard drives. Speed and memory, in other words, increased 160-fold in five years, and the cost of the systems were approximately equal.

Similar economies of scale have been experienced by corporate computer users. Speeds and capacities of mainframe computers have grown as rapidly as those of their miniature counterparts, and organizations have responded in predictable fashion. Computer applications have boomed, and many involve communication of one sort or another.

TELECONFERENCING

Electronic mail and conferencing systems of the sort described above also are among the more profitable computer applications in organizational settings. Where applications involve organizations and mainframe computers rather than individuals and microcomputers, electronic mail systems are private and proprietary rather than public and accessible to any modem-equipped computer owner. Systems and benefits otherwise are identical.

Organizations, like individuals, benefit from computer communication through savings in time and cost. Messages are transmitted more rapidly and less expensively by computer than through any other channel. Corporate electronic mail systems, in fact, played a large role in the demise of Federal Express Corporation's ZapMail system during the early 1980s. Facsimile technology developed so rapidly that company-owned facsimile machines made ZapMail irrelevant before the service could become profitable.

While playing a growing role in organizational communication, computers play only a small part in teleconferencing, a process through which groups of individuals at different locations come together electronically for shared experiences. Experiences may be aural, visual, or both aural and visual and may be conducted on regional, national, or international scales. They can be conducted in visual form by computer, as discussed above, aurally by telephone, or in aural and visual form through closed circuit television. Experimental systems also have been developed using (a) computers equipped with drawing tablets and (b) telephones on separate circuits to produce a different combination of aural and visual communication.

Telephone Conferencing

As the name implies, telephone conferencing is an extension of the conventional conference call. Telephone conferences are little more than conference calls on a grand scale. They can be arranged through telephone companies or through one of several entrepreneurial organizations that provide such services.   Commercial organizations involved in providing telephone conferencing services compete with telephone companies by offering a number of value-added features. A typical conferencing company, for example, provides an operator who places calls to individual participants, gets all of them on line, describes a verbal protocol to be used during the conference, and notifies the chairperson that the group is ready to begin. The operator thereafter may stay with the group to insure that no connections are broken and, perhaps, to make transcriptions that are available by prearrangement.

Telephone conferencing offers no significant advantages over computer conferencing. Telephone participants need not know how to operate computers. Computer conference participants, however, need nothing more than hunt-and-peck knowledge of typewriter style keyboards. Telephone conference transcriptions are more difficult to manage than the computer variety. Audio tapes must be transcribed, and transcribers may experience problems in identifying participants. Only where participants place inordinate value in being able to discern tonal inflections does the telephone conference become more attractive than the computer variety. Conferences conducted by television are another matter. They add a visual dimension to communication that can be of substantial value. Whether the radically increased costs involved can be justified by those considering the medium in any given circumstances is another question.

Television Conferencing

Television rather than telephone technology is what most individuals have in mind in using the terms *teleconference* and *teleconferencing*. By any name, the technology is more complex and much more expensive than that used in telephone or computer conferencing.

In videoconferencing, one or more sets of participants who may be separated by almost any distance come together in specially equipped conference rooms at predetermined times. Each group usually is seated around a table and equipped with microphones, television cameras, and television screens so that members of each group can see members of other groups. To as great an extent as possible, videoconferences therefore are conducted in the same pattern as face-to-face meetings.

The equipment intensive nature of the videoconference make it the most expensive and least used of conferencing alternatives. Telephone or computer conferences usually are preferable other than where the visual dimension is essential, as in the case of an equipment demonstration. All of the systems have been found relatively cost effective, however, because of increasing travel costs and the fact that most organizations are becoming more and more geographically diverse. Savings in transportation costs and in the time of individuals involved quickly offset the cost of the technology.

VIDEOTEXT AND TELETEXT

While essential to any complete list of new technologies, *videotext* and *teletext* are words that few consumers recognize and that most scholars in the United States would prefer to forget. They are names of two different systems of information transmission. Neither has proven economically viable in North America and the similarity in their names often is a source of confusion.

Part of the problem doubtless is semantic. *Videotext* and *teletext* are similar, and although the systems are different, few Americans have had any experience with them. The resulting confusion doubtless will persist despite the following definitions.

Videotext is an interactive system that enables consumers to request information from a central computer for delivery over telephone or cable television lines. *Teletext*, in contrast, is a system that enables users to view on request frames of information already being transmitted but invisible on their television screens. The difference between videotext and teletext, then, is in the manner in which information is handled by the originating computers. In videotext, information is stored for transmission at subscriber request. In teletext, information already is there and subject to viewing on request.

Teletext Systems

How can the information already be there? Signals are transmitted in the vertical blanking interval of conventional television broadcast signals. Television signals do not use all the lines of dots allocated for them (525 in the United States, 625 in Japan and most of Europe). Those left blank, and normally out of sight, are called the vertical blanking interval and can be used to transmit additional information in piggyback fashion on television signals.

Recipients use keypads similar to those on pocket calculators to select page numbers from a table of contents or menu. The teletext system grabs the selected page the next time it goes by, decodes it, and displays it on the television screen, usually after a ten to twenty second delay.

Teletext has several drawbacks, for reasons implied above.

First, capacity is limited. Most systems contain only a few hundred frames of information. System capacity is not physically limited, but delays in calling up specific frames grow with the number of frames in use. Teletext systems thus are less interactive than videotext. On the other hand, costs are relatively low. Consumers need only buy small decoding boxes. No monthly fees are charged because the service is supported by advertising.

Although little used, teletext already is in almost 100 million homes in the United States. CBS, NBC, and many local stations have been broadcasting teletext pages since 1983. Low-cost decoders remain to be introduced, however, and few Americans are aware the service exists.

Videotext Systems

In contrast to teletext, videotext is a simplified form of computer time sharing that allows almost unlimited numbers of individuals to call up information from a central computer. Videotext, in other words, is a sort of CompuServe by television rather than computer. Videotext offers several advantages and a few drawbacks in comparison with teletext.

Foremost among videotext's advantages from the user standpoint is that videotext response is far faster than teletext's. Videotext reacts in a fraction of a second where teletext may take half a minute to respond. On the negative side, long distance charges may be applicable in some instances because videotext uses telephone lines. A small charge also may be made for each frame of information requested, in much the same manner that CompuServe charges for on line time.

The word *frame* refers to the format in which information is provided by videotext and teletext. Rather than scrolling vertically or horizontally on the user's screen, as is the case with some televised news services, teletext and videotext present information in screen-sized frames. Frame size is limited, usually to about one hundred words.

Neither videotext nor teletext systems, despite lengthy and expensive experimentation, appear destined to become economically viable in the United States during the twentieth century or early in the twenty-first. Tests in Florida and California under newspaper sponsorship have been dismal and expensive failures. Canadian, French and British systems have been more successful, but only with considerable governmental support.

The primary obstacles to success in the United States appear to be the relative flexibility of newspapers and the relatively high cost of decoding devices. Microcomputer users, in addition, are not likely prospects for teletext or videotext. Equipped with inexpensive modems, their computers provide quick access to information utilities such as CompuServe and The Source, which contain essentially the same information that might be obtained by teletext and videotext. There thus appears little cause to believe that either of the latter technologies will move ahead with any significant speed in the United States.

INTERACTIVE CABLE SYSTEMS

While videotext and teletext appear to have little short term developmental potential, cable systems are another matter. Cable potential, in fact, is far greater than that of today's television networks. Two factors are involved, one technology-related, the other audience related.

The technology-related factor arguably is most significant. Today's cable systems are aging rapidly. With age comes deterioration in the wire cable with which systems were constructed.

While systems have been deteriorating, however, audiences have been improving. In the mid-1980s, some 40 percent of United States households were cable television subscribers. By 1990, the figure was approaching 60 percent, and forecasters were predicting a 70 percent market penetration by 2000.

Technological Change

Deterioration in cable systems installed tenor more years ago is remarkably well timed to produce quantum change in cable television. At least three factors are at work that appear to all but guarantee extensive change. First, in the technological arena, fiber optic cable is replacing wire, providing greater capacity at lower cost and in a form highly resistant to deterioration. Second, in the political arena, original cable franchises that restricted competition are expiring. Finally, the offspring of the Bell System are preparing to offer telecommunication services, probably in competition with cable systems as well as potential providers of in-home services.

The fiber optic revolution will provide problems and opportunities in equal part to cable system franchisees. The capacity of the new cable is far greater than that of the old. It can carry more channels or other consumer services, such as in-home banking or shopping. At the same time, however, fiber optic systems will at first be more expensive than wired systems, which means that original cable franchisers will have to invest large sums merely to stay in business.

The evolution of cable in individual communities for these reasons is likely to be a function of technological and economic variables working in combination. Telephone companies, like cable companies, are changing from wire to fibre optic cables. There is a significant difference, however, in the economic positions of the two groups. The Baby Bells are changing primarily to create more cost-efficient telephone systems. In the process, they gain additional capacity for services such as cable television at little added cost. Cable companies, in contrast, must spend large sums merely to replace deteriorating systems and to stay in business.

Perhaps most significant here are the implications of the two sets of circumstances as to competition. Given that the cost of telephone cable is built into telephone bills, telephone companies can launch into cable television with little additional capital investment. Cable companies, on the other hand, must pay for improvements through customer fees. Circumstances such as these readily can lead to rate wars of benefit only to cable subscribers and only in the short term.

Audience Change

From a longer timer perspective, rate wars of the sort logically in prospect in the cable arena could encourage conditions in which 80 to 90 percent of the population might become cable subscribers in the next few years, approximating a wired society in many geographic areas. Cable television, at that juncture, unquestionably would become the nation's primary mass medium, boasting the sort of market penetration claimed by daily newspapers during the pretelevision era. Perhaps more important, individual cable channel's audiences presumably will then have grown to a point at which they are of interest to advertisers.

Enhanced advertiser interest flows from growth in numbers of subscribers. Interest compounds where increases in subscribers are accompanied by audience losses among other media. Advertisers are anticipating that these circumstances will prevail in cable television for the remainder of the century. The primary reason: continuing proliferation in numbers of competing communication channels, producing more audience fragmentation and thereby enhancing the relative as well as the absolute position of cable television and individual cable channels.

SATELLITE SYSTEMS

Proliferation and fragmentation processes such as these are encouraged by advances in technology, especially those that expand system capacities. In recent years, while less than obvious to casual information consumers, satellite and cable technology have produced proliferation in the cable and telephone industries as well as in print and electronic media.

Technological improvements have increased the capacity and efficiency of cable systems. Improvement among satellites has permitted more of them to be concentrated in a limited area above the United States.

System Design

The functional benefit of satellites is a product of their ability to "stand still in space," to serve as fixed position platforms for receipt and transmission of radio signals. They achieve this objective from a position 22,300 miles above the earth, where they rocket through space at the same speed at which the planet is moving— 7,000 miles an hour.

Satellites first were positioned at least four degrees or 1,000 miles apart to avoid interfering with one another. As technology advanced, spacing was reduced by about half, but "parking spaces" remain limited, as is the capacity of individual satellites. Each satellite plays host to one to two dozen relay units or transponders, as they are called. Transponders receive signals from earth, convert them to other frequencies, amplify them, and beam them back to earth. One transponder can handle 1,300 telephone calls, 12 radio station signals or 1 color television signal.

Satellites add to communication productivity by enabling users to avoid greater costs than otherwise arise with greater distances.

In addition to lower telephone costs, satellites in the United States have contributed to growth in cable television; to development of national newspapers; and to flows of information for other media. Indirectly, satellites also have contributed, for better or worse, to diversity in mass mediated messages. Somewhat ironically, for example, the National Christian Network and the Playboy Channel use transponders on the same satellite—SATCOM F4.

Fiber Optic Applications

Advantages of the same sort are being created for many communication channels by the rapid replacement of conventional copper communication wires with fiber optic cable. Few recognize the extent to which fiber optic cable may fulfill the promise of the integrated grid society.

Three major advantages accrue to fiber optic cable users. First among the advantages is efficiency. A finger-sized fiber optic cable, more flexible than copper but equally amenable to splicing, can carry as many as forty thousand telephone calls. Second, but more important in some circumstances, is user flexibility. Fiber optic cable can carry messages simultaneously in both directions—a critical characteristic for interactive cable systems. Finally, messages carried by fiber optic cable are transmitted in light rather than electromagnetic waves. As such, they are immune from the sort of interference that arises as static, noise, or signal leakage.

Fiber optic cable also offers an economic advantage that may outweigh all the material's technological attributes: durability. While copper deteriorates over time, fiber optic cable resists corrosion. Investments in fiber optics therefore can be amortized over extended periods, making investment in systems using this technology considerably more attractive to those who provide capital to business and industry.

The investment economics of fiber optic cable can make a significant difference in entrepreneurial ability to facilitate the development of the integrated grid. If funds allocated to install fiber optic cable can be amortized over thirty or more years rather than five to ten years, entrepreneurs can reduce prices to consumers and gain market penetration, accelerating grid development while maintaining the economic integrity of their projects.

IN SUMMARY

The new technologies, as they are called, only now are beginning to make themselves felt in the United States. Popular definitions of the term *new technologies* usually are cast in terms far broader than appropriate. The new technologies are characterized by their interactivity, by the ability of users to interact with others through communication channels created by the technological devices involved. This standard is met only by computers, teleconferencing, teletext, videotext, interactive cable systems, and satellite communication systems. All other technologies are of earlier vintage or are not interactive.

Interactive media contrast strongly with contemporary mass media in information content. All are information intensive, while many of the mass media, especially in the broadcast category, are designed primarily to entertain rather than to inform their audiences. Interactive media also function as "many -to-many rather than as one-to-many communication channels. At the same time, they are capable of precise audience segmentation. Their interactivity levels are high, although, as in the case of computer-based communication, responses may be delayed. Finally, the interactive media permit equal access by all users.

Microcomputers are most used among the interactive media, although all microcomputer applications are not interactive. Interactive microcomputer applications include conferencing, electronic mail, and data base research. All require a modem as well as a computer.

Computer conferencing functions in the same manner as telephone conferencing. The two differ substantively in only two respects. First, computer conferencing is visual while telephone conferencing is aural. Second, computer conferencing is more amenable to production of verbatim transcripts in written form.

Electronic mail is one of three message services available through computer utilities such as CompuServe Information Service and The Source. The others are bulletin boards maintained by special interest groups and CB channels that perform in the same manner as citizen band radios.

Data base research conducted by microcomputer creates multiple user advantages. Direct access to mainframe information utilities brings more information within the reach of more researchers more rapidly and efficiently than ever before. Information can be quickly located and downloaded to microcomputers at nominal cost, although data obtained in this manner still must be assimilated, organized, and evaluated in conventional fashion.

Teleconferencing in many ways is similar to computer conferencing. As popularly used, teleconferencing refers more to systems based on television than to telephone technologies. Telephone systems to date have been more commonly used, however, because of the relatively high cost of television conferences. High costs are produced by the technology-intensive nature of television conferencing, which involves intensive use of costly satellites as well as complex studio facilities. In essence, computer conferencing is a visual medium while telephone conferencing is an aural medium, and television combines the attributes of the other two and adds pictures.

Videotext and teletext are interactive information systems that use television screens but otherwise share few technological similarities. Videotext enables consumers to request information from a central computer for delivery over telephone or cable television lines. Teletext content, in contrast, already is delivered to many homes but can be retrieved only with relatively costly converters. Teletext data is transmitted in the vertical blanking interval, the lines of dots not used by television broadcasters for commercial signals.

Interactive cable systems build on the videotext concept but can provide a far broader range of services to consumers. Remote banking, fire and burglar alarm systems, shopping services, and entertainment services of all kinds can be made available to consumers via cable systems. Either telephone or cable television systems can be used, and evolving technologies suggest that both telephone and cable companies ultimately will be competing in this arena.

Competing with the telephone and cable companies for consumers well may be satellite-based communication systems. Satellites already are in use in combination with other technologies, from teleconferencing and cable television to newspaper publishing. Their further development into areas such as direct broadcast of television programming and concurrent development of fiber optic systems quickly could bring many areas into what futurists have called integrated grid societies.

ADDITIONAL READING

Didsbury, Howard F., ed. *Communications and the Future: Prospects, Promises and Problems*. Bethesda, MD: World Future Society, 1982.

Rogers, Everett M. *Communication Technology: The New Media in Society*. New York: Free Press, 1986.

Williams, Frederick, ed. *Measuring the Information Society*. Beverly Hills, Calif.: Sage, 1988.

6 The New Newspapers

Newspapers superficially appear anything but new. They have been a part of United States society since the founding of the colonies. Today's newspapers, however, only physically resemble those of the past. Only the containers in which publishers deliver news realistically can be compared with those used by newspapers of more than a few years ago. All else has changed to a degree beyond the imagination of newspaper readers.

Much of the change, unfortunately, has been for the worse rather than the better. Newspapers' shares of the information and advertising markets have been in decline for more than a decade. They have experienced steady erosion in readership and advertising revenues, in relative if not absolute terms, despite extensive application of new technologies to reduce costs.

Most of the deterioration, also unfortunately, has not impressed typical newspaper readers. Few long mourn the passing of newspapers, many of which have expired since midcentury. Most of the survivors have become components of publicly owned corporations arguably more oriented toward profit than journalism. These trends, occurring in concert with explosive growth in television and among other competing media, are reshaping the newspaper world.

MARKET CONDITIONS

Basic change among newspapers is readily seen in data published annually by the public affairs department of the American Newspaper Publishers Association (ANPA). Information and figures published for 1977, 1982, and 1987 demonstrate the breadth and depth of prevalent trends, despite ANPA's best-foot-forward approach.

Most noticeably, the editorial emphasis of the publishers' annual reports over the ten-year period have turned from growth to social role. "Newspapers continued their dramatic growth in 1977," according to ANPA's 1978 report. Under a headline that read "Newspapers: A Growth Business," the association reported:

> Newspapers in the United States now reach more than 120 million readers daily. In 1977 all-time highs were recorded in newspaper advertising revenues, employment, newsprint consumption, and Sunday and weekly circulation.

> This record performance attests to the recognition by readers of the importance of newspapers in keeping them informed about things that affect their daily lives.

Five years later, in 1983, ANPA's tone was markedly less optimistic:

> Newspapers function as a unique and vital force in the daily lives of millions of Americans. They provide the facts and analysis that allow informed citizens to make effective and responsible decisions, not only in coping with the complexities of modern living, but also in protecting the rights and liberties of a free society.

ANPA's 1988 report was no more optimistic:

> Newspapers serve the people of a free society by providing the facts and analysis necessary to enable them to make responsible and effective decisions—to sustain good government and to lead full and successful lives.

The Hard Numbers

Behind these glowing generalities were two sets of data that demonstrated deterioration in newspapers' positions as leading disseminaters of information and sellers of advertising in the United States. The two factors—circulation levels and advertising sales—are primary indicators of economic if not journalistic success.

While readers buy newspapers, advertisers buy circulation levels. Newspapers' economic success is governed by the numbers of readers that editors attract for publishers to sell to advertisers. Advertising rates increase—or decline—with circulation levels.

Advertising rate structures also are influenced by relative audience levels. Television's ability to deliver larger audiences, for example, dampens publishers' ability to raise rates. Even where circulations grow, audience share, as it's called in the advertising fraternity, may be deteriorating.

Circulation data. In 1977, there were 353 morning, 1,433 evening, and 7,466 weekly newspapers in the United States. In 1987 there were 512 in the morning, 1,165 in the evening, and 7,498 appearing weekly. While morning newspapers had increased in number, there were more than 100 fewer daily newspapers at the end of the ten-year period.

Daily newspaper circulation increased by more than 1.1 million during the same period, but that was a percentage gain of less than 2 percent. Sunday circulation grew by 14 percent to more than 60 million. The average weekly newspaper's circulation increased more than 35 percent, however, from 5,075 to 6,894, and total circulation of all weeklies increased 36 percent, from 37.8 million to 51.6 million.

Even the prestigious *Wall Street Journal* was losing ground to competitors such as *Financial Times*, *Investor's Daily*, and *The New York Times*. The *Journal's* circulation for 1988 was 1.95 million, down from a 1983 peak of 2.11 million. *Barron's*, the *Journal's* Dow-Jones stable mate, also was losing ground. At least part of the losses were being attributed by media experts to developments such as NBC's new cable venture, the Consumer News and Business Channel.

While circulation problems plagued many newspaper publishers, revenues were continuing to increase. Total daily newspaper advertising revenues in 1976 were $9.9 billion. By 1986, the total had risen to $26.9 billion, an increase of 171 percent. While revenues were increasing, however, newspapers were steadily losing their hold on the advertising market.

Market Share. In 1976, daily newspapers captured 29.4 percent of all advertising dollars spent in the United States, 4.5 percent of all national advertiser expenditures, and 24.9 percent of local advertiser spending. Ten years later, advertising expenditures with newspapers had declined to 26.4 percent of total advertiser spending. National advertising was down from 4.5 to 3.3 percent and local advertiser spending was down from 24.9 to 23.1 percent.

Advertising industry components that had gained ground during the decade included television and direct mail. Many others, however, had bettered the record of the daily newspaper component in retaining market share.

Television revenues increased from 19.9 to 22.7 percent of the total. Direct mail revenues increased from 14.3 to 16.8 percent. While losing ground to television and/or direct mail, magazines, radio, farm publications, outdoor advertising, and business papers all performed significantly better than newspapers. Magazines' share of advertising revenues was down 0.1 percent. Radio and farm publication and outdoor advertising shares declined by the same amount. Business papers suffered a loss of 0.8 percent. Their revenues declined from 3.1 to 2.3 percent of total advertising expenditures over the ten-year period.

Competition among newspapers in part contributed to the overall problem. Many of today's stronger newspapers are relative newcomers. Long Island's *Newsday*, for example, has grown to become a power in the New York metropolitan area. The *Los Angeles Times*, which established a reputation for quality during the latter half of the twentieth century, is under continuing assault by the suburban *Orange County News* and *Daily News*. While the population of the Times' market has grown by 25 percent in a decade, the newspaper's circulation has increased by only 12 percent. The *Times* may be a less-than-perfect example of metropolitan dailies in decline. Some argue that editorial ineptitude may have contributed to the newspaper's decline. The same sort of decline has occurred, however, in most metropolitan daily newspapers. For better or worse, the trend is apt to continue.

Circulation Patterns. Newspaper circulation patterns reported by the Audit Bureau of Circulation (ABC) and published as part of ANPA's reports for 1982 and 1987 underscored an implied threat to traditional daily newspapers. *USA Today* was only a footnote to the 1982 data. By 1987, the newcomer ranked second among the nation's daily newspapers in circulation.

The footnote for 1982 indicated that the accounting firm of Price-Waterhouse had reported *USA Today* circulation at 531,438, which would have placed the paper thirteenth on a list of the nation's largest newspapers. ABC had not audited *USA Today* circulation for that year. The 1987 audit placed *USA Today* second only to *The Wall Street Journal* in circulation. *USA Today* had 1,324,223 readers versus 1,961,846 for the *Journal*.

Also noteworthy in the 1987 data is that three of the five largest newspapers (in circulation), *USA Today*, the *Journal*, and *The New York Times*, were nationally circulated. All were printed in multiple plants using content transmitted through computer-satellite systems.

Ownership Concentration. Finally, the ANPA data for 1982 and 1987 reflect a continuing trend toward concentration of newspaper ownership in the United States. In 1982, the dozen largest newspaper companies owned 336 newspapers with a total circulation of 26.5 million. Five years later the twelve largest owned 400 newspapers with 29.9 million circulation.

The largest newspaper companies in total circulation in 1987 were Gannett Company, Knight-Ridder, Newhouse Newspapers, Tribune Company, Times-Mirror Company, and Dow Jones and Company, all with combined circulations in excess of 2.5 million. Gannett led with 6.02 million and Knight-Ridder was second with 3.8 million. The ranking had changed in only one respect over the prior five years. Dow Jones and Times Mirror had exchanged places.

The overall result of ownership concentration has been a decline in numbers of cities with two or more separately owned newspapers. There were fewer than fifty at last report, and the number was continuing to decline. Whether the survivors serve readers with the same alacrity that once was the case is open to question. The Newspaper Preservation Act, passed by Congress in 1970, permits newspapers to share printing, advertising, and circulation functions to their economic advantage. News and editorial operations must remain separate, but some question whether such arrangements encourage the aggressive competition that once prevailed among competing newspapers.

Factors leading to the decline in numbers of newspapers in the United States are open to question. Loss of advertisers rather than of readers appears to have been the primary cause of newspaper demise. Few major city newspapers that closed in recent years were experiencing major circulation losses. In some cases, the reverse has been true. The *New York Mirror* closed down, for example, with a circulation of some one million.

Cause for Optimism?

On the other hand, declines have been recorded in both daily and Sunday readership. Numbers of individuals who read a newspaper any given weekday declined during the 1970s from 78 percent to 70 percent of the population. Numbers who read a Sunday newspaper have declined from 72 percent to 69 percent.

The bulk of the decline, according to experts in the field, is produced by one of several trends. More hectic lifestyles, the inroads of competitive media, and declines in readership among younger audiences are most often cited. Those who assign blame to demographic trends see potential for improvement in the fact that the United States population is aging. Significantly larger numbers of older individuals read newspapers than is the case with younger groups. Therefore, they reason, the graying of America will bring increases in newspaper readership.

While the facts are, indeed, as specified above, the argument is open to question in one critical respect. Will those who have not become readers in their youths turn to newspapers as information sources in the later years? Today's older generation of newspaper readers was reared before the advent of television. Tomorrow's older generation will have had a different experience. Their lifelong predispositions toward television may not change as rapidly as the optimists believe. Their relatively high educational levels, on the other hand, indicate greater reading skills that might be more extensively exercised in retirement.

Two schools of thought conflict over the readership issue. One suggests the group raised in the age of television is accustomed to assimilating information in the form of images and no longer is comfortable with the print media. The other argues that increasingly bureaucratized work places have spawned occupational demand for more and more reading, thus equipping today's workers to read for leisure or information.

Also overlooked among most who express optimism over the future of newspapers are multiple studies of reader preferences. The studies indicate that readers more and more turn to newspapers for what can better be called entertainment rather than information. Advertisements, advice columns, comics, features, and the like rank higher than news. Newspaper publishers once assumed that television would serve those who seek entertainment and superficial information, while newspapers would continue to serve an active, news-seeking population. That population is proving too small to support newspapers. Publishers are being forced, as a result, to emulate the pattern popularized by *USA Today*, which uses short articles, large illustrations, and a great deal of "soft" information to attract readers.

Underlying Factors

Greater impacts on the economics of newspaper publishing probably were created by basic changes in the family and in retailing in the United States. Neither families nor retail establishments exist today in the form that prevailed a few decades ago. The changes that have been experienced almost inevitably were transmitted through them to newspaper publishers.

Research data demonstrate that potential for newspaper subscription increases with numbers of adults in households and with the amount of time adults have available to dedicate for reading. Prevailing trends during the 1980s ran in opposite directions. The number of traditional nuclear household units was declining. In addition, more and more women were coming into the work force.

Changes in retailing were even more pervasive and, economically, more devastating to newspapers. Concentration of ownership and geographic dispersion became the principal characteristics of retailing, once primarily a "mom and pop" enterprise in the United States. Chain organizations became the dominant players in the retail market as family firms went out of business and were not replaced.

With growth, chain organizations tightened control over advertising and marketing and centralized those functions at their headquarters. Responsibility for the operation of local stores, including advertising and marketing, was placed in the hands of professional managers committed to climbing corporate ladders rather than to their communities. Buyer-seller relationships between media and major retail accounts changed accordingly, and the changes influenced retail advertising. The result, in part, has been far greater increases in television advertising at the expense of newspapers.

Technological Change

Concentration of ownership contributed to two other trends prevalent among newspapers in the United States during the latter part of the 1980s. One involved increased use of the new technologies. The other, probably a result of the first, was a relative decline in industry employment.

Technological change was most evident in mechanical production of the newspaper. Most of the nation's newspapers by 1987 had made the transition from hot metal to computerized production systems. The new technologies also created change in other departments, however, and still more changes are in prospect.

Work Force Changes. Employment in newspapers in the United States was estimated by the Bureau of Labor Statistics at 462,200 for 1987. That total was 17.6 percent higher than the 392,900 the bureau had estimated for 1977, but the data are misleading.

The 1977 total was about 4.3 percent of a United States labor force then estimated at 90.5 million. The 1987 total, in contrast, represented 4.1 percent of a work force estimated at 122.4 million. The decline, although apparently small, is significant in that it occurred during a time when the work force as a whole had increased by 73.9 percent.

New Technologies. Although data are lacking, work force reductions appear to have occurred almost exclusively in connection with the newspaper production process. Sales, news, and administrative staffs appear little changed, although small reductions in the administrative sector may have resulted from growth among newspaper chains.

The nature of the technological changes, almost all of them computer-based, are illustrated in figure 5.1, which compares the hot metal and computerized production processes. The hot metal process had prevailed in newspaper printing for decades, since the linotype machine and rotary press replaced hand set type and the flatbed press. Type set on linotype or head casting machines then was proofed and corrected before being placed in page forms. The forms were converted to curved plates for use on rotary presses through molding and casting processes.

Contemporary computer systems enable writers and advertising personnel to create newspaper content with keyboards and scanners.

Photocomposition processes are becoming sufficiently sophisticated to handle full pages as well as their component parts, and hardware involved soon may be able to generate negatives as well as "type." As the computerized process becomes more sophisticated still, what once required fourteen steps in the hot metal process may well be reduced to as few as seven in computer-based systems.

An Old Problem. While technology was reducing production expenses, material costs continued to increase. Newsprint, the paper on which newspapers are printed, continued a steady increase in cost with no end in sight. The price of newsprint increased from $147 a metric ton in 1965 to more than $650 in 1989. The cost of every copy of every newspaper increased apace. *The New York Times'* Albert Scardino explained the phenomenon in this fashion.

> A pound of newsprint delivered from the paper mill to a news paper warehouse costs about 21.7 cents at today's market price. That pound of paper will become 96 pages of printed material . . . but only after a publisher spends 60 cents or so to pay journalists, advertising sales representatives, accountants, and others who work in the process.

> In other words, it costs almost a penny a page to produce a standard-sized paper. At that rate, a ten-pound Sunday issue, common in Los Angeles and New York and occasionally sighted in metropolitan neighborhoods in between, is an $8.70 product. Of that, paper accounts for $2.70. Yet papers that size typically sell for $1.25 in their local circulation area.

Publishers use such reasoning to justify ever-higher prices but not entirely without cause. As Scardino pointed out, the price of newspapers by 1989 had almost reached the level at which they could be sold as scrap paper. Publishers, however, are reluctant to raise prices. They assume, perhaps with some justification, that there somewhere exists a consumer resistance level and that prices may be so close to that level that increases could produce lower sales levels. Their rationale is not without merit. Price increases that would probably not discourage the typical reader of *The New York Times* could be another matter another city.

CONTENT PATTERNS

Whether technological advances will be sufficient to overcome increasing newsprint costs and save traditional newspapers from long-predicted extinction remains to be seen. As is the case with any commercial medium, newspapers' economic viability is a function of ability to attract and retain audiences of sufficient size and quality to earn advertisers' support. Every newspaper editor, indeed, every executive of every mass medium, is attempting to achieve that objective.

Editors and their publishers universally have been seeking to retain or improve their market positions with what might best be described as "niche" strategies. Each newspaper attempts to identify one or more groups of prospective readers and tailor content to their needs. The practice is evident in the content of virtually every newspaper regardless of degree of success achieved.

Some publishers also attempt to achieve economic security through diversification. Many have established or acquired additional newspapers or other properties in order to assure their companies' long-term survival.

Niche Players

Almost every newspaper has become a "niche player" over the past decade. Some long have been narrowly oriented, as in the case of *The Wall Street Journal*. Others only recently have found it necessary to specialize, but specialization has become the order of the day. Seldom can any newspaper any longer be called a traditional daily.

The traditional daily attempted to meet all of the informational needs of its readers. Local news was supplemented with information concerning state, regional, national and international affairs. General news, in other words, was the staple component of the traditional newspaper.

The appeal of general news started to decline, for readers of traditional newspapers as well as editors and publishers, with the onset of competition from two sets of sources. One set, within the newspaper industry, consists of more specialized publications that attempt to carve away some of the traditional newspaper's readers. The second set consists of other media bent on the same objective.

Competing Newspapers. Competition for traditional newspapers' audiences developed on national and local levels. At the national level, *The Wall Street Journal* made itself indispensable to almost every business person as local, regional, and national economies gave way to a global business environment. *The New York Times* and the *Christian Science Monitor*, in like manner, gained dominant positions in national and international news. At the other end of the scale, *USA Today*, or "McPaper," as it has been called, took what some consider "the low road," delivering the equivalent of television newscasts in printed form. Other than the *Monitor*, all of these newspapers are available in many cities through home delivery as well as on news stands and by mail. The same distribution plan was to be used by a new, national sports daily announced in early 1989 by former *New York Post* publishers Peter O. Price and sportswriter Frank Deford.

At the other end of the geographic spectrum, aggressive local competition has developed for the once-dominant metropolitan dailies. Business and entertainment newspapers have proven to be especially effective competition for local dailies. Most are published weekly, as are many of the suburban weeklies that long have existed in smaller communities and on the fringes of many large cities.

Other Competitors. Still more competition, especially for advertising revenue, has developed in major markets in the form of specialized publications. General merchandise "shoppers," some produced by weekly newspaper publishers and a few published by daily newspapers, have been joined by merchandise-specific publications. Some are physically more akin to magazines than to traditional newspapers, but all are in competition for the same advertising dollars.

Many of the specialized publications deal in real estate and motor vehicles of all kinds. Residential real estate publications have been joined in many markets by others specializing in multifamily dwellings. Newspapers specializing in automotive advertising have spawned truck and boat publications. All of them, to a greater or lesser extent, drain advertising dollars away from traditional newspapers.

The Daily Niche
These trends, in most cities, have forced traditional daily newspapers to return to their journalistic roots: local news. The trend is

logical and may prove essential to survival as new and existing media continue their efforts to lure away newspaper readers.

Dailies long have been their communities' primary sources of local news. Their only significant competition has come from television, but the nature of that medium works in favor of newspapers. Television stations lack adequate time to deliver information in the depth and breadth many individuals demand. Broadcasters may skim some of the cream from the potential audience, especially where subject matter is amenable to visualization, as with fires, disasters, and the like. Where information is less visual and more complex, as with politics, governmental policies, and budgets, newspapers have a distinct advantage.

DEVELOPMENTAL PATTERNS

Will "niche playing" prove adequate to preserve newspapers as we know them? A number of elements have been identified that will influence the destiny of the daily newspaper. None individually will control it, however, and any effort to predict the future on the basis of available evidence is risky.

End of an Era?

The heyday of the daily newspaper appears to be over. After almost a decade of revenue and profit growth, newspapers have joined other media in what *The New York Times*' Albert Scardino described as "a swamp" of declining revenues. Advertising and circulation revenues have increased marginally, if at all, since 1986, Scardino says. Reported increases often result only from price increases.

In many markets, circulation levels are stable at best and often decline despite newspapers' best efforts. Data compiled by the American Society of Newspaper Editors suggest household penetration (as opposed to circulation) has declined some 10 percent during the past ten years.

Can newspapers reverse this trend? If reversal is possible, there exists no consensus among executives as to how the task is to be accomplished. A special report by *Advertising Age* in 1987 dealt more with what will not work than what will. Among newspaper executives' comments were the following:

We got into trouble because we didn't pay as much attention to the product as we should and we didn't pay as much attention to service as we should have.

For years the industry ignored those special-interest segments. Instead we thought, "There is a ninth-grade graduate out there that needs to be told certain things."

Sometimes we all behave like pamphleteers. We put out newspapers that we think are good and we don't bother to see what the reader thinks of it.

These are not the industry's only problems. Advertising volume in general is expected to grow more slowly than has been the case in the past, and newsprint costs are increasing. The decline in advertising is being fed the business community's merger mania. When two airlines or two grocery store chains merge, one set of advertising expenditures is eliminated, to the benefit of the merged firm but to the detriment of the media.

Growth in classified advertising, which long has been the one bright spot on publishers' revenue horizons, also is starting to decline. Classified spending increased 10.1 percent in 1988 as opposed to 14.9 percent in 1987 and 11.1 percent in 1986. The 1988 figures were the lowest reported since 1985.

Industry Change?

How might the industry best respond? An almost limitless number of options exist, and publishers are exploiting almost all of them to a greater or lesser extent. Some are expanding publishing activities. Others appear intent on broadening their activities to encompass other communication sectors or, at minimum, on preventing denizens of those areas from getting too close to publishing.

Still others seem to be looking for new and better ways to do what they have always done, apparently in the belief that there remains a market for the traditional daily newspaper. Which of these techniques, if any of them, will prove successful remains to be seen.

Expansion Trend. Newspapers are expanding their publishing activities in two areas: by adding editions and by adding newspapers. A number of daily newspapers have acquired suburban weeklies in areas they serve. Others have been launching Sunday editions in an effort to capitalize on larger circulations on that day of the week.

Among more recent prospective acquirers of weekly newspapers have been *The Chicago Sun Times* and *The Baltimore Sun*. The Chicago newspaper in early 1989 moved to acquire thirty-eight weekly newspapers owned by Pioneer Press while the *Sun* acted to purchase four weeklies owned by the Susquehanna Press. Such transactions enable newspapers to offer group buys to advertisers, provided that publishers do not run afoul of the courts in the process, as was the case a few years ago for the *Orlando Sentinel* in Florida. The *Sentinel* was required by the Justice Department to divest itself of weekly holdings.

The Sunday publishing trend is less risky and apparently equally profitable. Sunday editions are important to publishers because newspaper reading is a more popular activity on Sunday, when the pace of life is slower and more people have time to read. Retail advertisers have been shifting more and more of their budgets to Sunday editions, and Sunday has become a big shopping day as well.

Sunday has become so attractive a publishing day, in fact, that Sunday competition has started to appear for the daily newspapers. A chain of free weeklies ringing St. Louis in summer of 1989 announced plans to compete with the city's daily newspaper in the Sunday market. One industry analyst described the move as ". . . a brilliant strategy, and one other suburban newspapers are apt to emulate."

Protecting Turf. While Sunday editions may help for a time, long-term development of publishing enterprises may depend on the extent to which publishers succeed in protecting existing turf and capturing new territory in several areas. In 1988, for example, publishers gained a competitive advantage through an increase in postage rates for third class mailers. Third class mailers include a number of organizations that distribute promotional coupons, depriving newspapers of what publishers' perceive to be their revenues. The postal rate change followed an extensive campaign on the part of publishers to induce postal authorities to change their rate structures.

Publishing interests have been less successful in the courtroom than in the administrative arena. While the postal service was agreeing to modify its rates, a series of court decision freed telephone companies to become involved in electronic publishing. Federal District Judge Harold H. Greene, who oversaw the breakup of the American Telephone and Telegraph Company ruled that AT&T could could become involved in electronic publishing and that the regional "Baby Bell" companies can set up mechanisms to store, handle, and deliver electronic information, including services such as "phone-in yellow pages." Publishers fear the telephone companies ultimately might be authorized to generate as well as deliver such information, giving them an entry point into the lucrative classified advertising market.

Rearguard Action. While waiting for Sunday editions or electronic delivery systems or both to enhance their economic positions, publishers have not proved averse to using traditional methods in efforts toward product improvement. More often than not, however, these efforts are less than optimally productive.

Consider, for example, the many dailies that have attempted through redesign to "look more like *USA Today*." Former editor William Kovach, of the *Atlanta Journal and Constitution*, a hard-nosed newsman of the old school, departed the Georgia city after a dispute with publisher Cox Enterprises over precisely that issue.

In an even more striking response to publisher efforts to remold their products for economic reasons, three senior editors resigned from the staff of the prestigious *Christian Science Monitor* in late 1988. Editor Katherine W. Fanning, managing editor David Anable, and assistant managing editor David Winder submitted their resignations in the face of management plans for layoffs and a redesign of the newspaper.

Future Development

While individual publishers' responses to change have been somewhat inconsistent, a reinvigorated ANPA is taking some steps that the association hopes will assure the future of members' businesses if not that of newspaper publishing in the traditional sense. Two steps have been taken, for example, to protect newspapers' advertising revenues by making it easier for advertisers to place their advertising.

National standards are being established for remote entry of classified advertising in order to enable large advertisers to place orders by personal computer for any newspaper in the country using a single format. A draft of the proposed standards was being reviewed by an industry committee in 1988, and the system was to be formally installed in 1989. Even more innovative than the classified system was AD-SAT, a venture launched in 1987 that uses satellite transmission systems to deliver color or black and white advertising simultaneously to newspapers.

Long-Term Prospects. These technology-based services represent a small part of the potential publishers may exploit over the remainder of the century and beyond. "New technology," in the words of management consultant John Diebold, "will bring newspapers either a serious erosion of readership and revenues—or an explosion of opportunities—according to how well it is managed." Diebold's recommendations to the 1988 meeting of the American Society of Newspaper Editors follow:

> Stop trying to block the role of others in providing electronic services . . . . Think instead in terms of joint efforts with communications companies and other enterprises . . . or launch your own electronic information services.

> Study where you might take better advantage of your current distribution channels to supplement your advertising. Merchants who can't afford newspaper advertising are turning to flyers and direct mail. Information technology . . . could be used to target those merchants with finely zoned advertising, and recoup those advertising losses.

> Experiment with the challenging editorial problem of treating a similar subject on print and on television, or on videotext.

> Mount a serious effort at achieving research and development in this country on electronic printing.

Diebold concluded by repeating a statement he had made to the editors during another talk twenty years before: "Far from fighting a rear-guard action as every new technology allows other media to encroach on your business, you can use technology to open an era in journalism. . . . The new technology . . . can make possible . . . a new and golden age of newspapers in this country and throughout the world."

Unfortunately, newspaper publishers appear little disposed to follow Diebold's advice. In the wake of failed electronic publishing experiments undertaken by Knight-Ridder and the Times-Mirror Company, publishers have concentrated on resisting potential competitors, especially the telephone companies. American Telephone and Telegraph Company and its offspring, the Baby Bells, all were attempting to gain access to electronic publishing in the late 1980s through legislative and legal channels. Specifically, they were seeking changes in rules that permitted them to distribute but not provide information. Publisher resistance was based primarily on concerns that the telephone companies might offer electronic yellow pages, capturing a portion of newspaper advertising revenues in the process.

Publishers' concerns at least to some extent may be well founded. New York Telephone in 1989 launched an information service called InfoLook that offered consumers business news and excerpts from *USA Today* and *Newsday* in addition to other services. New York Telephone was one of six of the seven Baby Bells that had announced plans for such "gateway" services. With such systems in place, the Baby Bells could become formidable competitors to newspaper publishers, especially if they are granted permission to become electronic publishers as well as gateway operators.

Short term prospects. Veronis, Suhler and Associates is more optimistic than Diebold concerning the newspaper industry's short term prospects. Veronis, Suhler data are based primarily on changing demographic patterns, which will produce greater numbers of individuals in older age groups. These conditions suggest prosperity for newspapers through the early 1990s, but offer no insight into potential changes that might occur if the telephone companies succeed in entering the electronic publishing field.

"The maturing population and a health economy will lead to 10 percent gains in circulation and advertising over the next five years," the company says. "Assuming good economic growth, classified advertising will become an increasingly important source of revenue for newspapers."

Projections based on research data, including those of Veronis, Suhler, universally assume other factors are equal. Whether such assumptions are valid where newspapers are involved is open to question. Members of the International Newspaper Advertising and Marketing Executives organization in 1987 were expressing substantive concerns over the future of their publications. Speakers at the group's annual meeting universally espoused reader-oriented strategies, and most expressed concern over the ability of newspapers to hold their own in increasingly competitive environments.

IN SUMMARY

Newspapers have been in decline in the United States for more than a decade, and there appears little reason to believe that the trend soon will be reversed. Circulation levels have been declining steadily in relative if not absolute terms in most markets,although advertising revenues have been relatively stable and profits have been strong.

The industry has been losing market share to competing media, and significant shifts have been occurring within the newspaper sector as well. National dailies have gained strength, as have the major newspaper chains. Publishers have taken comfort from demographic trends, but these may not produce hoped-for changes in newspaper readership patterns.

Newspapers have taken advantage of advancing technology to reduce their costs. Lithography has supplanted letterpress production techniques. Computers have replaced typewriters and hot metal composition systems. Satellite systems have permitted the development of national newspapers. Production costs continue to climb, however, fueled in large part by the price of newsprint, the paper on which newspapers publish.

Like other media, newspapers have become "niche players." Business newspapers and suburban weeklies have maintained strong market positions. Each of the national newspapers has focused its attention on specific audience segments, and the metropolitan dailies appear to be moving in the same direction, emphasizing local news in efforts to maintain readership levels.

The extent to which these techniques will succeed remains to be demonstrated. Publishers continue to jockey for position within the information industry, moving into other forms of communication to expand on or protect their publishing positions. Their futures will depend in large part on their ability to adapt to changing industry circumstances.

ADDITIONAL READING

American Newspaper Publishers Association. *Facts About Newspapers '88*. Washington, D.C.: American Newspaper Publishers Association, 1988.

American Newspaper Publishers Association. *Facts About Newspapers '83*. Washington, D.C.: American Newspaper Publishers Association, 1983.

American Newspaper Publishers Association. *Facts About Newspapers '78*. Washington, D.C.: American Newspaper Publishers Association, 1978.

Bogart, Leo. *Press and Public: Who Reads What, When, Where and Why in American Newspapers*. Hillsdale, N.J.: Erlbaum, 1981.

Diebold, John. "Newspapers and Information Technology: Some Strategic Options." Paper presented to the annual meeting of the American Society of Newspaper Editors, Washington, D.C., Apr. 15, 1988.

Emery, Edwin, and Michael Emery. *The Press and America: An Interpretive History of the Mass Media*. 5th ed. Englewood Cliffs, N.J.: Prentice-Hall, 1984.

Gaziano, Cecilie, and Kristin McGrath. "Segments of the Public Most Critical of Newspapers' Credibility: A Psychographic Analysis." *Newspaper Research Journal*, Summer 1987.

Gold, Allan R. "Editors of Monitor Resign Over Cuts." *New York Times*. Nov. 15, 1988.

Hulin-Salkin, Belinda. "Stretching to Deliver Readers' Needs." *Advertising Age*, July 25, 1987.

Jamieson, Kathleen H., and Karlyn K. Campbell. *The Interplay of Influence: Mass Media and Their Publics in News, Advertising, Politics*. 2nd ed. Belmont, Calif.: Wadsworth, 1983.

Jones, Alex S. "Newspapers Ponder Electronic Rivals," *New York Times*, Apr. 24, 1989.

—, "Sunday Papers Facing New Rival for Ads," *New York Times*, June 12, 1989.

Markoff, John. "Nynex Offers Broad Data Service," *New York Times*, Apr. 26, 1989.

Roberts, Johnnie L. "Newspapers Are Facing Tougher Times." *Wall Street Journal*, Sept. 21, 1988.

Rose, Frederick. "Los Angeles Times, a Publishing Power, Is Beset by Small Rivals." *Wall Street Journal*, Feb. 7, 1989.

Scardino, Albert. "After Years of Swimming, Newspapers Tread Water." *New York Times*, Nov. 21, 1988.

—. "Higher Cost of Newsprint Is Part of an Odd Equation." *New York Times*, Sept. 26, 1988.

Schiffman, James R., and Timothy K. Smith. "An Editor Quits, On Losing End of Old Struggle." *Wall Street Journal*, Nov. 7, 1988.

Selnow, Gary W., and William D. Crano. *Planning, Implementing, and Evaluating Targeted Communication Programs: A Manual for Business Communicators*. New York: Quorum, 1987.

Sharkey, Joe. "Daily Sports Paper To Be Launched Later This Year." *Wall Street Journal*, May 3, 1989.

—. "More Newspapers Plan Sunday Edition." *Wall Street Journal*. Jan. 19, 1989.

—. "Newspapers Are Facing Slower Growth In Classified Advertising, Survey Finds." *Wall Street Journal*, Apr. 24, 1989.

Sims, Calvin. "Information Please: Phone Companies vs. Newspapers." *New York Times*, May 7, 1989.

Veronis, Suhler and Associates. *Second Annual Five-Year Communications Industry Forecast, 1988-1992*. New York: Veronis, Suhler and Associates, July 1988.

7   New Magazines

Magazines fast are becoming the strongest of the mass media. While individual magazines may find their growth limited by greater competition for advertiser dollars, magazines as a group are more prosperous in readers and in revenues than at any time in their recent history. Not since the so-called golden age of magazines in the late 1800s has this mass medium been so strong.

Three factors contribute most to the collective strength of magazines: specialization, technology, and innovation. Specialization refers to a continuing trend away from general interest publications and toward magazines ever more tightly focused on narrowly defined subject matter. Technology has supported the trend toward specialization by reducing the cost of publishing, primarily through use of computer-based systems. Innovation involves progressively more creative concepts to produce audiences attractive to prospective advertisers and therefore rewarding to entrepreneurs.

These factors yet may produce another golden age in which magazines are the nation's preeminent mass medium. Industry performance since 1962, as described by the Magazine Publishers of America (MPA), suggests that magazines at minimum are becoming the nation's primary source of contemporary information. While MPA is a partisan source, the association's data are persuasive. The persuasiveness is heightened when the data are examined in the context of information published by independent sources.

At least one negative factor also is introduced by an independent source, however, in the form of data regarding the comprehension of print communication. Researchers working under the sponsorship of the Advertising Educational Foundation have found print communications—specifically, magazines—to be less effective communication vehicles than some believe to be the case.

MISCOMPREHENSION

The researchers, Jacob Jacoby and Wayne D. Hoyer, examined a series of questions critical to advertisers and others who depend on the efficiency of mass media:

1. What is the average level of comprehension among magazine readers?
2. Does comprehension level vary with type of content?
3. Do sociodemographic differences influence comprehension?

Research data were gathered by administering quizzes to readers after they were exposed to magazine communication. Results were not reassuring to those who depend on the effectiveness or efficiency of printed communication.

Comprehension Levels

Only 63 percent of the questions posed by the researchers were answered accurately. Twenty-one percent of respondents misunderstood the messages to which they had been exposed, while the remainder indicated they did not know.

Among the 1,347 who participated in the study, only 10 percent answered all questions correctly. Seventy-four percent misunderstood a part of what they had read. The remainder of responses were in the "don't know" category. In general, the researchers found, only 63 percent of messages in magazines are understood.

A small but significant variation in comprehension was found between advertising and editorial content. Normative miscomprehension of advertisements ranged from 15 to 23 percent while miscomprehension of editorial content was in the 19 to 28 percent range.

Sociodemographics

Differences in comprehension recorded among respondent subgroups were small. Miscomprehension tended to increase slightly in those over the age of fifty-four. Those with less than ninth grade education experienced more miscomprehension than others, and a small inverse relationship was found between income and miscomprehension. No significant gender difference were detected, but facts were found to be markedly less prone to misconception than inferences.

Perhaps most interesting in terms of sociodemographics are differences between the findings of this study and data gathered by the researchers during a similar project dealing with the electronic media. Sociographic and demographic factors accounted for far greater variation in comprehension in the electronic media than among magazines (see chapter 8).

SPECIALIZATION

Although less than perfect as channels of communication, magazines exert a growing influence among mass media. The most persuasive data concerning the influence of magazines arises out of a trend toward specialization. The depth and breadth of the specialization trend is most apparent in the several magazine directories used by advertisers and others. Standard Rate and Data Service's consumer magazine directory, for example, is little more than a third the bulk and weight of the company's directory of trade magazines. Within the consumer directory, in addition, are found a relative handful of what might be termed general interest publications. Magazines today might be better categorized as general interest, special interest, and super-special interest, with the latter category consisting of publications catering to business, the professions and academia.

Publications is the critical word in the sentence above. The word encompasses newspapers and newsletters as well as magazines. Definitions that might permit accurately sorting out the components of those categories are another matter.

Journalists generally are strict constructionists in defining the word *newspaper*. They apply broader definitions to *magazine* and *newsletter*, and the results can be confusing to lay persons. Many publications that appear to be newspapers are classified by professionals as magazines and, as a result, numbered as magazines by those who publish media directories.

Definitional Characteristics

Much of the definition problem has to do with criteria used in sorting out or differentiating between and among newspapers, newsletters, and magazines. Ambiguity is the prevalent characteristic of contemporary definitions, regardless of source.

Webster defines a magazine as "a periodical that usually contains a miscellaneous collection of articles, stories, poems and pictures and is directed at the general reading public" and as "a periodical containing special interest material directed at a group having a particular hobby, interest or profession (as education, photography or medicine) or at a particular age group (as children, teenagers)." The two definitions more or less adequately cover general and special interest magazines.

A newspaper, in contrast, is defined as "a paper that is printed and distributed daily, weekly, or at some other regular and usually short interval and that contains news, articles of opinion (as editorials), features, advertising, or other matter regarded as of current interest. A newsletter is defined as "a printed sheet, pamphlet, or small newspaper containing news or information of current interest to or bearing upon the interests of a special group."

Variables that these definitions address include (a) frequency or regularity of publication, (b) nature of content, and (c) nature of audience. None of these characteristics, unfortunately, can be defined with sufficient precision to circumscribe any media group. All publications that appear daily are newspapers but the newspaper category also encompasses weekly and biweekly publications. Many magazines and newsletters also appear at weekly intervals.

Differences in content between articles, as specific to general interest magazines, and news, as specific to newspapers, are more difficult to define. Much of the content of the major weekly news magazines—*Time*, *Newsweek*, and *U.S. News & World Report*—would be as much at home in newspaper as in magazine format. In like manner, much of the content of a Sunday edition of *The New York Times* or *The Washington Post* could be published by one of the news magazines without departing from any apparent content standard.

Newsletters usually are readily identified by their relative brevity and format. Much of their content, however, could make the transition to a magazine or newspaper with little difficulty. A number of magazines in special and general interest categories, for example, contain pages composed in a manner resembling the typewriter format of the *Kiplinger Washington Letter.*

Other Approaches

Presumed experts have taken divergent approaches to defining types of print media. Some have managed to write extensively about newspapers and magazines without venturing concise definitions. Others who made the effort fell short of establishing all-encompassing categories to make discussions more easily managed.

Author and media critic Ben Bagdikian, himself a former print *(New York Times)* journalist, defines a newspaper as a publication that carries information on newsprint for a general audience that is issued daily, weekly, or on Sunday. (There have, in the history of U.S. journalism, been several newspapers that printed only on Sunday.) Bagdikian's definition would exclude some publications that virtually every authority considers to be newspapers and would include others that few would consider worthy inclusion. *The Wall Street Journal*, for example, would have to be excluded from a Bagdikian list in that it is not directed toward a general audience. Many shoppers and advertising circulars would have to be included.

Among those who manage to successfully avoid definitions while dealing effectively with extensive descriptions of the media are two teams of textbook authors. Warren Agee, Phillip Ault and Edwin Emery describe newspapers and magazines at length in *Introduction to Mass Communications*, as do Ray Hiebert, Donald Ungurait and Thomas Bohn in *Mass Media V.* In neither of these books are individual media precisely defined, and probably for good reason. No debate over the nature of specific mass media is apt to be productive in an era of rapid change. Historically, the word *magazine* was derived from the French and referred to a warehouse or storehouse. Early magazines, in fact, were compendia of information previously printed elsewhere. Newspapers, in contrast, usually contained originally written material.

Distinctions such as these today have blurred to a point at which they are all but meaningless. The blurring, moreover, is proceeding at a rate that raises questions as to the meanings of basic media language. Consider, for example, some of the publications serving the media industry. *Editor and Publisher*, most would agree, is a magazine. *Advertising Age*, however, appears in tabloid format and uses a makeup style more akin to traditional newspapers than to magazines.

Any two individuals who agree on the basic nature of *Editor and Publisher* and *Advertising Age* may want to entertain themselves by attempting to characterize *TV Sports*. This advertiser supported magazine was launched by ESPN, the cable television station sports station, primarily to carry broadcast listings. Is the result a competitor to *TV Guide*, an item of direct mail advertising, or a printed version of television content akin to the soap opera magazines?

The Magazine Mix

Your conclusion concerning an appropriate label for *TV Sports*, or any other magazine, is unlikely to detract from the evident trend toward specialization in the magazine sector as a whole. Of the almost 500 magazines launched in 1987, only 180 were of the consumer variety and only 10, or about 2 percent of the total, were categorized by the Magazine Publisher Association as general interest. Largest numbers of start-ups in the consumer group were as follows:

City and regional interest	20
Business	16
Travel	14
Sports	12
Health	11
General interest	10

MPA data are straightforward but may be somewhat misleading, as indicated by the definitional questions addressed above. This is especially so in MPA's city and regional interest category. Broadly defined, *city and regional interest* can cover a host of publications that might as readily be assigned to special interest categories. What category, for example, is logically home to an entertainment magazine oriented to a relatively small geographic area? Both city and regional interest and entertainment categories would be defensible choices.

Trend Origins

While numerical estimates vary, history and logic suggest that only a small percentage of magazines launched each year will survive. New launches continue, however, because of magazines' ability to target and deliver specific audiences to waiting advertisers.

Targetability or selectivity is the most attractive feature of magazines from the viewpoints of publishers and advertisers. Magazines also are attractive in that they are better "attended" than competing media. Magazines are sought out and selected by their readers. Rather than being casually watched or scanned as a matter of course, magazines tend to be closely read. More than three quarters of all magazines are purchased by subscription rather than in single copies. In addition, magazines equal or outperform newspapers in exposure to white collar readers.

Finally, magazines are best equipped to deliver complex information and provide high quality reproduction. Magazine audiences are interested in the in-depth treatment of subject matter in which their publications specialize. The nature of magazine production processes enables publishers to provide better reproduction than is possible in newspapers for advertisers and readers. These attributes collectively have triggered a growth pattern that continues to accelerate.

PATTERNS OF GROWTH

Magazines have increased consistently in number, in total circulation, and in advertiser patronage through the last half of the twentieth century. The growth pattern apparently persists because of the relative quality of magazine audiences from user as well as advertiser standpoints.

Both perspectives were illustrated by a 1986 study of magazine and television advertising conducted by Audits and Surveys. Men and women both rated magazines superior by significant margins.

Growth Trends

Magazine circulation in the United States has grown more rapidly than the nation's population since midcentury. From 197 million in 1962, magazine circulation increased to 236 million in 1972 and 291 million in 1982. By 1987, the total had reached 336 million.

Advertising revenues grew at approximately the same rate as circulation during the 1960s and early 1970s but increased rapidly during the 1980s. From $850 million in 1962, revenues grew to $1.3 billion in 1972 then more than tripled to $3.42 billion in 1982. The 1987 total was $5.39 billion.

Numbers of magazines increased by almost 28 percent during the same period, from 9,062 to 11,593, and the pattern promised to continue. A total of 477 new magazines was published in 1987. More impressive than numbers of magazines established, however, are data about magazine circulation in comparison with the national population. While the population increased by less than 70 percent between 1952 and 1987, magazine circulation more than doubled on a per-issue basis.

Magazine reading, as a result, is pervasive in the United States. Ninety-four percent of the population eighteen years old and older read an average of 9.6 magazines each month. More than 96 percent of readers attended or graduated from college, and the same percentage enjoy household incomes of $40,000 or more. The extent and affluence of readers, in fact, doubtless is the primary factor that motivates publishers to launch more and more magazines. As long as advertisers are interested in publishers' affluent audiences, proliferation of magazines will continue.

Proliferation Patterns

The magnitude of the proliferation pattern was described by *New York Times* columnist Wayne Curtis in early 1989 with a summary of the previous year's statistics:

> Magazine publishers seem undaunted by the fact that only two out of 10 new magazines survive beyond their fourth year. Indeed, in 1987, 477 new consumer magazines appeared on the newsstands, a 28 percent increase over new launches in 1986.
>
> Growth continued apace in 1988, although figures have yet to be tabulated. And the activity shows no sign of abating. In recent days, the information hot line at the Successful Magazine Publishing Group, an association of magazine executives, fielded one phone call a day from prospective publishers requesting details on how to start a new magazine.

Most of them are bent on developing specialized publications to develop narrow reader groups for waiting advertisers. Only rarely will a publisher launch a magazine as broadly oriented as *People*. Among 1987 start-ups, sports, music, and automotive magazines were among the most popular, but entrepreneurial publishers are prone to move quickly from one area to another in keeping with perceived profit potential.

Levitt Communications is exemplary of the sort of entrepreneurial organization often found in magazine publishing and elsewhere in the communication industry. Founded by American Stock Exchange Chairman Arthur Levitt, Jr., and consultant James K. Glassman, Levitt Communications took a broad-spectrum approach to publishing. The firm publishes *Roll Call*, a newspaper for Congress, and owns University Press, an academic book publisher, as well as half of *Battery News*, a weekly serving Battery Park City in New York.

Entrepreneurism is no less prevalent, however, in other sectors or niches. Observers of the mass media during the late 1980s have found no shortage of material concerning new publishing ventures. The start-ups came so frequently, however, that editors were discouraging articles other than those that focused on some trend or otherwise newsworthy development.

Media Coverage

Battles for market position or circulation then became media reporters' favorite subjects. Magazines oriented to soap opera fans, teenagers, homemakers, the over forty woman, the wealthy, the computer user, and the business community proliferated. Media writers and critics responded accordingly. Their efforts also included a number of lengthy features concerning the major media organizations' efforts to prosper in increasingly competitive environments.

Among the more aggressive of the media moguls is S. I. Newhouse, Jr., who inherited Conde Nast Publications in 1979 and proceeded to build on that base. Newhouse launched *Self* and *Vanity Fair* and acquired *New Yorker*, *GQ*, and several others. By 1989, Newhouse owned more than a dozen magazines and probably would own more. Unlike those building media empires for their own sake, he selected publications based on his own interests and took a long developmental view rather than aiming for short term profits.

Newhouse nevertheless was in the thick of the battle for magazine markets. His *Vanity Fair* and *Conde Nast's Traveler* (the Diner's Club magazine renamed) fought for circulation with the likes of *Elle*, *M*, *Connoisseur*, and *Millionaire*. Similar turf wars raged over the over-forty woman, the soap opera fan, the business executive and others. *Lear's*, *Memories*, *Modern Maturity*, *50 Plus* and others are competing aggressively for a growing "seniors" market. *Soap*

Opera Update, Soap Opera Digest, and *Daytime TV* are among major competitors for the soap viewer. In New York, *New York City Business, Manhattan, inc.*, and *Crain's New York Business* compete with *Business Week, Nation's Business, Barron's, Dun's Review*, and a host of other publications for the business market. The same pattern prevails in the business sector across the country, with more than one hundred publications
competing for executive attention.

While battling for new audiences, publishers also were competing for increased shares of existing markets. Competition for homemaker readers, for example, accelerated sharply during the late 1980s. The field had been dominated by the so-called seven sisters: *Ladies Home Journal, Good Housekeeping, McCall's, Better Homes and Gardens, Family Circle, Redbook*, and *Woman's Day*. Bauer Publishing, a division of Germany's Heinrich Bauer Verlag, then announced plans to introduce *First for Women*, aiming at a circulation of two million. At about the same time, Newhouse's Conde Nast announced plans to buy *Woman*, and News Corporation announced plans for *Mirabella*, an upscale fashion monthly.

Battle lines even extended into magazine design, once an area ruled by tradition. Successful designs then changed rarely and at a glacial pace, presumably to avoid offending existing readers. Fresh faces became the rule in the late 1980s, with magazines undergoing almost wholesale restyling. During 1988, for example, *Ms, Esquire, H.G., Mademoiselle, Good Housekeeping, Glamour, Fortune, Self*, and *Mother Jones* were only part of the horde of new faces that appeared on newsstands. The flurry of redesign projects was prompted by a perceived need to adhere to contemporary standards and by competitive factors. Advertisers' reactions are as important as those of readers, especially in the early months of a refurbished format. Redesign can help or hinder in advertising sales as well as on the newsstand.

Day-to-day competition among magazines within and across reader categories in the 1980s partly obscured the passing of the era of general interest magazines. Something of an epitaph appeared in *The New York Times* on September 10, 1985. In an article written by advertising columnist Philip H. Dougherty, *The Times* recorded *Reader's Digest*'s decision to reduce its circulation rate base by 1.5 million to 16.25 million and, thereby, yield circulation leadership to *TV Guide*. The *Digest*'s move, in a sense, marked the end of an era in magazine publishing. Not only did few mass audience magazines remain, but no longer did one of them lead in circulation.

INNOVATION

Redesign, as mentioned above, is a basic competitive strategy in publishing. Magazines and newspapers long have sought to capture reader attention with more attractive type dress or graphics. In recent years, innovation has moved beyond graphics and content formats to several nontraditional areas. In magazine publishing, most such efforts have taken one of two forms: other components of the communication industry have used magazines as extensions of their services, and magazine publishers have extended their operations into other communication sectors.

There remains one other area, however, in which magazine publishers have become increasingly active: innovation within traditional magazine formats. Innovation here refers to relatively radical departures from traditional mechanical processes to enhance the attractiveness of publications to advertisers and/or readers.

Mechanical Innovation

The origins of the first mechanical innovation—peel-apart advertisements containing perfume samples—are lost in time, although the technology continues in use and presumably remains productive for users. With scent strips now commonplace, advertisers are introducing a broad range of what some term high tech advertisements. Some consist of nothing more than pop-ups of the sort long used in preschoolers' story books. Others are more innovative.

Advertising pop-ups first appeared in the mid-1980s. Honeywell was among the first users with a model of a factory complex that appeared in *Business Week*. Pop-ups since then have been used by Disney World, Dodge trucks, Transamerica, Corporation, Chicago's Northern Trust Company, and Hennessy cognac.

Toyota Motor Sales went beyond traditional pop-ups in 1987 by inserting 3-D viewers in advertisements introducing a new model of the Toyota Corolla. Carillon Importers, and Brown-Forman Beverage Company used microchips to create musical advertisements playing Christmas carols. IBM used music and blinking lights in an advertisement introducing its PC microcomputer in France, and there seems no end in sight.

Publishers are using computers to insert subscribers' names into magazine advertisements. The process is tricky in that mailing labels must match advertising content, but the technique has been applied successfully by several publishers.

Where does it end? *Business Week*'s Amy Dunkin reports that some expect microchips to someday permit magazines to mimic television and quotes advertising executive Jerry Della Femina: "The limit is when a pair of hands reaches out of the ad, grabs you by the throat, and pulls you in."

Media Innovation

Publishers' openness to new technology in advertising is more than equaled by their internal applications of technology. Many have become involved in electronic information distribution and some firms in the electronic sector have expanded into magazine publishing. In other cases, magazine entrepreneurs first have developed innovative published products and have subsequently moved into the electronic sector.

New Approaches. Perhaps most innovative in the latter group has been Christopher Whittle, chairman of Whittle Communications of Knoxville, Tennessee. Whittle in 1988 launched *Special Report*, a quarterly magazine that comes in six parts and is circulated exclusively through physicians' offices. *Special Report* departed from tradition by

- selling category advertising directly to producers rather than by working through advertising agencies, and allowing only one company in any retail category to advertise in each of the six magazines;

- guaranteeing advertisers that magazines would be placed in the waiting rooms of at least fifteen thousand obstetricians, pediatricians, and family practice physicians, all of whom would be required to have no more than two other magazines in their waiting rooms;

- selling advertising in twenty-four page units (one page per year in each of the six magazines) at $1.25 million per unit.

The magnitude of Whittle's enterprise was unprecedented, but he was not alone in applying the free circulation principle to magazines. Many others have done the same. Ford Motor Company's *Ford Times* was a pioneer in this area. Farmers Insurance Group distributes *Friendly Exchange* to some four million policyholders, and United Healthcare is publishing *Healthscenes* for distribution by member hospitals to their patients.

The same pattern is followed in somewhat different fashion by magazines such as *Avenue* and *Seven Days* in New York and *Dossier* in Washington. These magazines cater to the affluent. Their publishers, who prosper by delivering large affluent and/or well-educated audiences to advertisers, have elected to use free or controlled circulation to boost their distribution figures and support high advertising rates. The technique thus is neither new nor innovative.

While the jury was still out as to the long term success of *Special Report*, Whittle was in the process of launching "Channel One," a broadcast product intended for high school audiences. Whittle Communications proposed to provide receivers free of charge to participating schools. The schools would agree to have students watch educational programming and accompanying commercials that Whittle presumably would sell to sponsors.

"Channel One" brought a small deluge of protests from authors and others concerned over the future of literacy, literature and reading but Whittle appeared little concerned. Time, Incorporated had agreed to pay $185 million for a half interest in Whittle Communications and an option to purchase an additional 30 percent. Within months, in addition, both Turner Broadcasting of Atlanta and the Discovery Channel had announced plans for similar projects aimed at the high school market. The destiny of classroom-oriented broadcasting remains uncertain, however. "Channel One" has been banned by the New York Board of Regents from schools in that state, and California authorities have discouraged schools from using the program.

Other Techniques. Whittle's was not the only move on the part of a publisher from print to electronic media. Several others attempted to follow the same path, in one direction or the other. While publishers were moving into the electronic sector, some in the electronic world were moving into publishing.

Some moves across traditional media boundaries were logical in light of other factors involved. Whittle Communications' "Channel One" effort, on the other hand, appeared motivated purely by economic factors. The logical category included moves from publishing into the electronic world and from the electronic area into publishing. *PC Magazine* organized "PC MagNet," an interactive magazine extension that readers can dial up on computers by accessing CompuServe Information Service. The magazine's editorial involvement with every aspect of personal computers, including communication, made the move quite logical. McGraw-Hill, doubtless for similar reasons, offers Bix (Byte Information Exchange), primarily for readers of *Byte*, the company's computer magazine.

PC MagNet and Bix both have been productive for their sponsors in nonmonetary terms. *Byte* has recruited writers from among Bix users, and *PC Magazine* has used MagNet to conduct user surveys subsequently incorporated into the magazine. Most magazines have not sought to develop cash flows from their electronic ventures, viewing them instead as contributors to magazine growth.

The same sort of motivators apparently prompted *Online Today*, a monthly printed version of CompuServe Information Service's *Online Daily*. *Online Today* is published to encourage subscribers to expand their use of CompuServe. Content consists primarily of feature articles about CompuServe services and advertising for computer-related products and services.

Online Today is not the only publication for users of on-line computer services. Most of the magazine's competitors are entrepreneurial publications seeking to capitalize on growing interest in computer utilities. *Link-Up*, for example, is a bi-monthly tabloid newspaper that calls itself "the newsmagazine for users of online services." Other computer publications also dedicate significant amounts of space to online services and technologies of concern to the magazine publishing industry.

Yet another innovation came from the nation's catalog publishers, who were experimenting with publications that resembled magazines. Lands' End, Inc., was among pioneers in the area, adding employee profiles to clothing catalogs in 1981. Williams-Sonoma's cookware catalogs feature recipes, and Spiegel, Inc., produces self-improvement video tapes designed to sell items in its catalogs. Alternatively called "Magalogs" or "Catazines," they are yet another experiment in a fast-changing media world.

TECHNOLOGY

Some similar events have been spawned by changing technology. Most technology influencing the magazine industry relates to processes used in magazine production. In at least one case, however, technology has spawned a competitor. "Videozines," as they have been called, are nothing more than magazines delivered on videocassettes. They are designed to be watched and listened to rather than read. And while they "have some problems" at the moment, they someday may be part of the world of magazines—video or otherwise.

Most early videozines dealt with sports although one "publication" called *Travelquest* was aimed at travel agents. All face major developmental obstacles, primarily in high costs and equipment limitations. Costs of twenty dollars a copy are not unusual, and magazine publishers wonder whether readers can be attracted to "publications" that limit "reading" to rooms equipped with videocassette recorders. A portable player might encourage greater acceptance, however, as has been the case in Japan.

IMPACT OF COMPUTERS

Any new technology that erodes traditional magazines' market shares will be insignificant when compared with technologies that help publishers. Magazine proliferation has been fueled in large part by the microcomputer and the tools that it made accessible to writers and editors.

Microcomputers put magazine publishing within the economic reach of a large percentage of the population. These conditions result from the fact that tasks now performed by microcomputers once could be accomplished only by skilled workers through extensive manual labor, or both. The work of designers, writers, editors, advertising sales persons, commercial artists, and printers has been reduced in volume, has increased in productivity, or has in part been replaced through the workings of the microcomputer.

Designers

Computers enable designers to easily create as many different looks for existing or proposed magazines as owners or publishers care to contemplate. Once loaded into a microcomputer, through a scanner or otherwise, every component of the magazine readily can be modified for management review. Each resulting version can be quickly reproduced in hard copy form through laser printers. Where editors or publishers experience difficulty in visualizing results, slides or photo positives can be made from computer screens. Slides or photos can be reproduced in any size using state-of-the art copying equipment. Publishers or editors considering changes in the look of their publications thus can have almost any number of graphic variations in front of them in minutes.

Further modifications are just as easily accomplished. Microcomputers permit every proposed design to be saved in electronic form for subsequent use. Each can be further reviewed and modified through additions or deletions. Two or more features from separate versions can be combined to create still another variation. Finally, entire pages can be produced in nearly finished form for final review.

Preparing final review versions usually involves executing preliminary designs in virtually the same form in which they would be prepared for printing. Articles are set in type and placed in page form by computer. Alternative type faces may be used in the pages. Computers permit both processes to be completed in minutes at negligible cost.

Illustrations can be prepared separately or as a part of final review copies. Photos and artwork can be quickly and inexpensively edited and resized by computer. Graphic elements can be maintained as separate electronic files and integrated with others to create final products.

Computer-generated photographs have yet to achieve the clarity necessary to the final product. Some illustrations require alternative production techniques as well. Computer-managed illustrations are more than adequate for review purposes, however, and production technology is advancing at a rate that soon should overcome the last barriers to high fidelity computer graphics.

Photographers

Devices that ultimately will overcome the photo fidelity barrier already exist in a new imaging technology that replaces photographic images with computer files. The process requires a device externally resembling a 35 mm camera and equipped with a lens. The resemblance stops with the lens, however, in that the "camera" records images on miniature floppy disks rather than on film. Resulting files can be loaded into computers, shown on video display terminals or television screens, printed out on laser printers, and combined with words to create newspaper or magazine content.

Images also can be transmitted in digital form via microwave or telephone lines.

The technological feasibility of the system was demonstrated during the national political conventions of 1988, when a University of Missouri team transmitted images to their campus for reproduction in student newspapers. Image quality arguably was inadequate for magazine reproduction, but advancing technology can be expected to soon overcome these deficiencies.

While imaging technology will continue to improve, the process will not soon eliminate the photograph. Results will remain inferior to professional photography for some time to come. The cost of computer imaging, in addition, will be beyond the reach of individuals for some time. Equipment necessary to reproduce images in a form similar to photography costs several thousand dollars. Images can be displayed on television or VDT screens at lower costs, but television images fall short of photographs in many respects.

Photographers and photography at a minimum will continue to prosper as artists and an art form. Photographic training doubtless will be necessary to those using imaging equipment during a transitional period. Photography ultimately will probably disappear, however, as a mass media technique.

Mechanical Artists

Computer technology already is leading mechanical artists to the brink of extinction. Magazines and, to a lesser extent, newspapers long have employed mechanical artists to handle paste-up duties. Paste-up involves taking reproduction proofs of type set in metal or by photo typesetters and, literally, pasting them up in final page form.

Type for articles and advertisements today is more easily and more rapidly manipulated by computer than in proof form. Sizes and leading, the space between lines of type, can be changed at the stroke of a computer key. Where necessary, type faces can be changed with equal ease. The finished product can be printed out on a laser printer in camera-ready form for use in lithographic printing or, through more sophisticated equipment, can be converted directly to negative or plate form.

Mechanical artists, as a result, have become or have been supplanted by computer operators. Writers and editors who came first into the computer age more often than not have been replacing mechanical artists in their traditional roles. Specifications prepared by graphic designers are readily followed by writers or editors, eliminating the need for mechanical artwork.

Writers

Adaptation to computers came easily to writers because of advantages they derived from the technology. Computers permit rapid and efficient reorganization of work in progress. Changes can be made easily in words, sentences, paragraphs, pages, chapters and books. Consider, for example, the doctoral candidate making last minute changes in a dissertation. Pages and footnotes in such documents must be consecutively numbered and precisely positioned. Minor changes, in the precomputer era, often required retyping dozens of pages of manuscript. Computers eliminate such problems. Footnotes are renumbered and repositioned, pages are renumbered, and indexes are modified in keeping with other changes, all in a matter of moments. A few key strokes then direct the computer to generate a revised manuscript.

The benefits are even greater for those who write books or engage in projects of similar magnitude. Paragraphs, pages, and entire chapters can be moved about at will. Changes that must be carried out repetitively throughout a manuscript, such as those in which specific words must be replaced, can be accomplished automatically.

Writers who prefer their own typographic specifications to those imposed by graphic designers or others also find the computer environment hospitable. At little cost beyond the time required to learn a graphics program such as PageMaker or Ventura Publisher, writers can specify type faces and sizes to their hearts' content.

Finally, writers enjoy the portability of computers and the capability to transmit files by telephone. Portable computers are smaller and lighter than typewriters. More important, they can be equipped with internal modems—modulator-demodulators—that permit them to be quickly plugged into telephone lines.

Editors

Ease of content management by far is the most attractive attribute of computers from the standpoint of magazine editors. Where writers find computers helpful in transmitting information, editors find them even more beneficial after information has been received. What earlier would have been a typewritten document that would have to be rekeyed by a typesetter now is an electronic file that needs no rekeying. Editors can examine and revise electronic files on their computers, hold them in electronic form for further revision, or convert them almost instantaneously into page form for printing.

Advertising Sales Persons

Those in advertising sales enjoy the same benefits that computers create for writers and editors, and others as well. All writing, editing, and file management attributes that assist editors and writers help advertising sales personnel and managers. Perhaps the most productive computer-based devices for those in advertising, however, are software packages that permit several individuals to work on the same electronic file at the same time from different locations. An advertising sales person and his or her client, for example, together can make changes in a proposed advertisement, each from his or her own office.

The sales person can transmit an electronic file containing an advertisement to an advertiser in the same way that the writer transmits an article. The two of them then link their computers by telephone using a two-party editing program and employ a second telephone line for accompanying conversation. Each sees the advertisement on his or her computer screen while the other makes changes. When final changes have been made and approved, the finished file becomes camera-ready copy ready for insertion into the appropriate publication page.

Savings in time are considerable in the exchanges between advertising sales persons and their prospects alone. Savings increase when computers also are used in preparing copy and converting that copy into advertisements. Where start-up magazines are involved, computers and software enable the same personnel to handle editorial and advertising content with equal ease and economy.

Printers

While helping the advertising department, computers replaced printers. *Printer* is a term with multiple meanings. Traditionally, the printer is an individual who operates a printing press. In the magazine industry, however, the printing press operator is a pressman, or press person if you prefer. The printer, in contrast, was the individual who took metal type prepared by typesetting machines and placed it in forms from which press plates ultimately were made. The printer, in other words, did what the writer and advertising person now can do more rapidly and more cleanly by computer. The printer and the typesetting machine operator were displaced by the computer.

IN SUMMARY

Until general introduction of interactive media will remake the face of mass communication, changes in magazines during the 1980s will stand as the most radical upheaval among mass media since the appearance of television. By the time the interactive media come into common use, in addition, magazines well may have adapted to those media as well.

The only substantive problem on the horizon for magazines only recently has been isolated by researchers. Substantial portions of the messages transmitted through magazines are miscomprehended. Fewer then 10 percent of those involved in the study answered all questions correctly, and as much as 63 percent of messages apparently were misunderstood.

Comprehension problems aside, magazines have gained in strength as well as numbers over the past decade and more, primarily through specialization. Entrepreneurial publishers have become adept at identifying prospectively productive audience groups and designing publications to meet their needs while creating new audiences to sell to advertisers. So strong has been the entrepreneurial boom in specialized magazines that circulation losses occasioned by the disappearance of mass magazines has been absorbed without slowing the overall pace of growth in the industry.

Publishers have used a broad range of innovative techniques to fuel the economic growth of the magazine industry. These range from advertiser-oriented devices such as scent strips, pop-ups, and the like to computer-based production technology. Product innovation has ranged from development of publications for specific audiences to creation of on-line versions of magazines and so-called videozines.

Microcomputers have come into extensive use in the magazine publishing world in the writing, editing, advertising and production processes. Still more innovation is expected as imaging replaces photography.

ADDITIONAL READING

Agee, Warren K., Phillip H. Ault and Edwin Emery. *Introduction to Mass Communication*. 9th ed. New York: Harper and Row, 1988.

Alter, Johnathan. "Boom in the Business Press." *Newsweek*, Jan. 7, 1985.

Barmash, Isadore. "A Magazine with a Profit at its Debut." *New York Times*, Sept. 30, 1988.

Blau, Eleanor. "Soap Opera Magazines Fight for Fans' Hearts and Dollars." *New York Times*, Oct. 24, 1988.

Bulkeley, William M. "Battle of the Computer-Magazine Titans: Ziff Pulls Ahead of Main Rival in U.S. Market." *New York Times*, Feb. 24, 1989.

Crossen, Cynthia. "Magazine for Homemakers Aims to Avoid Ad Clutter." *Wall Street Journal*, Nov. 16, 1988.

—. "Magazines Offer 'Extras' in Battle for Ads." *Wall Street Journal*, Jan. 4, 1989.

—. "Magazines Use Free Copies to Attract Affluent Readers." *Wall Street Journal*, Feb. 13, 1989.

Curtis, Wayne. "What's New in Magazine Publishing." *New York Times*, Jan. 22, 1989.

—, "A New Personality and Name: Say Hello to 'Magalogs.'" *New York Times*, May 14, 1989.

Dougherty, Philip H. "Reader's Digest Cuts Rate Base." *New York Times*, Sept. 10, 1985.

—. "Special Ad Section Debated." *New York Times*, Oct. 9, 1985.

Dunkin, Amy. "Print Ads That Make You Stop, Look–and Listen." *Business Week*, Nov. 23, 1987.

Fabrikant, Geraldine. "And Now, A Magazine For the Over-40 Woman." *New York Times*, Feb. 7, 1988.

—. "Si Newhouse Tests His Magazine Magic." *New York Times*, Sept. 25, 1988.

—. "Time and Whittle Form Alliance." *New York Times*. Oct. 21, 1988.

—. "Wooing the Wealthy Reader." *New York Times*, Oct. 4, 1987.

Hiebert, Ray E., Donald F. Ungurait, and Thomas W. Bohn. *Mass Media V*. New York: Longman, 1988.

Husni, Samir. *Samir Husni's Guide to New Magazines*. University, Miss.: University of Mississippi Department of Journalism, 1988.

Jacoby, Jacob, and Wayne D. Hoyer. *The Comprehension and Miscomprehension of Print Communications: An Investigation of Mass Media Magazines*. New York: Advertising Educational Foundation, 1987.

Magazine Publishers of America. "A Documentary on the Power of Magazines." New York: Magazine Publishers of America, Dec. 1987, (no. 55).

——. "Magazine Almanac: Facts, Trends and Perspectives That Can Work for You." New York: Magazine Publishers of America, Mar. 1988 (no. 56).

——. "Magazine Almanac: Information Is Your Competitive Edge." New York: Magazine Publishers of America, Nov. 1986 (no. 53).

Miller, Michael W. "Computer Magazines' Electronic Spinoffs Give Readers a Quick Way to Talk Back." *Wall Street Journal*, Oct. 19, 1988.

Mills, David. "Publications At No Charge Are Subtle Ads." *Wall Street Journal*, Aug. 5, 1983.

Plutka, Gary. "Discovery Channel Is Latest to Offer TV Show to Schools," *Wall Street Journal*, May 17, 1989.

Rothenberg, Randall. "The Media Business." *New York Times*, Nov. 9, 1988.

Selnow, Gary W., and William D. Crano. *Planning, Implementing, and Evaluating Targeted Communication Programs: A Manual for Business Communicators*. New York: Quorum, 1987.

Stevenson, Richard W. "A Sports Magazine from ESPN." *New York Times*, October 13, 1988.

Toth, Debora. "What's New in Magazine Redesign." *New York Times*, Jan. 1, 1989.

8 Narrowcasting Revisited

A growing volume of special interest programming years ago prompted the suggestion that the electronic media were dealing in narrowcasting rather than broadcasting. Diversity in cable programming and further audience fragmentation make "narrowcasting" an even more appropriate descriptor of contemporary conditions. Although once dominated by three major commercial networks, television is coming to resemble radio in numbers of outlets and variety in programming. Independent television stations are increasing in number, and the advent of low power stations will further that trend. Perhaps most significant, competition for existing cable systems is taking shape among the offspring of American Telephone and Telegraph Company.

Technological progress in radio and television is fostering diversity and accompanying audience fragmentation while undermining network dominance. Deterioration in network influence is especially noticeable in television, where advances in satellite technology have enabled stations to improve remote news coverage and reduce dependence on networks. Network investment in news programming has declined for this and one other reason: network news budgets have come under increasing pressure as advertising revenues decline with audience shares.

News budget reductions underscore the entertainment orientation of the electronic media. Radio and television, with few exceptions, are committed more to entertainment than to information. The principle applies equal to radio and television, to broadcast and cable outlets, and to network and independent stations. News and weather channels available through cable systems are not exceptions to the rule. Their informational programming is a small percentage of each system's daily fare. In the broadcast sector, National Public Radio and Public Broadcasting System television offerings are still smaller islands of information in large seas of entertainment.

These conditions are overshadowed, for those interested in the broadcast media as information channels, by a growing body of evidence suggesting that these media are less effective in communicating information than earlier was believed to be the case. Research in the United States and abroad suggests that a large percentage of information presumably conveyed to listeners or viewers is not received. Additional research shows that significant portions of what is received is misperceived or misunderstood.

Contemporary circumstances suggest that these trends will persist, that the informational efficiency of electronic media will further deteriorate. Audiences apparently will continue to fragment. Technology will further the fragmentation process, especially in dissemination of information. The efficiency of electronic media as mass communication channels will deteriorate. Only the speed and magnitude of these developments appear open to question.

COMMUNICATION EFFICIENCY

Efficiency among electronic media as channels of communication is governed by two audience variables: comprehension and memory. A growing body of research indicates that significant differences exist in the extent to which recipients recall and understand electronically mediated messages.

Much of the research has been summarized in two recently published works, one by Barrie Gunter, the other by Jacob Jacoby, Wayne D. Hoyer, and David A. Sheluga. Gunter's work includes an extensive summary of research data in the field. Jacoby and his colleagues reported only on a study sponsored by the Educational Foundation of the American Association of Advertising Agencies.

Historical Data
Research dealing with radio and summarized by Gunter is not as plentiful as that relating to television, but the data involved are consistent. They suggest variation in news knowledge occurs by

education, class, age, and sex. Variation across the sexes appeared to be more a matter of content than any other factor but nevertheless has been consistently observed. Programming involving violence, for undetermined reasons, is less memorable to females.

While presumably interesting to communicators, the data involved are less significant than those dealing with recall of electronically transmitted messages. As many as 31 percent of television viewers and 46 percent of radio listeners cannot recall news bulletin content approximately an hour after broadcast.

Message recipients' ability to comprehend electronically delivered messages is worse than their ability to recall. No more than 50 percent of respondents with university degrees comprehended broadcast messages. The percentage was as low as 17 percent among unskilled and semiskilled recipients.

Gunter found variation in memory and comprehension related to several variables. Social class, intelligence and educational levels, and occupation all appear to be related to individual memory and comprehension of broadcast information. In general, recall is greater for television than for radio, probably as a result of television's added visual dimension.

Other researchers have confirmed that large parts of the information to which radio and television users are exposed are retained inaccurately if at all. Among radio bulletin listeners, 36 to 46 percent have been found unable to recall subject matter about an hour after a broadcast. Recall is only slightly better among television viewers, of whom 9 to 31 percent fail to recall bulletin subject matter.

Foundation Study

Gunter's research objectives differed from those of Jacoby, Hoyer, and Sheluga. Gunter sought to synthesize a substantial body of knowledge acquired by researchers over time to provide new insights into the ways in which individuals handle electronically transmitted messages. Jacoby, Hoyer, and Sheluga were commissioned to assess the efficacy of messages. Gunter's data dealt with radio as well as television, and exclusively with news or informational broadcasts. The Jacoby study focused on advertising.

Results of the Jacoby research nevertheless are important to communicators. Differences between sets of results are small and readily explicable, as discussed below. The Jacoby, Hoyer, and Sheluga findings raise major questions, however, as to the effectiveness of electronic media in message delivery. Their findings can be best summarized as follows:

Some miscomprehension occurs in more than 96 percent of televised communication.

Approximately 30 percent of relevant information content is miscomprehended in each communication.

The typical or normative range of miscomprehension for televised messages is 23 to 36 percent.

Miscomprehension levels are significantly higher for nonadvertising than for advertising messages, but differences involved are relatively small.

Miscomprehension occurs at approximately equal rates whether factual statements or inferences are involved.

There appear to be no major demographic variables associated with miscomprehension.

Differences between study reports concerning demographic variables can be attributed to differences in methodologies and content. Gunter summarized all pertinent field and laboratory research concerning memory and comprehension of information conveyed by television. Jacoby, Hoyer, and Sheluga dealt almost exclusively with the study they undertook on behalf of the American Association of Advertising Agencies. Where Gunter was concerned primarily with news, Jacoby and his colleagues focused on advertising. Individual interest in news varies more strongly with demographic factors than is the case with advertising. Social class, education, and age consistently have been found to influence interest in information. These circumstances may explain why Gunter found demographic factors related to memory and understanding while the Jacoby team found no similar correlations.

Another Perspective

Further research at the University of Iowa confirmed the relative inefficiency of television without dealing with causal factors. A sophisticated statistical model developed by Gerald Tellis suggests that television exposure has a minimal impact on buying patterns. Tellis' research indicates that in-store displays and coupons exert greater short-term influence and that television advertising is not effective, even in the long run.

Started in the mid-1980s, Tellis' studies have produced controversy among advertisers and agencies. Early reports in scholarly journals generated criticism that prompted him to refine and repeat much of his research. Follow-up studies indicated, however, that television effectiveness was even lower than suggested by the original data. The debate continues, but such diverse organizations as A.C. Nielsen Company, a leader in market research, and D'Arcy, Masius Benton and Bowles, one of the nation's leading advertising agencies, are closely watching Tellis' continuing research. As Neilsen's Robert Bock was quoted in *The Wall Street Journal*, "We're searching for the Holy Grail in marketing here: Does marketing have an impact? We're finally getting to the point where there is data available to find out."

COMPETITIVE FACTORS

Growing competition is no less a problem to radio and television executives than is audience comprehension. The new technologies are but a small part of the competitive forces besieging established organizations. The future of electronic communication in the United States ultimately will be decided by governments, regulators, and perhaps the courts. These are the entities that will determine whether regional telephone companies or cable television operators will provide consumers with a vast array of communication and entertainment services. Resolution of outstanding questions concerning newer television systems also will influence the economic welfare of the old.

Impending legal, regulatory, and technological developments were reflected in the late 1980s in a marked ambivalence on the part of potential investors in broadcast television. Numbers of stations continued to increase, but market prices for existing stations were less than robust. There appeared to be more profit potential in establishing new stations, the market suggested, than in operating existing television outlets.

Numbers of commercial television outlets continued to grow in the United States at a rate of about 6 percent a year during the latter 1980s. There were 1,030 commercial stations in operation in 1988, up from 968 the previous year, according to *Television Digest*. Of the 1,030, 539 were VHF and 491 were UHF as compared with 424 and 444, respectively, for 1987. Most of the growth occurred among independent stations, which had more than doubled in number during the prior five years.

At the same time, however, the market for television stations had weakened significantly. More network (as opposed to independent) television stations were being offered for sale than at any time in recent history. Some 5 percent of the nation's 600 network stations then were on the block, with few prospective buyers in sight.

Uncertainties then existing concerning future development of cable and other television delivery systems doubtless were discouraging to potential buyers. Broadcast stations that had been selling at fifteen times annual cash flow, as a result, were changing hands at ten to thirteen times cash flow, and some were predicting further decline. If market prices, as economists assure us, accurately reflect external conditions, buyers and sellers apparently had agreed that broadcast television would become less profitable than had been the case earlier.

At least one straw in the wind early suggested that pricing trends are an accurate indicator of industry conditions. NBC in 1989 announced plans to start paying affiliated stations on the basis of their performance in attracting audience to the network. Total compensation to affiliates was to remain the same under the network plan but the dollars would flow to those stations that best serve the network's economic interests.

Battle Lines Established

Uncertainty concerning the value of broadcast stations in part was influenced by the escalating warfare between cable systems and telephone companies. These entities were locked in battle on two fronts, arguing the scope of services to be provided to consumers as well as which of them would be the primary provider.

Telephone companies contend they should provide services and delivery systems because they already serve most homes. Cable operators, in comparison, serve some 60 percent of the nation's dwellings. The Baby Bells, as they've been called, also argue that the economics of fiber optic system installation requires that they be allowed to compete with cable operators.

The Federal Communications Commission in 1988 proposed lifting a ban on telephone company involvement in cable television on grounds that resulting competition would benefit consumers. Cable operators contend, however, that the Baby Bells would use their telephone monopolies and economic resources to unfairly subsidize their cable ventures.

The stakes are high. Cable television revenues totaled $12 billion in 1987 and will increase as operators offer a broader range of services. Revenue growth probably would accelerate were the telephone companies, with their advantage in market penetration, to offer cable services. Telephone company ability to offer such services was improving in the 1980s with the continuing replacement of copper wire with fiber optic cable, creating no little apprehension among cable operators.

Fiber optic systems will provide benefits for consumers regardless of ownership, but telephone company systems would compound those benefits. High definition television and high speed data services require fiber optic cable. Copper wire is inadequate to transmit pictures as clear as those captured on 35 mm film and sound equal to that available on compact disks. Unlike cable systems, however, telephone companies readily could offer on-demand video programming. Telephone company or third parties' programs could be provided on request rather than only at predetermined times. Cable companies would have to restructure their networks at considerable expense to offer on demand programming.

AUDIENCE TRENDS

Radio and television are highly competitive media, as indicated by the contentiousness described above. Internecine battles aside, however, industry audiences continued to grow through the twentieth century and are expected to continue to grow in the twenty-first. Growth in recent years has been characterized by changes in audience distribution, and the trend is apt to continue.

Network television audiences, for example, have been in steady decline since the late 1970s, according to the A. C. Nielsen Company. Audience totals declined by almost 12 percent in the five years ending in 1985-86, and the trend continues. The combined prime-time rating for the three networks for the 1988-89 season was 41.3, as compared with 42.8 the previous year. Since each rating point means 904,000 homes, losses for 1988-89 approached 1,360,000. One bright spot appeared in the market data, however, in the form of greater stability in volume of television usage.

Television 'Watching'

Although network audiences continued to decline, "people meter" data showed that television watching per household was seven hours per day during the first nine months of 1988. Data generated by the older diary system for the same period in 1987 showed television sets were on for six hours and fifty-nine minutes daily. Over the air (as opposed to cable) television continued to dominate with 82 percent of all viewing, according to the people meters.

Data compiled by A. C. Nielsen and reported by the Television Bureau of Advertising indicated that hours of television usage for 1988 as a whole would be close to those of 1987. The industry's record was set in 1985, when average viewing time was seven hours and ten minutes. The total declined to seven hours and eight minutes for 1986 and seven hours and one minute for 1987.

The apparent slowing in the rate of decline in television use was not consistent, however, from one part of the nation to another. Audiences were smallest in some cities that are among the most coveted by advertisers. Residents of Washington, D.C. and San Francisco, for example, spent more time with activities other than television. Arbitron Rating Company data for October 1988, for example, showed only 60 percent of Washington's television sets were turned on during prime time hours (8:00 to 11:00 P.M. Monday through Saturday). In San Francisco, only 58 percent were watching. Data from Arbitron competitor A. C. Nielsen were similar. Washingtonians spent an average of forty-six hours and thirty-seven minutes watching television during October of 1988. In San Francisco, the total was forty-six hours and forty minutes.

These circumstances produce two results: higher costs for advertisers and more difficult conditions for communicators generally. Media representatives cited audience buying power and other demographic characteristics to justify higher than average advertising rates. That position will be difficult to sustain, however, unless the claimed purchasing power produces sales proportionate to expenditures. More creativity and ingenuity will be necessary among public relations consultants, advertising agencies, and others whose livelihoods depend on productive communications.

The VCR Variable

Purchasing power claims may be especially difficult to validate in light of the growing use of videocassette recorders (VCRs) and their contribution to audience declines. About 60 percent of households were equipped with VCRs by the end of 1988, according to data compiled for the Television Bureau of Advertising by A. C. Neilsen. The total represented a gain of about 12 percent from 1987, and the penetration rate was expected to increase as VCR prices continued to decline. About 76 percent of all households are expected to have VCRs by 1996.

Survey data indicated the average VCR was used 151 minutes a week for recording and 256 minutes for playback. Daytime and prime time were the most popular recording times, while playback time was more evenly distributed over daytime, early evening, and prime time. More than half (55 percent) of VCR users reported doing some commercial "zapping," but only six percent reported zapping on an average day.

In terms of information flows, VCR usage is most damaging during afternoon and evening weekday time slots, when newscasts are most prevalent. Data for 1988 show that 16 percent of television viewers were watching recorded programming during the 4:30 to 8:00 P.M. segment and that 23 percent were watching recorded programming during the 8:00 to 11:00 P.M. segment. Between 16 and 23 percent of surveyed households therefore were missing newscasts broadcast between 4:30 and 11:00 P.M.

Continuing decline in audiences due to VCR use probably was destined to continue even if numbers of the devices did not significantly increase as anticipated. Advancing digital technology in 1989 resulted in production of a VCR that could be programmed with owners' viewing preferences. Armed with this profile, the VCR then would scan incoming programs and record those that met specified criteria. With or without such devices, increased VCR use was tantamount to audience loss from an advertiser standpoint.

Cable Trends

Although the ultimate shape of the television marketplace remained in doubt during the last decade of the twentieth century, cable households continued to proliferate at a rate of 2 to 3 percent a year. The Television Bureau of Advertising estimated that 52.8 percent of households would be hooked to cable systems by 1989, with 28.9 percent subscribing to premium services.

The bureau's predictions assumed stability in relative cost factors, however, and that assumption may or may not be fulfilled. While cable television audiences were growing, user fees were increasing in many areas at rates that may prove sufficient to dampen growth rates. United States Commerce Department data released in December of 1988 showed that cable charges had increased 13.6 percent for the twelve months ending in October 1988. Rate increases had been endemic in the industry since the courts freed cable systems from local government control in 1984. In the ensuing four years, rates in Manhattan increased 53 percent. In Los Angeles, the average basic rate increased 44 percent.

Audience Gains. At the same time, however, the cable networks were gaining in audience and revenues. Data published by advertising agency McCann-Erickson indicated that cable had captured 18 percent of the total prime time audience by 1988, as compared with 8 percent in 1982 and 11 percent in 1986. Advertising revenues of the primary cable networks were improving even more rapidly. Superstation WTBS, the foundation of Ted Turner's Atlanta-based empire, had revenues of $95 million for 1988, as compared with $46 million five years earlier. WTBS' improvement, moreover, was relatively small by cable industry standards.

ESPN, the sports network, also had $95 million in 1988 revenues, but that figure compared with a $26 million negative cash flow five years earlier. Turner's Cable News Network had moved from a $4 million negative flow to $85 million in revenues. MTV Music Television recorded $45 million in revenues, as compared with a negative $5 million cash flow in 1983, and Nickelodeon reported similar improvement. The USA Network's $12 million negative cash flow in 1983 contrasted with $28 million in revenues for 1988. Similar turnarounds were recorded by the Nashville Network, Lifetime, and CBN Family Channel.

At about the same time, Turner Broadcasting and others across the nation were launching into aggressive expansion of sports programming through regional networks. Turner was a relative latecomer in announcing plans for a Southeastern sports network. Two major network groups already were in place, one with 9.5 million subscribers, the other with 6.3 million.

Two Denver firms, Daniels and Associates and TeleCommunications, assembled the larger group, covering parts of a scattered dozen states. Rainbow Program Enterprises, a joint venture of Cablevision Systems Corporation and National Broadcasting Company, operated the smaller group. Concentrated in the New York, Chicago, and Los Angeles areas, most group members operated under the name SportsChannel America.

Software System. In Denver, Tele-Communications, which operates that community's cable franchise, also was experimenting with a system to transmit software into homes via cable. The firm's X-Press Information Services subsidiary was offering two software packages: a job search program with a data base of listings and a program for planning airline flights. The company previously offered services that distribute news, market data and other information via cable to some fifteen thousand personal computers.

Taken in the context of networks' losses, cable system revenue gains sent broadcast interests back to Congress with a plea for at least partial re-regulation of the cable industry. The broadcasters denied interest in rate setting but asked Congress to limit cable operators' ability to (a) elect to carry or not carry broadcast stations and (b) to reassign cable channels to broadcast stations at will. Some in broadcasting suspected cable operators were moving their stations' cable channel assignments to discourage viewers.

With or without congressional intervention, growth rates of the sort cable systems enjoyed in the 1980s are not likely to continue. Cable television is a maturing industry, and two other factors, both at least equally important, will influence growth patterns. First, the networks will not yield their positions without a fight. More important, few cable franchises remain exclusive, and competition apparently will develop from the Baby Bells.

Strategic Shift. The networks' readiness for battle was demonstrated in early 1989 when they collectively shifted from defensive to offensive strategies. After years of silence in the face of cable claims, the networks and the Television Advertising Bureau together launched a coordinated counterattack. The Cable Television Advertising Bureau termed some of the broadcasters' claims "ridiculous" and the battle was joined.

Viewed pragmatically, television broadcasters were fighting an aggressive rear guard action against cable and other electronic dissemination systems. The heads of the three major networks agreed in early 1989 that their audience shares would continue to decline. One went so far as to suggest that the slide might bottom at below 60 percent of the prime time audience. All contended that network television remained superior to its competitors.

The networks' admissions came amidst new efforts by cable television, syndicated programming and independent stations—the three primary competitors—to capture more advertising revenues. Members of the Association of Independent Television Stations were the cause and the beneficiaries of part of the networks' difficulties, reporting progressively higher ratings in most markets. The Cabletelevision Advertising Bureau claimed its members had almost doubled their subscribers and prime time audiences since 1985 and was delivering 22 percent of prime time viewers during 1988.

The Association of Syndicated Television Advertising, whose members create programming for stations for a portion of the advertising time involved, reported similar growth. Members' revenues totaled $875 million in 1988 as compared with $50 million in 1980. Amounts involved presumably would have been collected by the networks before the advent of the syndication industry.

Profits at Stake. The network versus cable fight was a matter of profits; more specifically, of declines in profits. The networks appeared to be committed to regain lost ground. While reducing costs, the networks increased marketing staffs and relaxed restrictive rules on tie-ins. CBS went so far as to permit use of brand name products in prime time shows. NBC went farther, launching a cable channel of its own. The content of the Consumer News and Business Channel, or CNBC as it was named, was oriented to consumer economic news. Contrary claims notwithstanding, the new channel was in direct competition with two long-established Cable News Network channels. Among CNBC's resources, however, was access to the product of NBC's international news-gathering organization. The availability of this resource, together with NBC's deep pockets, portended a long competitive battle.

While joining forces to recapture advertising from cable systems and syndicators, the networks launched aggressive promotional efforts in support of their programs. Programs were reoriented to upscale audiences and the networks started producing more programming of their own to capture rerun revenues that otherwise accrue to syndicators.

The networks also were buying more advertising time than ever on the cable channels. Their objective was to recapture audience. The three networks' audience share is about 75 percent of noncable subscribers but only 50 percent in cable homes that subscribe to pay services, according to the Cable Advertising Bureau.

Revenue Losses. More was involved, however, than numbers of viewers. The cable systems were starting to erode the networks' advertising revenue base. Part of the erosion was driven by demographic data. Managers in the 1988 political campaign shifted significant portions of their television budgets from network to cable. They found the major cable networks—CBN, CNN, ESPN, and FNN—had captured large numbers of voters who are better educated, better paid, and older than average—all characteristics of those most likely to vote.

While the economics of broadcasting require that networks and local stations deal in lowest common denominator programming, cable systems can cater to diverse tastes. These circumstances contribute to programming diversity in several ways. Cable operators early delivered programming that ranged from news and music to religion and shopping and that was designed for national audiences. Regional sports programming now is being added to the menu, as described earlier.

More is involved, however, than additional programming for sports junkies. Regional programming means more audience fragmentation and enhanced potential for regional advertising oriented to fragmented audiences. Successful regional programming also implies continuing decline in network advertising revenues.

Cable systems and regional programmers, in addition, were not alone in attacking the network treasuries. A new set of "networks" was being established by independent broadcasters in 1989 with that same goal in mind. These new networks consisted of sets of stations organized to sell advertising at advantageous rates. "Advantageous" means profitable to and competitive with network stations and cable operators. As many as two hundred independent television stations in almost as many markets were organizing in 1989 to offer time to advertisers in this manner.

The Radio Market

Competition for audience and revenues is no less a factor in radio than in television. Industry size, in fact, tends to make competition more intense. Radio is an industry of almost incredible scope in the United States. More than 10,000 stations are broadcasting to more than 450 million radios located in more than 99 percent of all of the nation's homes, offices and vehicles. The station total in 1989 included 4,863 commercial AM, 3,944 commercial FM, and 1,263 non-commercial, most of them on the FM dial.

As implied by the number of stations, radio is intensely competitive, generating more than 26 percent of total broadcast revenues but earning less than 10 percent of overall profits. Profits remain low despite technological progress. Satellites have added to the efficiency of radio networks, for example, to an extent that has encouraged development of networks targeted to specific audiences.

Satellite Music Network (SMN) of Dallas demonstrates the advantages that new technology has created for radio broadcasters. SMN offers nine music formats to radio station owners via satellite for the price of a full-time employee. SMN was servicing more than 1,000 stations in 1988, and experts were predicting that SMN and similar organizations could be delivering programming to four times that many stations before the turn of the century.

ABC also has launched multiple networks targeted to specific audiences, and further networking is in prospect. More than two dozen existed in 1989 and the number was growing. Satellite-based systems can provide a relatively inexpensive entertainment product. Local broadcasters need add little more than advertising to the satellite-delivered product. Broadcasters incur only minor risk in that change in audience tastes can occur with some speed. Most satellite system vendors, however, stand ready to provide new "products" as conditions warrant.

Changing consumer tastes in part account for nearly constant jockeying for position and audience among stations. Changing tastes spawn new and modified broadcast formats that network entrepreneurs hope will attract station managers seeking to enhance audiences sizes and station profitability.

The largest changes in audience distribution between 1987 and 1988 occurred in three programming areas: rock, religious, and news/talk (see table 8.1). Stations offering rock programming declined by 3 percent. Those offering religious programming almost doubled in number, perhaps as the result of a decline in television evangelism resulting from the well-publicized difficulties of Jim and Tammy Bakker and others. In other significant changes, the number of stations with news/talk formats was reduced by about one-third and all news stations declined apace.

The latter changes are significant for communicators, especially in the context of the chart above. News/talk stations provide a disproportionately large percentage of most communities' informational broadcasting. Many stations offer little or no news. Decline in numbers of stations using news formats thus enhances the value of news delivered on other stations. Values may be especially great in that radio, to a greater extent than television, can engage the attention of specific audiences. Each of the broadcast formats specified above appeals to an audience with more clearly defined demographic characteristics than can be found in television.

TABLE 8.1
PERCENTAGES OF AUDIENCE BY BROADCAST FORMAT
IN TOP 100 RADIO MARKETS, 1987-88

Format	AM		FM		Total	
	1987	1988	1987	1988	1987	1988
Adult contemporary	19.5	18.3	20.4	21.3	20.0	19.5
Country	16.8	17.8	15.0	13.8	15.9	16.1
Rock	4.1	2.9	19.4	16.7	11.8	8.8
Album rock	0.7	1.3	13.4	13.0	7.1	6.2
Nostalgia	13.1	11.8	1.5	1.4	7.3	7.4
Easy listening	1.5	1.8	10.5	8.8	6.0	7.4
Religious	8.0	14.1	3.1	6.1	5.5	10.3
News/talk	12.0	7.0	0.9	0.5	6.5	4.2
Black rhythm/blues	5.1	4.4	2.2	2.3	3.7	3.5
Urban contemporary	1.9	2.5	4.4	3.4	3.2	2.9
Golden oldies	5.2	6.6	1.1	1.8	3.2	4.6
Spanish	4.4	4.4	0.8	0.9	2.6	2.9
Classical	1.2	0.5	2.1	4.0	1.7	1.1
All news	3.4	2.0	0.0	0.0	1.7	1.1
Soft contemporary	1.4	1.1	4.1	4.6	2.8	2.3
Variety	1.3	0.9	0.4	0.5	1.0	0.7

Source: Radio Facts, 1987-88 and 1988-89 editions. New York: Radio Advertising Bureau.

The decline in news programming in part may have accounted for a resurgence by National Public Radio. From near bankruptcy and a $3 million deficit in 1983, NPR rebounded to a $7.8 million surplus in 1988. Member stations increased from 260 to 365, and the network was offering more news and cultural programming than ever before.

NPR's news audience alone had grown to some five million, and contributions by corporations and foundations increased from $2.7 million in 1983 to $10.6 million in 1988. NPR shares a public weekly radio audience of eleven million with a variety of other networks as well as hundreds of unaffiliated public radio stations, many on college and university campuses.

TECHNOLOGICAL CHANGES

Contemporary diversity in radio and television appears likely to increase through the early part of the twenty-first century. Technological change will be the driving force behind broader distribution of information and entertainment through these media, but not all change will necessarily be beneficial.

New technologies of several types will be introduced in radio and television, and existing technologies will be applied to expand the reach of radio in unusual directions. Some of the innovations in each sector, however, will be of greater significance to retailers than to broadcasters.

Hardware Improvements

Retailers and their customers, rather than broadcasters, will reap most of the benefits from the new technologies. In television, the principal advance will be in high definition television, a system that puts more "lines" on the screen to produce pictures of nearly motion-picture clarity. Beyond improved screen images, television also will benefit from enhanced sound technology and reduced bulk.

High definition television (HDTV), as the improved picture system is called, potentially will be one of the strongest generators of change in the industry. HDTV uses digital rather than analog technology. Television will share the language of computers with telephones, radios, recordings, and even movies.

The digital technologies ultimately may combined in any number of ways for greater consumer benefit. At the outset they will serve primarily to produce enhanced television pictures and increased equipment sales. HDTV at first will mean only expense, however, for broadcasters and cable companies. Those distributing television signals will need more sophisticated and more costly equipment to produce optimum results for the consumer. Whether the expense involved can be recovered through higher advertising rates is questionable.

Radio Technologies

Circumstances in radio are quite different. New technologies are waiting in the wings, as it were, but some of them will lead to new markets as well as improved products. In early 1989, for example, "broadcasters" were looking toward a new audience: bus riders. At least two companies were competing to install systems to deliver information, entertainment and, of course, advertising, to passengers on municipal buses. One of the companies was using cellular technology; the other was using FM.

Transit officials liked the idea of gaining more revenues but expressed reservations on several points. FM and cellular-driven systems both can encounter dead spots where signals fade. More important to transit operators, however, are potential equipment problems. Presumably sensitive hardware aboard buses would take a consistent pounding from potholes, passengers, and clean-up crews.

The public transportation market ultimately could be a source of considerable revenue for radio, especially if renewed energy problems encourage transportation system development. Like television, however, radio is not without new systems that will be of greater benefit to manufacturers and consumers than broad-casters.

One such technology is a new method of FM broadcasting called FMX. FMX is designed to expand stations' signal coverage areas while improving signal reception. Already adopted by about one hundred stations, the FMX system maintains contemporary FM-quality reception with existing receivers but produces improved performance only with FMX receivers.

A debate over FMX system quality developed in 1989 when Amar B. Bose, a Massachusetts Institute of Technology professor and chairman of Bose Corporation, a stereo equipment manufacturing firm, warned consumers and broadcasters against FMX. System developers denied Bose's charges, and the issue remains unresolved.

Should FMX meet the performance standards established by its owners, including the National Association of Broadcasters and CBS, a miniresurgence in radio well might result. FMX technology developed out of research at CBS, which closed its research laboratory in 1986. Two former employees of the laboratory then joined with CBS and NAB as Broadcasting Technology Partners to market the new system.

Television Technology

Improvements in radio technology are apt to move more slowly than those in television because of the greater potential for new or improved services through television. Some of the potential is being demonstrated in Cerritos, California, where extensive fiber optic facilities had been installed in conjunction with the 1988 Summer Olympic Games. A year later, GTE Corporation, launched an experiment under which selected cable subscribers were to get considerably more than standard cable services.

The selected few were to be able to receive almost any movie at any hour. If plans being developed by the City of Cerritos materialize, subscribers will also be able to use the system to sign up for tennis courts and to get dog licenses and temporary parking permits. The Cerritos system also will provide home shopping through a device that appears similar to a television remote control unit. Banking services will be available by cable as well.

The benefits generated by the Cerritos system will extend beyond customers, however. Advertisers, for example, will be able to tell how many sets are tuned to specific shows and how many commercial are zapped by viewers. System operators and their vendors, such as Home Box Office, also will benefit in that the system will preclude signal piracy.

Systems like those that GTE is installing in Cerritos will join an increasingly diverse set of television delivery methodologies. Two others already exist, and still more are expected to develop in the near future. The existing systems are subscription television (STV) and multipoint distribution services (MDS). Both are over-the-air systems that depend on subscriber fees for income. Neither STV nor MDS are major competitors for cable, but both can develop by serving areas so sparsely settled as to prevent cable penetration. MDS systems also are practical alternatives to cable in large cities, where cable installation would be prohibitive in cost. Some sixty such systems exist, but signal problems and limited program offerings have made them only marginally competitive.

Direct broadcast satellite (DBS) and low power television (LPTV) systems also may ultimately gain significant market shares. DBS exists only in the form of applications pending before the Federal Communication Commission and would consist of programming transmitted via satellite directly to subscriber homes. LPTV, for which the FCC also has accepted applications, can include teletext and pay systems as well as low-power stations in traditional formats and in networks. Some four hundred LPTV licenses have been granted and construction permits have been awarded for an additional fourteen hundred stations.

Regulatory Developments

Future development of television systems in competition with networks and cable depend largely on the extent to which regulators and courts permit telephone companies to enter this arena. The growing competitiveness that appeared to be developing in the marketplace was underscored in 1989 through the activities of American Telephone and Telegraph Company on the one hand and the American Newspaper Publishers Association on the other.

AT&T petitioned a Federal court in 1989 for permission to create as well as transmit computerized information services over its long distance network. The company then was prohibited under a 1982 court decision that broke up the Bell system from offering services such as electronic shopping, banking, or news.

The petition, as subsequently approved, will permit AT&T to collect, compile, and edit information. Company spokespersons declined to be more specific for competitive reasons but said AT&T had no current plans to offer electronic yellow pages. Such plans doubtless would have provoked the wrath of the newspaper publishers, who long have been concerned over the possible development of electronic classified advertising on the part of newspaper's competitors.

IN SUMMARY

The electronic media are enmeshed in an era of change greater than any they have experienced to date. Multiple battles for audience shares and revenues are occurring in radio and television, while a growing body of evidence suggests that the electronic media are inefficient message delivery systems.

Television audiences continue to fragment as programming becomes available from a growing number of sources, and the same trend now may be developing in radio. Deterioration in network audiences has sparked a virtual war for television viewers. New and existing technological developments threaten to add to these difficulties.

Evidence of inefficiency in information delivery is contained in two recent works, one by Barrie Gunter, the other by Jacob Jacoby, Wayne Hoyer and David Shaluga. Gunter's survey of pre-existing research in radio and television suggested significant variation in media ability to convey information successfully. As many as 31 percent of television viewers and 46 percent of radio listeners can not recall news bulletin content an hour after it is broadcast, Gunter found.

Jacoby and his associates reported similar findings after concluding a study of the efficiency of television. They found that miscomprehension occurs in more than 96 percent of televised communication, that about 30 percent of relevant information is miscomprehended, and that the normative range of miscomprehension is 23 to 36 percent.

From the standpoint of broadcast and cable executives, however, increasing competition is as much a problem as information delivery. After years of attempting to ignore the threat that cable systems posed to their positions, the three major networks have experienced intolerable audience losses and have started to fight back, promotionally and practically.

Their collective advertising and promotional efforts, which have included larger expenditures in cable television advertising, have been supplemented by expansion into what earlier had been competitors' turf. Directly or indirectly, all of the networks have become involved in cable, satellite, or emerging transmission systems. Perhaps in part as a result of their efforts, deterioration in television watching generally has slowed, although VCRs continue to increase in market penetration and cable systems have become more and more profitable.

For the long term, the future of television probably will be determined more by legislative, regulatory, and legal action than by competitive or technological developments. The extent to which telephone companies are permitted to become involved in development as well as delivery of services to consumers is especially critical.

Radio markets are expected to change little in relative terms. Intense competition is apt to continue, however, with more and more stations using syndicated entertainment packages delivered by satellite across the nation. Prepackaged entertainment reduces operating costs and, presumably, enhances potential for greater profit.

Improved sound and picture technologies soon should be available to consumers, but these will create no benefits for broadcasters or managers of other delivery systems. Emerging television and radio systems may enable radio and television outlets to capture larger audiences and generate greater profits, but these systems remain some years away in most markets.

ADDITIONAL READING

Amparano, Julie, and Mary Lu Carnevale. *Phone Firms Battle Cable-TV Operators over Providing Fiber-Optic Home Links.* Wall Street Journal, Sept. 9, 1988.

Blau, Eleanor. "National Public Radio Gets By with Help from Its Friends." *New York Times*, Feb. 27, 1989.

Bulkeley, William M. "GTE Test Offers View of Video Future: Optical Fiber Boosts Services to Subscribers." *Wall Street Journal*, Dec. 29, 1988.

Carter, Bill. "NBC Tightens Grip on Lead, but Networks Lose Viewers." *New York Times*, Apr. 19, 1989.

Cox, Meg, "NBC Plans to Link Pay of Affiliates to Performance," *The Wall Street Journal*, May 23, 1989.

Fabrikant, Geraldine. "For Cable Networks, the Road Gets a Little Steeper." *The New York Times*, Feb. 26, 1989.

—. "In Free Rein of Cable TV, Fees Are Up." *New York Times*, Dec. 11, 1988.

Fahri, Paul. "Area Residents Tuning Out Television: Affluent Market Poses Challenge to Advertisers." *Washington Post*, Dec. 8, 1988.

Fly, Richard, and Frances Seghers. "Campaign '88 Makes A Cable Connection." *Business Week*, Nov. 23, 1987.

Gunter, Barrier. *Poor Reception: Misunderstanding and Forgetting Broadcast News*. Hillsdale, N.J.: Erlbaum, 1987.

Jacoby, Jacob, Wayne D. Hoyer, and David A. Sheluga. *Misconceptions of Televised Communications*. New York: American Association of Advertising Agencies, 1980.

Kleinfield, N. R. "Glut of TV Stations for Sale Being Met by Buyer Apathy." *New York Times*, Nov. 30, 1988.

——, "Stung by Cable Audience Claims, Networks Retaliate." *New York Times*, Jan. 9, 1989.

Landro, Laura. "Independent TV Stations Assume Bigger Role in Broadcast Industry." *Wall Street Journal*, May 11, 1984.

Lazar, Ellan A., ed. *The Video Age: Television Technology and Applications in the 1980s*. White Plains, N.Y.: Knowledge Industry Publications, 1982.

Lieberman, David. "How Do You Spell Pain? ABC, NBC and CBS." *Business Week*, Dec. 7, 1987.

Lipman, Joanne. "As Network TV Fades, Many Advertisers Try Age-Old Promotions." *Wall Street Journal*, Aug. 26, 1986.

——. "Networks Bash Cable but Still Buy Ads., *Wall Street Journal*, Mar. 10, 1989.

——. "TV Ads' Influence Found Wanting." *Wall Street Journal*, Feb. 15, 1989.

Prescott, Eileen. "The Networks Fight Back, Finally." *New York Times*, March 5, 1989.

Rothenberg, Randall. "Three Networks See Declines Continuing." *New York Times*, Feb. 8, 1989.

Sims, Calvin. "A.T.&T. Is Proposing to Offer Electronic Publishing Service." *New York Times*, Apr. 22, 1989.

——. "New FM System is Challenged." *New York Times*, Feb. 22, 1989.

Waldman, Peter. "Testing the Limits of Sports on Cable TV." *Wall Street Journal*, Apr. 25, 1989.

9 Organizations as Laboratories

Organizational communication is only marginally a component of mass communication within the usual definitions of those terms. Insight into change in organizations nevertheless is important to trend watchers in mass communication in that organizations often are the laboratories of society. Organizations, more than individuals, have the resources and will to become early adopters of new technologies. The nature of organizations also tends to make them more responsive than individuals to developments in their environments. Organizations must maintain a high state of preparedness to capitalize on innovation and maintain competitive position.

The latter attribute especially makes organizations predisposed to adopt and adapt to change among audiences, technologies, and media. The process necessarily varies among organizations. Some are led by early adopters. In others, the early adopters are well down the organizational ladder, as demonstrated with the advent of the microcomputer. Innovators in some large corporations found themselves forced to bootleg the new technology into their organizations to avoid corporate barriers of one sort or another. Adoption generally proceeds more rapidly in organizations than in society as a whole, however, because organizational resistance to change more readily gives way to demonstrated performance or productivity. Individual failure to apply new techniques in organizations to strengthen competitive circumstances can endanger career potential. Individual environments are less competitive and more cost sensitive. Organizations, for these reasons, often become the applied technology laboratories of contemporary society. Innovative managers struggling to gain competitive advantage are most disposed to accept risks where potential rewards are great.

Rewards have been demonstrated beyond question in recent years where organizations have ventured into extensive use of several new technologies. Organizations have successfully adapted several of the new interactive media to corporate purposes, although commercial ventures involving the same technologies have fallen short of economic success. Satellite-based teleconferencing and interactive computer systems have been applied productively by corporations ranging from the long-established and relatively conservative to the young and aggressive. Examples include 3M among the pioneers in using teletext/videotext systems as information exchange systems, and Federal Express Corporation, an early adopter of satellite-based videoconferencing.

The same underlying pattern prevails among smaller organizations. Technologies—communication and otherwise—are adopted and adapted as rapidly as their benefits increase or their costs decline. These conditions also suggest one other reason for close observation of communication trends in organizations: both trends and their results are apt to develop later in the society as a whole.

COMMUNICATION RATIONALE

The extent and complexity of organizational communication systems is a product of two social trends. First, according to *pr reporter*, workers are better educated, more independent, more worldly and knowledgeable, and less awed by authority. They want information about their organization from senior managers. Second, workers, especially younger workers, become fewer and fewer in number as the so-called baby bust supplants the baby boom in the work force. As such, they are becoming an increasingly rare and progressively more valuable commodity in the United States.

Organizations, in these conditions, must design communication programs characterized by the following:

1. Openness expressed in organizational decisions, policies, and budgets as well as in words on paper.

2. Mutual trust and confidence, which can be engendered only by fairness and consistency in management performance.

3. Two-way, as opposed to unilateral communication. Workers must be heard and heeded. They must be originators as well as receivers of messages.

4. Careful selection of communication channels. Media must be selected in keeping with audience preferences rather than managerial fiat.

Building trust and credibility requires frequent and candid communication in as personal a manner as possible. "Management by walking around (MBWA)," as it's been called, is the best approach. It is especially effective where senior managers provide candid answers to questions and share the bad news as well as the good with their personnel.

Workers' sense of security can be enhanced where managers become personally involved in communicating organizational information concerning policies, procedures, and behaviors that affect on personnel. Speeches, meetings with employees, personal letters and telephone calls are among media of choice in an era in which "the grapevine" often is an organization's most credible medium. Recognizing special employee contributions to organizational success also is important. Awards, letters, telephone calls, and recognition through internal media can be productive.

Worker knowledge and safety also require attention in the context of management communication. Information that workers need must be provided to them on timely bases through publications, bulletin boards, videotape, and any other applicable media. Accurate and timely information is even more important during crisis conditions and when employee safety might be threatened. Senior managers under these conditions must spend their time in communicating, using every channel at hand to convey information to personnel, shareholders, customers, media, and others.

The breadth and depth of these needs, coupled with contemporary competitive circumstances, have encouraged organizations to remain on the leading edge of communication technology. The technologies often are amenable to small-scale internal application prior to extensive external use. Organizations therefore have often become laboratories for the communication technologies.

COMPUTERS IN ORGANIZATIONS

No technology is more generally applied in organizations than the computer. From free-standing microcomputers to mainframe-based networks, organizations have pioneered in developing and applying computer hardware and software. As microcomputers became a commodity during the mid-1980s, they became an almost essential tool in almost every business environment, large and small. Originally used almost exclusively for data management tasks, microcomputers now also have been harnessed to serve as word processors, communication devices, and addressing systems; in typesetting and printing, audiovisual production, and information management; and as remote extensions of offices large and small.

Advancing technologies are producing computer proliferation at both ends of the size/capabilities scale. Introduction of Intel's 80386 and 80486 microprocessors in the late 1980s put more computing power into machines physically configured for desktop use. Microcomputers were advancing to become minicomputers. At the same time, large organizations were making multimillion-dollar commitments to global computer-based information systems. American Airlines, for example, in 1989 announced plans for InterAAction. The system was designed as an "electronic platform" to all but eliminate paperwork, minimize numbers of middle managers and clerical workers, and move decision making down the organization.

The evolution of large and small computers from information warehouses to multipurpose tools is typical of the manner in which the machines have been exploited in organizations. As originally introduced in relatively cumbersome form, computers could do little more than store and manipulate columns of numbers. Today, microcomputers and mainframes are equally adept at managing information in sentence and paragraph form. Tomorrow, intelligent systems will be doing more and more of the thinking now handled by humans. Insight into the developmental pattern involved and, especially, into the speed with which development has progressed is helpful in understanding precisely how close to reality "the future" may be.

Information Applications

The bulk of computer functions in most organizations are most readily described as information applications in which equipment is used to store and retrieve data in numerical or other form. The information involved traditionally has been loaded into computers by users but this pattern is starting to change. The relatively recent development of high-capacity storage media, especially read-only optical disks, is leading organizations to purchase information in computer-readable rather than printed form.

Virtually any directory or periodical, for example, could be issued on optical disks rather than on paper. The Thomas Register, the several publications of Dun and Bradstreet's credit reporting service, and the multiple directories of Standard Rate and Data Service are but a few examples of information that ultimately can be expected to become available on read-only optical disks. The technology involved has not advanced to a point at which users can economically put information on optical disks, but the disks are ideal for directory purposes, especially in large offices where multiple subscriptions might otherwise be required. Information provided on optical disks then could be loaded into office computers for use by all involved.

Computers also are used to manage organizational information of every kind. Research and development, sales, marketing, personnel, inventory control and virtually every other type of data can be maintained by computer for immediate access. The computer's major advantage is currency. All data is up to the minute. Inventory figures can be adjusted, for example, as orders are entered. Change in inventory levels can automatically trigger issuance of purchase orders to vendors. Data bases used in these processes can be applied with equal ease to generate customer mailing lists, analyze developmental patterns; and monitor the performance of any and every organizational component.

Communication Systems

The value of information contained in computers is limited or enhanced by the extent to which it is or can be made accessible inside and outside the organization. These circumstances led to the development of another of the computer's major attributes: communication.

Communication can be accomplished in any of several ways. Organizations can maintain extensive centralized computer systems with hundreds or thousands of hard wired terminals. In the alternative, large numbers of microcomputers can be linked together in local area networks. Finally, and most importantly, computers can be joined intermittently by telephone and microwave systems.

Most organizations use one or more of these systems to increase the value of information by making it readily transferrable across organizational boundaries. American Airlines' InterAAction system is representative of those used by larger organizations. Often global in scope, these systems often are made accessible in part to outsiders, especially journalists, financial analysts, and others whose behaviors can influence organizational welfare. Organizations often address these needs by providing computer codes that admit users to libraries of news releases, briefing papers, annual reports, product information, and other data that can be helpful to those involved. 3M pioneered in this area while establishing its own computer communication system.

Smaller organizations attack the communication problem in one of several ways. Floppy disks are passed from hand to hand and may be mailed where stand-alone microcomputers are used. As organizations grow, local area networks usually are installed, linking all microcomputers to a file server, another computer not necessarily more powerful than the micros but with greater storage capacity. Networking can provide for small, single-site organizations all the benefits that American Airlines' $150 million investment will create for that international company. Information becomes immediately accessible to all organization members, subject to any hierarchical access system that management may prescribe. The movement of paper to transport information, and the delays that the paper process necessarily entails, are eliminated.

Mainframe and networked microcomputer systems are supplemented in most organizations through the use of modems (modulator/demodulators), inexpensive devices that enable computers to exchange data over conventional telephone lines. Modems also give users access to national and international electronic mail systems operated in part by telephone companies and in part by computer utilities. MCI Communications, CompuServe, and The Source are among those offering electronic mail and, in some cases, facsimile services as well. The facsimile services enable computer users to send directly from their computers rather than creating paper copies and feeding them into facsimile transmitters.

Potential computer-based communication system applications are almost limitless. These systems are used extensively in the communication disciplines for transmission and receipt of information of all kinds and, of late, in all shapes as well. Among types of information commonly moved through computer systems are news and information for the mass media as well as public relations, advertising, and sales promotion materials.

Graphics Applications

Even the graphics that computers can create are amenable to transmission through their communication systems. In more sophisticated forms, the systems permit simultaneous visual and aural communication, enabling advertisers and their agencies, for example, to simultaneously examine and make changes in sketches on computer screens. The same sort of technology has even been used by Harvard University in providing interactive continuing education in such sophisticated areas as medicine.

Ability to transmit is but a small part of computer capabilities in graphics, however. Equipped with appropriate software, computers can generate monotone and color graphics of all kinds for a broad range of applications. Abstract art created by computer has become a small industry in its own right. Drawings once provided through clipping services to newspapers, printers, and others are now generated by computer and distributed on floppy disks.

The graphics capabilities of computers expanded with the advent of optical scanners in the late 1980s. These devices enabled computer users to "load" drawings and photos as well as type from printed materials. Early scanned photo quality was less than optimal, but drawings were readily loaded into computers, edited where necessary, and reused. Extensive reuse is encouraged in that computer images are readily transferred to slides, overhead transparencies, videotape, and other media.

Publishing Applications

The other media mentioned above include every form of printed material. Newsletters, catalogs, brochures, and books all have been produced in large part by computer. "In large part" means replacing designers, typographers, mechanical artists, and, to some extent, printers with computer operators. Equipped with computers, writers can accomplish all or part of what once required the efforts of other skilled personnel.

The transition is not necessarily easy for any of those involved. Writers often struggle to learn desktop publishing procedures. In addition, as Memphis State University Professor Arthur A. Terry points out, equipment does not equal artistry. "Buying a camera doesn't make you a photographer," says Terry, a former *National Geographic* editorr who has become expert in desktop publishing.

Where computers are used for writing, as almost invariably is now the case, writers increasingly are becoming involved in subsequent production steps. The transition became virtually unavoidable in the late 1980s when WordPerfect Corporation and other word processing software developers introduced a set of innovative products. Conventionally referred to as "upgrades" in the software industry, the new generation of programs quickly became known as "word publishing software." They occupied a niche between sophisticated desktop publishing and conventional word processing, combining some of the features of each.

Any of these programs, used in combination with an appropriate microcomputer and laser printer, can generate what is known in printing as camera-ready copy. The latter term refers to black-on-white prints from which offset printing plates can be made via photographic processes. Writers operating microcomputers and laser printers can provide such copy for products ranging from newsletters and leaflets to catalogs and books. The book you are reading was produced in precisely this fashion. It required no typesetting and no composition other than that accomplished by the author on the same computer on which the manuscript was prepared.

Boundary Spanning

As the foregoing should make evident, one of the computer's major advantages is flexibility in application. The same equipment is used for multiple purposes. Equally important, computer content is just as flexible. Illustrations produced for printing readily can be printed on paper and converted for use with an overhead projector. Conversion to color slides for use in audiovisual presentations also is easily accomplished. More sophisticated systems are necessary to transmit printed pages, as in the case of nationally circulated daily newspapers published in multiple plants, but the principles are identical.

Content flexibility extends to words as well as illustrations. Pragmatically, words are the more flexible of the components of printed products. Where necessary, words can be more quickly edited than illustrations for multiple media or for different audiences. Essentially identical information, for example, quickly can be recycled for use in news releases, employee newsletters, bulletin board announcements, annual reports, and elsewhere. Rephrasing may be necessary to cope with variation in audience demographics or differences in media, but such changes are easily accomplished.

Alternative Environments

The flexibility that computers create in manipulating words and illustrations is equalled by their ability to destroy barriers created by time and distance. Computers are turning homes into work places and enabling workers to take their offices wherever they go. Two distinct trends have developed as a result of this flexibility. First, more and more individuals are working at home. Second, those whose work requires travel are becoming more productive than ever before.

These trends are a product of multiple computer capabilities. The most obvious among them is the computer's ability to transmit and receive messages. Transmission and reception can be accomplished wherever users can find telephones. Ideally, the telephones can be readily disconnected from their jacks, permitting modem wires to be plugged in instead. Acoustic modems can be attached to telephone receivers, but they usually are more bulky than their electronic counterparts.

With computers connected to telephones, travelers can transmit and receive messages at any hour of the day or night. Correspondence, reports, and memoranda can be transmitted to their offices for processing and distribution, in electronic or printed form. Information needed for clients or customers can be similarly handled. Computer data banks in many organizations are maintained to fill information requests from field personnel. In other organizations, secretaries provide personal response services. Computers reduce response times from days to minutes in either case.

Portable computers also enable those who travel to carry and apply more information than earlier was possible. Complete records concerning customers and projects are more readily contained and managed in computers than in briefcases. Often, in fact, computers permit engineers and other technically oriented travelers to take with them the equivalent of more paper than ever could have been transported.

These capabilities are created by a portable computer much different from early "transportable" models. Today's portable computers have been reduced in size and weight and expanded in capability to a point at which they can perform almost any task for which a desktop machine is necessary. Sophisticated portables can be equipped with multiple disk drives, modems, and other accessories necessary to permit use in almost any environment.

The overall result is more productivity. Field personnel apply computers to better use their time, putting more "on the road" hours to productive purposes. Time used in this way replaces time that otherwise would have to be spent in home offices catching up on paperwork. The savings can be translated into more time in the field, more time with the family, or both. Organizations and their employees benefit in either case.

THE AUDIOVISUAL REVOLUTION

A revolution of a magnitude at least equal to that triggered by the microcomputer has occurred relatively quietly in the audiovisual sector. The revolution has occurred quietly for a several reasons. While comparable to the computer revolution in magnitude, the audiovisual revolution at first involved more organizations than individuals. Only recently have some of the hardware improvements involved been made available in equipment used by hobbyists. In addition, many of the organizational needs fulfilled through sophisticated audiovisual technologies seldom arise for individuals or families.

The audiovisual revolution encompasses several areas most easily identified with the technologies involved, although the technologies often are used in combination. Perhaps the most significant component of the audiovisual revolution is business television, the commercial application of television technologies to benefit specific industries or companies. A number of networks have developed, in fact, to provide regular programming for groups involved.

Individual organizations use the same technologies, consisting primarily of computers and satellites, to transmit information around the globe in audiovisual form. Federal Express Corporation, for example, broadcasts daily to all personnel and conducts an annual employee meeting via satellite-based television links.

Network and corporate programming, coupled with more conventional uses of improved videotape and related equipment, together have also induced organizations and their vendors to make large investments in audiovisual production facilities. Federal Express maintains production studios at its headquarters in Memphis, Tennessee, for example, while Burson-Marsteller, one of the world's leading public relations firms, installed state-of-the-art facilities in its new headquarters in lower Manhattan during the mid-1980s.

Audiovisual Technologies

The nature of the audiovisual revolution is most readily understood when viewed from two perspectives, both dealing with messages. One is message preparation. The other is message distribution. Preparation involves one set of technologies, while distribution requires another.

Given necessary words, usually in the form of a speech or script, messages usually are recorded in preparation for delivery. Preparation options historically have included an audio tape with slides or film strip or a motion picture. The latter approach usually was too time consuming and too costly, while the former tended to be crude and relatively inefficient. Early videotape systems were only marginally better, but videotape technology has radically improved over the years. Video images nnw can be combined with graphics to create the sort of sophisticated visual effects to which television watchers have become accustomed.

With taped messages in hand, organizations select from among a broad range of distribution options. The original tape can be circulated for showing to multiple groups or quickly duplicated for shipping to distant points. A satellite transponder alternatively can be rented to broadcast the message live or via tape.

Using these technologies, Federal Express produces daily internal television reports concerning route conditions. Others, such as Texas Instruments, use television to introduce products. Still others use the medium as a teaching device, showing workers in fast food establishments, for example, how to prepare their products. Organizational needs, time requirements, and budgetary limitations together usually determine which of the options is selected.

Audiovisual Applications

Need for sophisticated audiovisual production and distribution facilities evolved in keeping with two parallel trends. First, work forces increasingly are populated with individuals who have been weaned, as it were, on audiovisual rather than printed messages.

Where the workers of the past grew up with newspapers and magazines, today's workers are members of an electronic generation. Second, the capabilities of audiovisual media have developed with the introduction of the new technologies, especially with the maturing of videotape systems. Videotape slowly has supplanted overhead projection and slide projection in most settings and long ago replaced the motion picture as a matter of economics.

Technological improvements have not, however, been the driving force behind the organizational trend toward audiovisual technology. The trend developed instead from basic change in populations with which organizations seek to communication. Workers, customers, and almost every other group today are more at home with electronically mediated information. In addition, electronically delivered information can be illustrated in ways that make it more memorable and more useful.

Usefulness often is especially important in organizations, where audiovisual presentations have become more common components of orientation and training programs. Mechanical procedures especially are more productively demonstrated than described. Audiovisuals, particularly videotape, make this process more easily accomplished than with other media. Audiovisuals also are readily applied in sales and marketing, in personnel recruiting as well as orientation and training, and in a host of other settings.

Computer Enhancements

Improved audiovisual technologies are even more productive where linked to computers, as is the case in interactive video systems. Companies in the automotive, insurance, and duplicating industries, to name but a few, also are using sophisticated interactive video systems to train sales personnel. The systems are designed to provide personalized instruction, thereby improving user performance. Trainees "talk" with video displays through computer keyboards or touch-sensitive video screens, using responses from lengthy lists stored on video disks. In some systems, trainees are taped while they respond to "customers'" questions or objections and later can play back the tape to analyze their performances. Trainees usually repeat such exercises until they are satisfied and then review the results with supervisors for additional coaching.

Savings involved in the use of these systems can be almost as dramatic as the profit potential in the interactive video marketplace. Chrysler Corporation estimates that it saved $1.3 million by using interactive video to instruct eighty-five thousand workers on the dangers of hazardous materials. IBM, after using the system internally for some years, entered the race for an estimated $50 billion to $70 billion in annual sales with a $9,000 unit oriented toward schools, banks, and insurance companies.

Educational Program

The most massive applications of new audiovisual technologies today are dedicated to worker education applications and are generally referred to as business television. Those who think of television in terms of news and entertainment or teleconferencing almost invariably are surprised to learn the extent to which the medium is used for business programming. A growing number of programming providers are generating real time broadcasts as well as taped presentations through multiple outlets. Some two dozen networks regularly broadcast business programs via their own or third parties' satellites. Many others offer a growing number of videotape programs, many of them from earlier broadcasts.

In 1983, there were four satellite-based business television networks. In 1988 there were more than sixty, and business was booming. Satellite television equipment and transmission services had become a $150 million market. The technology was not new but the cost was high—some $5 million for a studio, transmission center and fifty receiving sites.

The boom was a product of system efficiency and, some said, CEO vanity. "First we couldn't drag him in front of a television camera," said one public relations executive of his CEO, "but now he thinks he's a television star." More significant, however, was the development of a user's market in satellite-based communication during the late 1980s.

Conditions advantageous to this development were a result of changing technology. Fiber optic telephone circuits across the United States and under the Atlantic drew traffic away from the satellites, making transponders available. In October 1988, with 138 transponders available, demand required fewer than 100. At the same time, new technology shrank satellite antennas, transmitters, receivers and related equipment, concurrently making them less expensive to buy, operate, and maintain.

Economic factors. The boom was being stimulated by sheer economics. J. C. Penney Company executives estimated they recovered the cost of their $4 million, 700-site system in one year through savings in travel costs. First Union National Bank of Charlotte, North Carolina, projected $3 million in savings over five years.

Then there are the nontraining applications. K-Mart Corporation installed dishes at some two thousand stores to transmit business information. Chrysler Corporation uses a similar system to communicate with six thousand dealerships and plants in North America. Penney uses its network to deliver antidrug programming. Texas Instruments brought executives together with reporters in five cities to discuss a new technological development. Merrill Lynch uses a 450-site system to roll out new mutual funds. And Citicorp executives met with Hewlett-Packard officers via the bankers' television system to close a financing transaction.

J. C. Penney has also used its system to enable outlet personnel to select merchandise rather than having them come to New York for that purpose. Perhaps most impressive to newcomers to business television, however, is the fact that Penney has launched into the corporate communication business with J. C. Penney Communications, a subsidiary designed to capitalize on the company's experience.

The extent to which such systems can be used perhaps best can be illustrated through the Merrill Lynch example. During the 1987 market crash, top management conducted daily briefings for all personnel. The next week, the company responded in similar manner to another emergency. A customer had shot two Merrill Lynch brokers, and retail division heads used the medium to reassure other personnel.

Those who can not afford systems of their own increasingly are joining in industry networks. Some three thousand auto dealers, for example, have joined the Automotive Satellite Network (ASTN), which is earning revenues of almost $20 million a year. ASTN soon added a Law Enforcement Satellite Network to train police officers, and others have similar expansion plans. Industry experts expect almost 150 networks to be in operation in the next few years.

Networks Listed. Existing networks are sponsored by the American Hospital Association, American Law Network, American Management Association, American Rehabilitation Educational Network, Arts and Sciences Teleconferencing Services, Automotive Satellite Television Network, Bankers-TV Network, California State University, Chico Center for Regional and Continuing Education, Computer Channel, ComputerLand Corporation, Continuing Legal

Education Satellite Network, Executive Communications, George Washington University National Satellite Network, Hospital Satellite Network, Institute of Electrical and Electronics Engineers, Institutional Research Network, Inc., J. C. Penney Communications, National Technological University, National University Teleconference Network, Old Dominion University Network, Private Satellite Network, Satellite Conference Network, Triton College and VideoStar Communications.

Major satellite operators include the American Hospital Association, American Law Network, American Management Association, American Rehabilitation Educational Network, Arts and Sciences Teleconferencing Service, Bankers-TV Network, Continuing Legal Education Satellite Network, Executive Communications, George Washington University, Hospital Satellite Network, Institute of Electrical and Electronics Engineers, Institutional Research Network, National Technological University, National University Teleconference Network, Old Dominion University, and Triton College.

Videotape program providers include the America Hospital and American Management Associations, Barr Films, George Washington University, The Information Factory, Medical Care Development, and Medical Video Productions.

Programming Variation. Volume of programming available varies with the size and interests of groups involved. Larger groups, for economic reasons, generally are better served than their smaller counterparts. The size of the health care industry, for example, induced providers to offer multiple programs on an almost daily basis. Programming specifically designed for the legal profession, however, seldom involves more than a half dozen offerings each month.

How large will this industry become, and how effective will it be? Industry spokespersons are enthusiastic. Others, such as author Tom Peters, are less sanguine, suggesting that corporate television "dehumanizes the corporate world even further." Only the passage of time will resolve the conflict, but growth apparently will continue for the short term at least.

Educational Tapes

Videotape often meets the needs of organizations without the size and resources to use television. Videotape use among small businesses has been increasing at a rapid rate, according to the

American Society for Training and Development. Tapes can be inexpensively produced internally or obtained from business, trade, or professional associations.

Some organizations have used videotapes in internal and external applications. Manufacturers have used them to train distributor personnel and to assist customers. Others have applied videotape for training and other purposes. Costs tend to be relatively high whether tapes are produced internally or rented, but results usually are more than sufficient to justify the investments involved.

LONG-TERM IMPLICATIONS

The extent to which audiovisual and other technologies have been applied to enhance organizations' ability to communicate suggests three long-term outcomes. First, greater sophistication in internal communication systems is apt to compound the difficulties experienced by "external" communicators in reaching members of audiences involved. Second, organizations are likely to continue to be early adopters of innovative communication techniques, including those coming into use through the new media. Third, the collective results of these trends almost inevitably will hasten the onset of the information age.

Of the three outcomes, enhanced sophistication among internal communication systems can be expected to create the most durable and pervasive impacts. Organizational use of sophisticated systems to enhance the efficiency of internal communication programs orients workers to the hardware and processes involved. Many who now have computers at home, for example, first used them in occupational settings. Those who become familiar with interactive communication systems operated by their employers will be similarly preconditioned to accept the same sort of systems elsewhere.

The extent to which these trends may influence the evolution of public mass communication systems and the timing involved are difficult to predict. Organizational use of new technologies inevitably will eliminate psychological barriers to their external use. Elimination of potential user barriers can not, however, be taken as a valid indicator of prospective economic success. While computer-based communication systems have been highly successful within organizations such as the 3M Company, for example,

CompuServe, The Source, and similar public utilities have been slow to achieve the successes their operators had anticipated.

Mass communicators must remember, on the other hand, that they compete with employers and others for the limited time individuals devote to information processing. Time committed to assimilating information delivered by employer communication systems—print as well as electronic—is not available to commercial publishers and broadcasters. Organizational systems already displace the commercial to some extent where companies, for example, broadcast news and weather to their personnel.

Those anticipating the early demise of the mass media are ill advised. Organizational communication systems are no more likely to replace the mass media than televised shopping services are apt to cause the death of the shopping mall. Both mall and media nevertheless are losing small parts of their customer base, however, and the attrition at some point will become significant.

IN SUMMARY

Organizations, because of their profit orientation and greater economic capabilities, provide de facto testing laboratories for the new technologies. Copying machines, computers, facsimile machines and the like are representative of the technology-based devices that have spread from the corporation to the small business and thence to the home.

Computers have been the most prominent of these technologies. They have developed over time from being a relative rarity in large organizations to becoming an essential component of most businesses. In recent years, computers have reached more than 25 percent of all homes in the United States.

Once applied primarily as storage and retrieval devices for information in statistical and verbal form, computers now are used for research, communication, and information management as well. Most recently, computers have been used extensively in graphics and desktop publishing applications.

The organizational audiovisual revolution is no less pervasive. Rapidly improving videotape technology has been primarily responsible, enabling organizations to apply this tool quickly and economically in informational and educational settings. Computer-produced graphics readily can be incorporated into videotape as well as slides and printed materials.

Satellite technology has been as important as videotape, however, in the development of audiovisual capabilities in organizations. During the five years ending in 1988, satellite-based networks developed for business purposes increased from four to more than sixty, driven by the enormous savings that attached to use of the technology involved. Networks were established by business and professional associations as well as by individual organizations. Where economics precluded large scale application of the medium, videotape program producers bridged the gap. Business audiovisual programming promises to be one of the fastest-growing of the technology-driven communication processes of the twenty-first century.

ADDITIONAL READING

Berger, Warren. "TV for the Boardroom and the Factory Floor," *New York Times*. Aug. 21, 1988.

Boudette, Neal E. "And Now, A Word From Our Sponsor: Using The Tube for Business Communications." *Industry Week*, Feb. 6, 1989.

"Communication Climate Determines How Employees View Their Jobs, So They Want Information about the Organization from Top Management." *pr reporter*, Aug. 25, 1986.

Copeland, Jeff B., Vern E. Smith, Karen Springen, and Jodi Stewart. "Broadcast News, Inc.: Private Networks Are Becoming a Fixture in Many American Companies." *Newsweek*, Jan. 4, 1988.

Dougherty, Philip H. "How PC's Help Out an Agency." *New York Times*, Oct. 1, 1987.

Fisher, Lawrence M. "TV a Growing Corporate Tool." *New York Times*, Jan. 3, 1987.

Grunig, James E., and Kathryn T. Theus. "Internal Communication Systems and Employee Satisfaction." Paper presented to the Public Relations Division, Association for Education in Journalism and Mass Communication, Norman, Okla., Aug. 1986.

Kuzela, Lad, "Long Way to Go: Videoconferencing's Chief Drawback: Cost." *Industry Week*, July 4, 1988.

Modic, Stanley J. "Grapevine Rated Most Believable." *Industry Week*, May 15, 1989.

Neff, Robert. "Videos Are Starring in More and More Training Programs." *Business Week*, Sept. 7, 1987.

Pincus, J. David., and Robert E. Rayfield. "The Relationships Between Top Management Communication and Organizational Effectiveness." Paper presented to the Public Relations Division, Association for Education in Journalism and Mass Communication, Norman, Okla., Aug. 1986.

Ricklef, Roger. "Firms Turn to Videos to Teach Workers." *New York Times*, Dec. 6, 1988.

Sims, Calvin. "Satellite Use By Business Is Growing." *New York Times*, Oct. 26, 1988.

10 The Wired Society Arrives

Immaturity among the new media and apparent stability among their senior brethren suggest to many that communication today is much the same as it was a decade ago. There are more television channels, more magazines, and fewer newspapers, but little else appears changed.

Appearances, however, are highly deceiving. An increasingly entrepreneurial society has been caught up in a firestorm of communication fed by what might best be called almost new technologies. Major components of this group include cellular telephones, facsimile machines, and electronic mail systems. Individually, they appear to exercise little influence on mass communication. Collectively, and at close range, they appear to be producing significant deterioration in traditional channels of mass communication.

More important, enhanced telephone, facsimile, and electronic mail systems are moving rapidly toward the "wired society" of which futurists have been speaking and writing for more than a decade. Systems that will bind these seemingly separate networks into a cohesive whole already are in place or under development. Connected to computers and satellites, they will become the veins and arteries of the age of information.

The impact of developing communication systems on individuals was inadvertently demonstrated in late 1988 in a *Business Week* article describing how Westinghouse Electric Corporation executives use the newer communication technologies. The extent to which the firm's chief executive officer uses personal computers, cellular telephones, and electronic mail was impressive. He uses them at home and in his car as well as in his office. The Westinghouse system is considered among the best in the world.

But what is the impact on the individuals involved? Where does Westinghouse President Paul E. Leg find the time he spends communicating with business associates via personal computer from home on Sundays? What does he sacrifice to use cellular telephone to confer with other executives while en route to the office at 6:30 A.M.? What is he missing when he sits down at his desk and turns on his office microcomputer?

Business Week's description of Leg's weekend and early Monday activities imply significant levels of insulation or isolation from traditional mass media. His personal communication patterns appear to preclude his watching television newscasts before leaving home, hearing radio newscasts en route to the office, and reading a local morning newspaper. Leg's potential exposure to these media and the messages they contain is radically limited by extensive use of newer and more selective channels of communication.

This process of replacement remains to be assessed with any degree of precision. No researcher yet has attempted to measure any of several pertinent factors critical to mass communication: to what extent do newer, more selective media drive out older, more mass-oriented media? To what extent do users of the new media, as a result, become more isolated or more provincial in their perspectives? And what do these factors imply as to the efficacy of traditional mass media?

Research data to date indicate only that information consumption is growing at a rate much slower than information production. Massachusetts Institute of Technology Professor Ithiel de Sola Pool, after monitoring media from 1960 to 1977, reported a 9 percent annual increase in data availability but only a 3 percent increase in consumption. More important from the perspective of communicators, he concluded that while transmission costs are dropping, the cost of communication—having the message received and assimilated—is increasing.

NOT-SO-NEW MEDIA

Time and human capacity to assimilate information are finite and inflexible. While enhancing rates of productivity, no operational technology can produce more time or expand capacity for information. To the extent that humans voluntarily and consciously commit more time to one medium, then, they necessarily reduce their commitments to competing media.

The terms *voluntarily* and *consciously* are necessary in that some forms of mass communication are virtually unavoidable. Signs of all kinds assault individuals at every turn. From the highway to the supermarket, from the subway to the public toilet, advertising signs are everywhere. The numbers of newspapers or magazines one reads, or the number of newscasts tuned in, are another matter.

Time dedicated to traditional mass media almost certainly will dwindle as interactive media come into general use. In the interim, however, a set of not-so-new media systems already clamor for attention and a share of available time. Not-so-new systems employ long-established rather than new technologies. The technologies have been applied or adapted, however, to create innovative communication channels that are quickly adding to what has been called "information overload."

Most not-so-new technologies share a characteristic observed in early videocassette recorders. Elapsed time from their introduction to maturity has been remarkably short. The facsimile machine, for example, progressed from introduction to maturity in little more than two years. Electronic mail and voice mail systems are following the same pattern. Each of these technologies, in the process, will capture a small but significant portion of the time their users earlier had allocated to other pursuits, probably to other information sources.

THE FACSIMILE EXPLOSION

While invented in the 1840s, facsimile "arrived" in the United States in the late 1980s in a form that surprised some of the nation's more respected corporate planners. Federal Express Corporation, which had expected to capitalize on facsimile technology to capture a large share of the electronic message delivery market, found itself driven from the marketplace by the speed of technological progress.

Federal had launched its ZapMail system in light of one of two unstated but tenuous assumptions. The first and least probable of the two was that the cost of high-quality facsimile equipment would remain at levels that would make owning systems impractical other than in the largest organizations. The second and more probable was that the technology would not be readily available through multiple vendors. Those who needed immediate document transmission, Federal apparently reasoned, therefore would be forced to use commercial services.

Neither assumption was validated by events. Facsimile equipment first quickly came to market from multiple sources. Then, as competition increased, prices declined. By 1989, facsimile machines were selling for less than 20 percent of their original prices. Machines at the low end of most manufacturers' lines were selling at less than six hundred dollars, and the bottom did not appear to be in sight. Sales, as a result, were almost doubling with each passing year. In 1986, 191,000 facsimile machines were sold. In 1987, sales topped the 475,000 mark. By 1989, portable machines had become common, and forecasters were expecting to see more than 1.5 million machines in use in the United States by 1990.

The early sales explosion was fueled by a host of other developments. Facsimile was linked to mainframe as well as mini- and microcomputers. Plain paper machines quickly started replacing those that used thermal papers. Compact units incorporating telephones appeared for the home and small business markets. Still smaller units were designed for portable use. Encryptors quickly became available to ensure security. Perhaps most important, numbers of manufacturers continued to increase. By 1988, more than thirty vendors were in the marketplace.

The vendors also were doing more than merely selling facsimile equipment. Many of them, some primarily dedicated to producing computers and peripherals and some with other origins, also were offering add-on "cards" or "boards" that enable computers to serve as facsimile machines. At about the same time, computer utilities such as CompuServe, telephone organizations such as MCI, and a number of independent vendors joined the market with products specifically oriented to prospective facsimile users. CompuServe established a system through which microcomputer users could send messages to facsimile machines. MCI announced plans to establish a facsimile system separate from the firm's telephone system.

Why would MCI enter an arena in which Federal Express had stumbled? The telephone-oriented company was offering fiber optic lines to insure image quality for those who wanted higher quality transmissions. The facsimile network was designed to provide a wide range of services, including customized dialing plans, 800 -line service, delivery confirmation, and security features. MCI's announced objective was to capture a larger share of the total telephone market.

Not all facsimile-related developments, of course, were welcome. Like telephone and mail systems, albeit more akin to the former, facsimile could be bent to purposes for which it was not intended. The major problem, which quickly came to be known as "junk fax," consisted of unwanted messages advertising products or services. Junk fax tied up machines needed for business purposes, exhausted expensive supplies, and quickly became a costly nuisance. Use of facsimile for advertising purposes proved popular because messages are read where direct mail envelopes may go unopened.

The junk fax problem prompted a number of state legislatures to begin work on laws that would outlaw the practice. The key provision of a proposed Oregon statute read, "No person shall use a machine that electronically transmits facsimiles of documents, through connection with a telephone network, to transmit unsolicited advertising material for the sale of any realty, goods or services."

Other states, including Washington and Connecticut, soon followed Oregon's lead, but not without resistance. The Direct Marketing Association, while conceding that junk facsimile messages can be irritating, expressed the belief that a ban might run afoul of the constitutional right to free speech. A representative of the association proposed that junk fax transmissions might better be restricted to specific hours rather than banned in their entirety. One facsimile machine manufacturer offered a more effective but more expensive solution: a facsimile machine that would deny access to all messages not preceded by a three-digit code.

Facsimile transmissions also necessarily involved potential drawbacks. Paramount among them in many cases is the fact that they seldom are confidential. Unless encrypted, and perhaps even then, facsimile-transmitted messages can go through several sets of hands before reaching intended recipients. Facsimile messages without cover sheets indicating the identity of recipients are apt to be passed from hand to hand until recognized.

Another "benefit" lost in the facsimile explosion arose in connection with time factors. One of those benefits might best be labeled communication "float." In the prefacsimile era, messages dispatched by mail, and the problems that they addressed, would be off senders' desks for days. Even where express mail was used, at least forty-eight hours elapsed before the problem demanded renewed attention.

Another facsimile benefit first was gained, then lost. With facsimile, days were added to the time that could be used to get a job done. With documents subject to facsimile delivery in minutes, "the last minute" could be, and usually was, relocated on the calendar. Unfortunately, the added flexibility quickly was factored into delivery formulas, and time gained when the facsimile machine was installed soon was lost to the enhanced expectations of senders, receivers, or both.

FROM PAPER TO VOICE

Those who find junk fax a problem tend to become more than a little irritated when confronted with "phone mail," a system that uses a combination of telephone, computer, and answering machine technologies to route and store incoming telephone messages. The system works this way: The number you call is answered by a computer that gives you a set of alternate destinations for your call, each accompanied by a number. This process may be repeated several times before you reach the destination telephone, which may or may not be answered by the individual you called. If he or she is not at the desk, or is simply too busy to answer, you can leave a taped message.

"This new technology," said *The New York Times*' James Barron, " . . . is enough to make frazzled callers who just want to reach out and touch someone want to reach out and scream." He described the responses of voice mail systems in these words: "It is the voice of a machine. It tells callers that if they have a phone with a tone, they can punch various digits to reach the different departments. . . . 'To leave a message for customer service, press nine-four-zero-zero now,' the voice says. 'To leave a message for customer service, press nine-four-zero-two now. Or enter the extension of the person to whom you wish to speak . . . now."

Variation in owner-installed instructions can create varying levels of satisfaction or frustration among callers. Some callers can quickly find themselves in what's been called "phone mail jail," bounced from one recorded response to another and unable to break through to a human being. Others just as quickly route their calls to desired destinations, as system users intended. Potential for caller frustration is tolerated by system users because of the range of functions that systems can provide. Among them are the following:

- Recording personal messages
- Forwarding messages
- Distributing messages to several recipients
- Screening and holding calls
- Providing voice bulletin boards
- Serving as gateways to computer databases

All of the foregoing functions compound the complexity of the more conventional answering systems described above. Some also are more sophisticated than they first appear. Messages can be recorded that will be played back only to those who have special access codes. A travel itinerary, for example, could be made available only to members of the organization. Voice bulletin board systems also can transmit one message to any number of recipients. A sales manager, for example, could notify fifty sales representatives of a price change with a single call.

Call screening functions ask callers for their names. Responses are heard by prospective call recipients, who can respond or direct the voice mail system to take a message. Callers put on hold are told how many others are waiting and are given codes that enable them to leave messages should their patience become exhausted.

System Origins

Phone mail systems started to multiply in 1987 although technology necessary to install them had been available for almost ten years. A year later, phone mail systems reportedly were in use by more than 28 percent of large companies (with more than one thousand internal telephones) but less than 1 percent of small companies (fewer than forty telephones). Analysts then were predicting that numbers of systems would almost triple among large companies and grow six-fold among their smaller counterparts by 1992.

The technology used in voice mail consists of personal computer circuit boards and software that makes the computers say the right things. Only since 1987, however, has software been improved to a point at which answers sound like they are being given by people who know what they are talking about. In most systems, in fact, answers at individual extensions are taped by those who use the phones in question.

As with most technologies, voice mail system prices have been declining as the technology becomes more popular. Low-end systems, consisting primarily of add-on circuit boards for microcomputers, sell for as little as $300 in addition to the cost of the computer. Systems capable of handling organizations of ten to four hundred individuals range in cost from $40,000 to less than $10,000, and prices are continuing to decline. At these price levels, voice mail systems quickly can pay for themselves through savings in operator time and increased communication efficiency. Labor shortages created by national demographic trends, however, may provide the greatest growth stimulus. Voice mail presents only one source of potential difficulty. Those who use older, rotary telephone equipment cannot activate voice mail systems.

Voice Mail Stimuli

Mounting shortages of qualified personnel already have added impetus to the phone mail explosion, which already extends from railroad schedules to dial-a-porn services. Phone mail is used extensively by cable television systems, public utilities, and similar organizations that receive heavy volumes of incoming calls. Sears, Roebuck and Company has installed phone mail in many of its stores, and the Public Broadcasting System uses phone mail to handle broadcasters' job inquiries. Travelers Companies has installed voice mail in the insurance firm's Hartford, Connecticut headquarters, and the Vatican is installing a system that will deliver recorded messages from the Pope. Even the American Civil Liberties Union, self-appointed guardian of free speech, has installed a system on the grounds that it is necessary to insure that all calls are answered.

What does the future hold? Proliferation and problems both are likely developments. Proliferation probably will be created by the Bell companies, although commercial renters of voice mail boxes already are active in some markets. Voice Mail International and American Express have started limited public voice mail systems, and GTE Corporation followed a test in Dallas by installing systems in New York and Los Angeles. The Bell companies' dominance would logically result were they to offer voice mail as a one of a growing number of "bells and whistles" available at extra cost with basic telephone services.

Potential Problems

Potential problems in part are apt to be similar to those that followed the facsimile explosion. If junk fax was a headache, in other words, can "junk phone mail" be far behind? Hardware used in voice mail systems is similar to that used in telemarketing, where computers dial numbers and dictate messages. Some voice mail system vendors have restricted the ability of their systems to dial out, but others have been less cautious.

Security also may be a potential source of difficulty. Computer hackers have been known to break into phone mail systems and replace conventional greetings with obscenities. Less substantive but equally troublesome may be the absence of phone mail code protocols. Codes vary across systems, and the number that saves a message on one system can erase it on another.

Potential for problems is offset to some extent, however, by prospective benefits. Among the more promising developments waiting in the wings is a system that will link voice mail with electronic text mail. Using computer software that converts text into speech, Kodak is working on a system through which callers can have written messages read to them by a machine. This device could become a sort of interface between internal phone mail systems and the electronic mail systems that are growing externally with almost equally explosive force.

Other Technologies

As long has been the case in other technologies, telephone and voice mail systems are spawning an extensive aftermarket. Local telephone companies are starting to offer hardware that permits subscribers to identify callers before answering. Other manufacturers, already providing such devices as cellular phone extensions, doubtless will follow with similar appliances.

New Jersey Bell first offered caller identification systems in December of 1988. Pacific Telesis planned to start offering a similar system in 1989, and Nynex Corporation scheduled its system for start-up in 1990. Nynex concurrently will roll out several other less-than-essential services. They include an automatic redial system that will keep dialing a busy number for as long as a half hour, a call tracing service that records the numbers of obscene callers and transmits them to telephone security offices, and a callback service that calls the last person who called, whether the call was answered or not.

South Central Bell introduced most of these services and some others in 1988 and 1989. Among them was a call blocking service that enabled users to block incoming calls from predetermined numbers. Pacific Telesis is planning to extend this type of service by enabling callers to prevent the display of their numbers on caller identification devices. Numbers would be replaced by the message, "private call."

Caller identification services in some areas are beneficial and in others detrimental. Restaurants offering home delivery services, for example, can use caller identification systems to confirm callers' numbers and screen out costly crank calls. On the other hand, however, the ability to identify the source of incoming calls might discourage prospective users of crisis services.

New telephone company services have not been received with universal acclaim. Analysts blame apathetic audiences and poor marketing programs. Marketing problems can be overcome, however, and the telephone companies have the staying power to see their new products to profitability.

FROM VOICE TO DATA

Facsimile-to-telephone linkages permitting computer-driven systems to "read" facsimile messages to callers appear more or less logical to the casual observer. Both systems use telephone lines. They differ only in the manner in which transmitted information is packaged—on paper rather than vocally. Translation requires only a mechanism through which bits of information on paper can be converted to sounds, as can readily be accomplished by a computer.

At second, if not at first, glance, linkages between facsimile and electronic mail and between electronic mail and voice mail systems are equally logical. Facsimile and electronic mail systems almost universally converse in translatable language. Where differences exist, they can be readily overcome. Consider individuals using different word processing programs on their computers and experiencing difficulty in exchanging files. The problem can be solved by applying one of several conversion programs that translate one word processor's language to that of another or by reducing the files to common ASCII computer code.

Conversion problems are equally soluble in electronic mail, as probably will be evident by the time this book appears. Internal and external electronic mail networks can be made capable of talking to one another and probably will be doing so before the end of 1990. Translation problems apparently will be solved in much the same manner that the nation's independent telephone companies long ago agreed to link their systems together: under consumer pressure.

The Universal System

Convincing pressure was brought to bear on the independent and separately operated electronic mail systems in December of 1988, when representatives of the fifty-member Aerospace Industries Association (AIA) delivered an ultimatum: their members would deal only with companies that started work no later than February 1989 toward universal system compatibility.

The ultimatum produced results for two reasons. The reasons can be summed up in one word: profit. Faced with potential loss of profit if they failed to act and with the prospect of greater profit if they acted, electronic mail system operators decided to cooperate. Loss potential was a matter of mathematics and timing. Electronic mail system operators were confronted by representatives of some three hundred thousand electronic mail users, each of whom send an average of two to three messages a day. The bulk of the messages, in addition, then were being sent under electronic mail contracts due to expire in little more than sixty days.

The logic of compatible systems, in the circumstances, apparently proved overpowering. If further incentives were needed, they were created through an estimate by aerospace executives that access to compatible systems would encourage their companies to transmit an additional 35 million messages a year, producing an additional $35 million in revenue for system operators.

Representatives of seven electronic mail networks responded in something less than sixty days with a demonstration of a functioning interconnected system for AIA representatives. A six-month pilot program involving eight aerospace companies quickly was put in place. The pilot system involved no commitment among the electronic mail vendors involved to make the same technology available to the public, but industry sources indicated that movement in that direction might occur as early as 1990.

While apparently ignoring the compatibility issue, electronic mail vendors had been making limited progress toward compatibility for several years. A vendor international rules committee created an operating standard for electronic mail systems in 1984. In the next several years, MCI used the standard to link up with CompuServe, and American Telephone and Telegraph adopted it to link up with Dialcom in providing services to the federal government.

Some electronic mail providers in mid-1989 remained less than comfortable with the prospect of marketing wars that might be triggered by universal compatibility. Some may elect to avoid compatibility as a result, said *Business Week*'s Frances Seghers, but the industry's experience with AIA suggests "that approach is nothing but a ticket to oblivion."

Emerging Systems

Universally accessible electronic mail systems will be among the final links in the wired society in the United States. They will bring multiple preexisting components together to create a functional whole. System components generally fall into one of two categories: those which would be immediately operational and those which would remain to become operational.

The first category, the immediately operational, include all elements of the telephone system as well as computers and facsimile systems operated by individuals and organizations. The second category consists of domestic voice mail systems and foreign segments of the integrated grid that might require additional effort in integration.

In practical terms, however, the wired society would come into being with integration of electronic mail systems. While integration of voice mail systems will enhance systemic flexibility and cohesiveness, most businesses and some 25 percent of all households in the United States already are equipped with mainframe and/or microcomputers. Modem-equipped computers provide immediate access to electronic mail and facsimile systems.

Universally accessible external or public electronic mail systems would bridge the remaining gaps between private systems, organizational and individual. The transition will be much akin to those that developed as today's telephone network took shape years ago. Residents of individual communities who could speak only with one another suddenly found themselves capable of communicating with any telephone user anywhere.

As Eastman or other vendors provide software to translate voice mail into print, and vice versa, the final links of the wired society will fall into place. Print, verbal, and electronic communication systems will become a cohesive whole. Individual and organizational users will have uniform access to one another and to a world of information that continues to grow at an exponential rate.

The Down Side

Unfortunately, electronic mail systems will be more likely to exacerbate the problems of today's communication systems than create a new tomorrow. Internal and external electronic mail systems are as prone to junk messages as the United States Postal Service and facsimile systems.

The potential for internal difficulties is not unlike that which was demonstrated with early copying machines. They generated more paper simply by being there. The same principle applies where electronic mail systems are available. They make it too easy to send messages to everyone. The chairman of the board does not need to know about the new sales representative just hired in Hushpuckena, Mississippi, but a message to "everyone" inevitably will reach him. He would not be forced to respond, but he will have to dispose of the message, which can be almost as time-consuming.

External aspects of this potential problem at first appeared somewhat less threatening but will not necessarily remain relatively small. Junk messages in electronic systems have proven relatively few because electronic mail addresses are less readily available than telephone numbers and because commercial services have attempted to protect their users. These barriers to abuse already are deteriorating.

Deterioration results from efforts to enhance the value of communication systems for users. More and more organizations, for example, are publishing internal electronic mail addresses together with telephone numbers. Externally, professional and trade associations have published their members' facsimile numbers and electronic mail addresses. While helping members stay in contact with one another, however, some organizational directories fall into the hands of list brokers, individuals or firms who make a business of selling mailing lists. The result can be a flood of junk facsimile or junk electronic messages equal to the junk mail flows at home.

Researchers at the Massachusetts Institute of Technology and elsewhere are developing protective devices but their efficiency remains to be proven. Most consist of computer programs that screen messages in keeping with user-defined criteria. Conceivably, they may prove highly efficient. If technologically successful and extensively marketed, however, they will inevitably be defeated by electronic entrepreneurs.

The developmental pattern involved is similar to that which long has prevailed in the evolution of highway radar detectors and more recently has appeared in telephones. Each succeeding generation of law enforcement radar prompted a new generation of detection equipment. Telemarketers' continuing efforts have prompted a similar progression. Telephone companies first offered unlisted numbers, which now are used by almost 30 percent of all United States households. Some telephone companies also offer a service called Caller ID. With about $75 worth of equipment and a subscription that sells for something under $100 a year, users can see callers' numbers displayed on a screen. They can answer or ignore calls, or permit them to be handled by answering machines. The next step in the progression, initiated by New Jersey Bell, is a less complex system. For $48 a year, the company will accept a list of up to six calling numbers and block calls from those numbers to the subscriber's telephone. Calls from those numbers are shunted to a central office recording device that tells them, in effect, to get lost.

Growth Patterns

With all its problem potential, however, electronic mail is expected to grow more rapidly than was the case with facsimile as compatibility barriers fall. Even without universal access, in fact, experts are predicting an explosion in internal and external electronic mail over the next several years.

Some 500 million messages were handled by public systems such as CompuServe and MCI in 1987. The number is expected to exceed 2 billion by 1992. At the same time, a ten-fold increase is expected in the estimated 1 billion messages handled by private systems.

These estimates involve no assumptions concerning the growing cost of conventional postal services. Electronic mail vendors long have looked to rising United States Postal Service rates as a stimulus to their businesses. History, however, reflects relatively little rate sensitivity where the Postal Service is concerned. Mail volume has grown with remarkable consistency over the years at an annual rate of about 5 percent. The advent of electronic communication devices has proved threatening, instead, to those who have profited on the basis of speed.

Federal Express, the nation's leader in overnight delivery services, has experienced no overall loss in volume, despite the fact that as much as 50 percent of the company's volume might be handled by facsimile. The company's marketing efforts, however, have been reoriented from the envelope to the package market, where neither facsimile nor electronic mail pose substantive long-term threats.

Some forecasters predict that Federal Express, Western Union's telex business, the Postal Service's express mail service, and others competing in the letter market ultimately may lose as much as 30 percent of their letter traffic to electronic transmission systems. These predictions are based, however, on assumptions that barriers between electronic mail systems will come down.

ADDITIONAL SERVICES

For better or worse, competition among delivery services and information providers will continue to grow, qualitatively and quantitatively. While many computer-based electronic services have faltered, entrepreneurial organizations quickly roll out replacements of all kinds. More of them are almost certain to appear as the regional Bell companies take advantage of the relative competitive freedom they now enjoy.

Collectively, communication services have stimulated growth in "electronic commuting," through which workers perform their duties at home, linked to their offices in whole or in part only through the new technologies. Computers were the first components of these commuting systems, but facsimile added to the feasibility of the practice. Voice mail and electronic mail doubtless will help as well.

The Electronic Cottage

While many continue to commute to their jobs, researchers in 1988 estimated that some 25 million United States workers were working at home. Fewer than 30 percent of them were self-employed. The remainder were working for others.

Although a relatively new development, the home office has become the fastest-growing component of the computer market and is adding considerably to sales in other areas. Telephones, facsimile machines, copiers, modems, printers, and a host of other devices are being sold in ever-growing quantities for home use.

Growth has been so rapid, in fact, as to induce futurist Alvin Toffler to concede that he had grossly underestimated the magnitude of the home office trend. "The numbers today are vastly greater than the largest numbers we allowed ourselves to imagine," he told *The New York Times* in 1988.

Development of the electronic cottage is also is encouraged by efforts in California and elsewhere to demonstrate practical alternatives to vehicular commuting. The objectives of California's Telecommuting Pilot Project, for example, include exploring the potential of what might best be called satellite work centers. These are suburban or rural offices wired to central offices and designed to minimize commuting, which Toffler described as "the single most nonproductive thing we do."

Bell Services

Commuting inevitably will decline as the wired society takes shape and the numbers and types of services available through electronic networks increase. The Bell companies, led by South Central Bell, are planning to offer a broad range of entertainment as well as communication services on a direct basis and through electronic "gateways." The latter approach is necessary in that telephone companies remain constrained by court orders from supplying, as opposed to delivering, some services. Among services soon to be available via telephone lines are the following:

1. Voice mail, a sophisticated service essentially identical to that which organizations can maintain through their own telephone systems. Calls will be routed to personal "voice mail boxes" in company offices for subsequent retrieval at a cost of about fifty cents a call.

2. Electronic mail, through which documents can be sent from one computer to another by calling a telephone number, eliminating any need for modems (or other peripherals), or for computer compatibility.

3. Voice message services, through which information concern ing entertainment, religious events, weather, and the like can be provided at the touch of a button.

4. Gateway services for computer users, permitting access to more than one thousand data banks without becoming involved in individual subscriptions, passwords, compatibility problems, or the like.

5. Audio-to-text and text-to-audio services for those who want to communicate with the blind.

6. Pay-per-view cable television that would substitute for existing "premium channels" by enabling viewers to pick and choose movies and other programs from an extensive menu.

BellSouth's gateway was launched with a field test in which the company offered a host of database and other services under the name Transtext Universal Gateway or T.U.G. Conceived in keeping with limitations imposed by court orders, T.U.G. will serve only as a gateway, offering no services of its own.

The BellSouth service as launched provided access to CompuServe, Dialcom, and The Source. Prospective additional participants included Dow Jones News Retrieval, Eaasy Sabre for airline fares, and several electronic mail services.

The primary user advantage in T.U.G. is economic. Users pay $3.00 an hour plus $1.20 for each 64,000 bytes of data sent or received. Those rates include all database services. No individual subscriptions, many of which carry minimum monthly fees, are required.

Other Services

BellSouth and the other Bell companies are not alone in seeking to exploit electronic communication systems. A number of players have come and gone, including Knight-Ridder Newspapers, yet others continue to seek profits in the electronic marketplace. Among the more recent entrants, in different ways, are IBM and Sears Roebuck in a joint venture in on line service and American Express in a radically new billing system.

IBM and Sears are betting some $250 million on jointly owned Trintex and its Prodigy service, an on-line system that will allow consumers to send and receive data and graphics via personal computer and telephone line. Prodigy will differ in several significant ways from earlier videotext services. Complex graphics and sophisticated text fonts will be offered, and the system will include advertising as well. Several major auto manufacturers and large retailers made early commitments to use the advertising service, although considerable time will be required before Prodigy can be called a success or a failure.

The new American Express billing system is a different approach to contemporary technology. While other credit card companies were replacing copies of charge slips with summary statements, American Express opted for a system that provides customers with laser-printed copies of all of their charge tickets—an expensive approach.

The system does more, however, that merely provide copies of charge tickets. American Express also is capturing information on those tickets, creating profiles of members' buying patterns. This information can become a valuable resource, especially if offered for sale to merchandisers.

IN SUMMARY

Although little noticed outside the business community and less than universally recognized within that community, the so-called wired society long promised by futurists was rapidly coming to operational status in the late 1980s. Perhaps the most significant development in the process was accomplished by electronic mail vendors. Operating under duress but nevertheless productively, electronic mail firms bridged the gaps between their several systems, following a pattern established years ago by then independent telephone companies.

Major milestones such as this one have been overshadowed by the rapid development of what might be called communication conveniences spawned by nearly new or not-so-new technologies. The cellular telephone, facsimile machine, and electronic mail system all are examples of such devices.

Contemporary facsimile networks were produced by a fast-maturing technology spurred forward to a point at which several dozen manufacturers were competing for market share primarily on the basis of price. The result was a facsimile machine in almost every business place and many homes by the end of the 1980s. These conditions prevailed despite the fact that Federal Express Corporation once had anticipated earning a great deal of profit through a proprietary facsimile system. Despite temporary problems with "junk fax" and pending legislation to curb unwanted facsimile messages in several states, the technology was well established in a relatively short time. Almost immediately, in fact, facsimile was supplemented by phone mail.

Phone mail, as the term implies, is nothing more than a computer-based system used to route calls and provide other services within organizations. The services range from call forwarding to recording. Recorders can be used by callers to leave messages for those out of their offices or for callers by those who are out. Phone mail systems appear subject to the same sort of "junk" calls that have plagued facsimile systems but few problems were reported as the systems became more prevalent.

Phone mail and facsimile systems will become most productive as bridges occur that permit them to be linked to one another and to computers. The bridges were under construction in the late 1980s in several forms. The fifty-member Aerospace Industries Association pressured electronic mail vendors to make their systems compatible with one another, while organizations such as Eastman were hard at work developing software that would translate voice mail into print. With scanners capable of translating print into computer language and computers already "speaking" through phone mail, these would be the final links in a functional integrated grid.

ADDITIONAL READING

Alsop, Ronald. "Has the Time Come to Regulate Junk Fax?" *Wall Street Journal*, Dec. 27, 1988.

Amparano, Julie. "A Wide Variety of Information Services Will Soon Be Available on Phone Lines." *Wall Street Journal*, Mar. 11, 1988.

Barron, James. "Press 2 for Service, Press ? for a Real Human." *New York Times*, Feb. 17, 1989.

Berg, Eric N. "One Industry Is Cheered by Rising Postal Costs." *New York Times*, Dec. 16, 1984.

Bovard, James. "Zapped by Electronic Mail." *Across the Board*, June 1985.

Churbuck, David. "Prepare for E-Mail Attack." *Forbes*, Jan. 23, 1989.

Coates, Vary T. "Linking the Home to the Global Village." *Across the Board*, April 1987.

Fahey, Alison. "States Ponder 'Junk Fax' Rules." *Advertising Age*, Jan. 16, 1989.

Lewis, Peter H. "BellSouth Opens an Electronic Mall." *New York Times*, Sept. 25, 1988.

_____. "'Electronic Cottages' Take Root." *New York Times*, Oct. 16, 1988.

_____. "E-Mail Searches for a Missing Link." *New York Times*, March 12, 1989.

Lipkin, Richard. "Fax Fever Slams Business Hard." *Insight*, Aug. 22, 1988.

_____. "Postal Service Ponders Its Twenty-first Century Prospects." *Insight*, Aug. 22, 1988.

Lopez, Julie Amparo. "New Telephone Services Fail to Connect." *Wall Street Journal*, May 23, 1989.

Lu, Cary. "Getting the Message: Electronic Mail Is an Idea Whose Time Has Come—Sort Of." *Inc.*, Oct. 1988.

_____. "Hello? Hello? Voice Mail Can Solve Many of Your Telephone-Answering Problems—Provided You Get The Right System." *Inc.*, Mar. 1989.

Lublin, Joann S. "Postal Service Finds Little Demand for New 'Electronic Mail' Service." *Wall Street Journal*, Sept. 16, 1983.

Markoff, John. "American Express Goes High-Tech." *New York Times*, July 31, 1988.

Murr, Andrew, and John Schwartz. "A Mounting Pile of 'Junk' Fax." *Newsweek*, July 25, 1988.

Patterson, William P. "Try, Try Again." *Industry Week*, Jan. 15, 1989.

Pollack, Andrew. "Phone Machines Streamline Offices." *New York Times*, Aug. 20, 1988.

Seghers, Frances, Jeffrey Rothfeder, and Robert D. Hof. "Electronic Mail: Neither Rain, Nor Sleet, Nor Software . . ." *Business Week*, Feb. 20, 1989.

Sims, Calvin. "MCI Plans A Separate Facsimile Network." *New York Times*, Nov. 4, 1988.

_____. "Who's Phoning? New System Will Tell You." *York Times*, Mar. 1, 1989.

Solomon, Jolie. "Business Communication in the Fax Age." *Wall Street Journal*, Oct. 27, 1988.

Ticer, Scott, and Frances Seghers. "How BellSouth Is Plugging into the Information Age." *Business Week*, Oct. 31, 1988.

"Voice-Mail Is Going Public." *Business Week*, Sept. 24, 1988.

Woolley, Suzanne. "Turning Home, Sweet Home into Office, Sweet Office." *Business Week*, Oct. 10, 1988.

11   The Market Responds

The onset of the wired society is producing mixed responses among established mass media and those who use them. Media activity ranges from feverishly pursued strategic and tactical responses in the television camp to near lethargy in much of the print sector. Conditions are identical among the communication disciplines. Responses range from vigorous among advertising agencies, advertisers, and marketers to benign neglect in sales promotion and public relations.

Differences between and among groups appear too small to account for variation in efforts to adjust to changing conditions. The interactive media will be as much a threat to newspapers as to television stations. Public relations counselors will have as much at risk as advertising agencies. Yet intergroup differences persist.

Some of the differences may be a product of the waves of change that have inundated the electronic media since the end of World War II. While the basics of newspaper and magazine publishing have changed little, television has moved from black and white to color, from a single delivery system to multiple systems, and from inactive to increasingly interactive systems. Radio has survived, although perhaps less profitably than might have been the case without television, and newspapers may perceive themselves as being in similar circumstances.

There appears little to commend such disparities among the communication disciplines,but they nevertheless exist. All have adopted and adapted to new technologies on behalf of clients. Few, however, have attempted to extend the scope of their own activities in keeping with environmental change, and most of the innovators have been in advertising. The remaining communication disciplines—marketing, sales promotion, and, especially, public relations, remain essentially traditionalist in their approaches. They compare with advertising in much the same manner that newspapers and magazines compare with the electronic media.

THE PRINT MEDIA

The print media—especially newspapers—stand at something of a crossroads. While magazine publishers have become aggressively entrepreneurial (see chapter 7), newspaper owners have sought greater profits through acquisitions. With the exception of Gannett's *USA Today* and the computer- and satellite-assisted distribution of *The Wall Street Journal*, there has been little innovation in newspaper publishing. Few believe these conditions will continue into the twenty-first century.

Newspapers must move ahead to offer information in new forms or risk loss of market share as the wired society takes shape. Several larger publishing organizations, especially Knight-Ridder and the Times-Mirror Company, have lost substantial investments in videotext services. Dow-Jones Information Service, from the publishers of *The Wall Street Journal*, may have been a special case. What should newspapers do now?

Newspaper Alternatives

Newspaper publishers received some sound counsel in 1988 from John Diebold, president of The Diebold Group, in a talk to the American Society of Newspaper Editors in Washington:

> Technology should not be used to mechanize an existing process or product, but to open new possibilities altogether. In contrast with newspapers' past experience, advertising may be a much more important product to consumers than editorial content when it comes to new technological forms of delivery.
>
> This does not mean the pressure is off newspapers. The greatest danger for newspaper management lies in standing still. The status quo will not continue; newspapers that do nothing

will fall further and further behind. Competition continues to emerge from often unexpected sources.

New technology will bring newspapers either a serious erosion of readership and revenues—or an explosion of new opportunities—according to how well it is managed.

Diebold urged the newspaper executives to innovate, to launch electronic information services individually or through joint ventures, to exploit their existing distribution systems, and to use the new technology to produce "a new and golden age of newspapers."

Limited Innovation

One potential application of the new technology is facsimile distribution of newspapers or parts thereof. Connecticut's *Hartford Courant* announced plans in early 1989 to offer $2,500 annual subscriptions to *Faxpaper*, a newsletter containing advance copies of *Courant* articles and editorials. *Faxpaper* was scheduled to be distributed via MCI Communications Corporation at 5:00 P.M. daily, many hours before the *Courant*'s first morning edition was available.

Other signs of entrepreneurial spirit among newspaper publishers, with one possible exception, originated among weeklies rather than dailies. The exception occurred in St. Louis, Missouri, where Ingersoll Publications announced plans to launch a daily and Sunday newspaper in late 1989. The *Sun*, as the newspaper was to be called, would have been the first metropolitan newspaper started in the United States since 1982.

At about the same time, a publisher of some seventy-five free distribution weeklies on New York's Long Island announced that it was consolidating the publications under a single title with as many zoned editions and a combined circulation in excess of one million. At the same time, the company more than doubled—to 30 percent—the amount of the papers' total news content and announced that it would mount a direct challenge to *Newsday*.

Several hundred miles away, in Washington, American Stock Exchange Chairman Arthur Levitt, Jr., and former *New Republic* president James K. Glassman acquired and reinvigorated *Roll Call*, a weekly catering to those who work on Capitol Hill. Within a matter of months, they had made the publication profitable and moved up to twice-weekly editions.

Print Advertising

The advertising component of the primary print media has changed little, although significant testing has occurred in alternative print forms. Metropolitan daily newspaper advertising has changed in appearance with the growth of preprinted inserts and the use of more color in advertising. Some have gone so far as to promote their own coupon-filled envelopes to compete with those distributed by mail.

A relatively few newspapers but a great many magazines also have started to accept advertising positioned other than in keeping with conventional standards. Advertisements across the top of pages, or as islands in the center of pages, is becoming more common, although some media continue to resist. Magazines also have been using computers to print personalized messages to subscribers. On occasion, magazine advertising also has been personalized.

Magazines also have maintained more flexibility than newspapers in several other areas. They have been responsive to any potential for new "niche" publications and to innovations in advertising techniques. Three dimensional advertising techniques such as "pop-ups" have been employed in magazines with considerable success, and more of this type of advertising is expected as advertisers seek greater memorability.

An indeterminate part of the greater publisher flexibility is a result of competitive pressure induced by users of coupons and similar promotional devices. Advo Systems and other producers of preprints and direct mail materials have been capturing an increasing volume of dollars that earlier might have been allocated to newspapers. Newspaper preprints have been growing at a rate almost double that at which newspaper display advertising has been increasing since the early 1980s, and the trend shows no sign of abating.

Other forms of print advertising also are being developed to compete with conventional magazines and newspapers. Whittle Communications' magazines for physician waiting rooms (see chapter 7) are but one innovation in print. Many catalogs now contain advertising for noncompeting merchandise as well as the publisher's own products, as in the case of automobile advertising in a specialty merchandise catalog. Analysts have been forecasting a catalog "shakeout" after years of steady growth, but catalogs did not appear to be declining in numbers.

The Whittle organization, in still another incursion into print media territory, in early 1989 announced plans for advertising in books by well-known authors. The company announced it had signed John Kenneth Galbraith, David Halberstram and others to produce relatively short nonfiction works of 20,000 to 25,000 words, which would be published with advertising interspersed throughout. Early reports indicated that Whittle plans called for some fifteen pages of advertising in each book. Originally intended for distribution to 150,000 opinion leaders, the books ultimately may appear in bookstores as well.

Two disparate trends were taking shape at the same time among established book publishers. The industry more and more was becoming dominated by overseas interests, and book publishing was becoming more a marketing than a creative activity. British communications entrepreneur Robert Maxwell's purchase of Macmillan and the acquisition of Doubleday by West Germany's Bertelsmann were the most recent of more than a dozen similar transactions .

Competition among publishers also was producing an unprecedented surge in fees paid for first novels, often in competitive auctions. While advances for first novels usually are between $5,000 and $15,000, an increasing number were reaching the six-figure level. The trend arose in part over publishers' efforts to "capture" new authors and in part over the growing marketing orientation in publishing.

THE ELECTRONIC MEDIA

Whittle's innovative bent also was on display in the electronic sector, where Whittle Communications had launched "Channel One," something akin to a "Today" show for teenagers. Channel One was established as a twelve-minute program incorporating two minutes of commercials to be distributed to schools. Whittle Communications provided $50,000 worth of receiving equipment, including a satellite dish, videocassette recorder and color television monitors, to participating schools. Early returns were mixed. California educational authorities imposed an economic penalty on schools electing to use "Channel One" and the system was barred from New York public schools by that state's Board of Regents. The mixed reviews were not sufficient, however, to discourage competition. Not to be outdone by Whittle, Turner Network Television, the Atlanta-based organization that owns Cable News Network, soon announced a similar broadcast program. The Discovery Channel was planning to offer a program oriented to high school students as well.

"Channel One" was launched in 1989 with six advertisers paying undisclosed "test market" fees. Whittle hoped to be serving eight thousand schools by 1990 with an audience of six to seven million teenagers—double the size of a prime time television audience. At that point, Whittle expected to be charging advertisers about half the rates they would pay for network prime time.

Channel One and the Turner plan were but two elements in a pattern of change, structural and technological, with which broadcast executives are attempting to contend. Change at the structural level involves more than broadcasters' loss of audience share to cable. New networks have developed to challenge the old. Cable penetration continues to erode broadcast audiences.

Technological change appears to have slowed in recent years, but the appearance is deceiving. Enhanced satellite-based systems several years ago granted local stations considerable independence from network domination. Little apparently has occurred since then, but much has been accomplished toward development of what some have called Television II. Television II almost inevitably will involve extensive fiber optic systems now being installed by telephone companies (see chapter 5). A new generation of receiver technology also is in development, and new varieties of programming are evolving as well.

New Networks

Patterns of new network development have emerged over time in two areas. Cable News Network, ESPN, and the Weather Channel, all oriented to specific program content and all designed primarily for cable use, were precursors of developments to come. Multiple entertainment channels followed as broadcast entrepreneur Ted Turner and others demonstrated the public's apparently insatiable appetite for television programming.

The second developmental area that contributed to the network trend involved, despite the apparent contradiction, nonnetwork broadcast stations. Independent television stations quadrupled in number during the 1980s. The new stations—broadcast and cable—did more for the industry than dilute the total viewing audience. They also created a market for additional programming. A fourth network and a massive television syndication industry soon took shape to meet the need.

The new network, Fox, was a creature of Rupert Murdoch's News Corporation which lost $136 million during its first two years with limited programming. The third year, 1987-88, was another matter. Fox doubled its weekend audience share and recorded a half million dollar profit for the second half of the year. By summer of 1989, Fox occasionally was besting ABC in network rating competition. More important, with 125 affiliates signed, Fox was planning to expand programming into weekday evenings and, perhaps, afternoons as well.

While still a distant fourth in weekend ratings battles at about 10 percent of the market, Fox often was beating the competition among a prime audience group: urban eighteen to thirty-four-year-olds. By 1993, Fox expects to be broadcasting on a seven-day schedule and may become a fourth major network. Fox was aggressively pursuing that objective in 1989 by attacking the senior networks on several fronts.

Fox was betting primarily on what economists would call a contrarian strategy, which involves doing precisely the opposite of what conventional wisdom prescribes. In the fall of 1989, for example, Fox launched Monday evening movies against Monday night football. As a sort of "nonnetwork" to the extent that it is not regulated by the Federal Communications Commission (FCC), Fox also is free to go counter to some of the agency's dicta. It need not broadcast news and public service programming, for example, and can concentrate its resources in entertainment. The two-year-old network in 1989 was steadily gaining audience share while the established networks were continuing to lose.

Cassette and Cable

The world of television also is continuing to experience substantial change in other areas. Videocassette recorders (VCRs), now present in 60 percent of all homes, are gaining an increasing share of viewer audiences. VCRs influence viewing habits in two ways. They capture broadcasts at times convenient to owners and enable them to use prerecorded cassettes.

Americans purchased sixty-five million prerecorded cassettes and rented more than two billion in 1987. If purchased cassettes were viewed twice and rented cassettes viewed once, 4.25 billion person-hours were committed to cassette viewing during that year. That amounts to 17.78 hours for every man, woman, and child regardless of age and physical or mental condition. Some of the same motion pictures accessible on cassettes also were shown on cable, by independent television stations, or both.

The continuing growth of cable systems has outstripped the most optimistic of forecasts. More than half of all households in the United States are hooked to a cable system, and data show that cable households spend at least as much time with cable as with broadcast stations.

The videocassette and cable trends together have taken a severe toll among network audiences. During the ten years ending in 1988, the networks' prime time audience declined from 92 percent to 68 percent of all television viewers. Those figures represent a loss of 35.29 percent of all viewers and countless millions of dollars in revenues for the networks. On a given evening in New York in 1988, viewers could select from among 219 programs *in addition to* the few dozen offered by the networks. On some nights, as a result, the sum of the networks' audiences total less than half of all viewers.

A new breed of media planners has emerged to cope with the increasing complexities that advertisers encounter in dealing with these conditions. Consisting primarily of younger people, they have come to exercise tremendous power over advertising budgets and have diverted substantial sums to cable and magazines as opposed to broadcast television.

Resulting network losses are being compounded by a progressive weakening in their news sectors. The networks long had been dominant in international, national, and even regional news. That dominance was being eroded, however, as local stations discovered that they did not need the networks. Satellite dishes bloomed adjacent to broadcast towers as local stations joined forces to establish resource-sharing consortia and used satellite picture feeds to gain access to breaking news around the world.

The strength of these trends was perhaps best demonstrated as the most successful of the broadcast networks in 1989 launched a major cable venture. NBC moved toward its declared objective of becoming a major cable industry factor with the debut of the twenty-four-hour Consumer News and Business Channel (CNBC). The new channel began with a subscriber base of 13 million, second only to the 17 million captured by Ted Turner's TNT movie channel, which also debuted in 1989. NBC committed a reported $65 million to the new venture, which benefits from access to NBC News' worldwide information-gathering network.

Despite continuing growth in the cable sector, predictions of the death of the networks, like those that foretold the collapse of radio, remain premature. Deteriorating audience shares and declining revenues nevertheless can be expected to produce a steady weakening. Research data indicate that growing numbers of television viewers engage in an activity labeled "grazing" and described by *Newsweek* in these terms: "Permanently jittery, instantly bored, loyal to no network or station, grazers incessantly roam the dial in search of . . . Something Better. Imagine the grazer of the future confronted with the hundreds of channels envisioned by most televisionaries. There will be, you might say, no holding them."

Such viewer loyalty as still exists is being further eroded by the growth of pay-per-view or PPV television. PPV enables viewers to select from published menus and then push appropriate buttons on remote control devices or telephones to have motion pictures instantly delivered to the screen. A $3.00 charge at the same time is added to the subscriber's bill, but the incoming motion picture also can be recorded as received, albeit illegally, for future repetitive viewing. By 1988, almost 5 million of the nation's estimated 46 million homes were wired for PPV. Industry projections indicate that a fourfold increase in PPV households may occur by 1995, further eroding network strength.

War Begins

Progressive audience erosion by 1989 produced a sudden change in network strategies. After years of treating the competition as unworthy of attention, the networks mounted an all out assault on multiple fronts in an exercise in self-preservation. Virtually overnight, the networks established a trade group to attack the interlopers, acted to strengthen their economic positions, and launched new attacks in the regulatory arena.

The network counterattack was launched with the creation of the Television Network Association (TNA), organized to promote the industry in the same manner in which the Magazine Publishers Association and the American Newspaper Publishers Association promote their interests. The cable industry's Cabletelevision Advertising Bureau (CAB) welcomed TNA as a new voice for television but concurrently claimed dominance in the industry as a whole. Thirty-six percent of viewing time is spent with basic cable, CAB's Robert H. Alter said in 1989, while only 34 percent is spent with the networks.

While collectively attacking the cable industry, however, the networks were not averse to joining them elsewhere. Consider, for example, the case of General Electric Company's NBC subsidiary and Cablevision Systems Corporation, which joined forces in 1989 to market a national cable network, several regional networks, and pay-per-view programming from the 1992 summer Olympics in Barcelona, Spain. "Today, NBC is referred to as a network," said NBC Cable President Thomas Rogers. "In the future, we will be a networks company."

Sixty days later, a move of similar sorts brought Time and Warner Communications together in a move toward basic cable programming. The two want to run advertiser-supported channels similar to the USA Network, Cable News Network, and ESPN. Both long had been major cable operators, and the basic cable sector was an attractive area for expansion. Among their possible early entries is an all-comedy channel also coveted by prospective competitors. Time's HBO and Cinemax channels, coupled with Time and Warner cable operations, with more than five million subscribers, make their combined effort a force to be reckoned with in the industry. The combined companies also are active in book and magazine publishing and in television production and conceivably might ultimately offer advertisers a sort of "one- stop shopping" for advertising.

Broadcasters Attack

The Time-Warner move came as the National Association of Broadcasters, perhaps prompted by cable's growing popularity, sought legislative relief. The National Association of Broadcasters asked Congress to at least partly reregulate the industry. Specifically, NAB asked for legislation that would require cable operators to carry local broadcast stations and bar them from capriciously changing broadcast stations' cable channel assignments.

An NAB spokesperson said the request was prompted by complaints from broadcasters. The request followed by only a few weeks a Roper Organization poll in which viewers gave cable better marks than the networks for program quality. Cable was ranked better for sports, cultural and educational programming, and overall quality, although viewers said cable also shows more sex, violence and profanity.

The Roper data was not without other surprises. Despite growth in "tabloid television," numbers of viewers who consider television in bad taste declined to 21 percent from 24 percent three years earlier. The legislative request and Roper report came at a time when syndicators were producing television programming not unlike the National Enquirer in content and audience appeal.

Changing Markets

There was little unanimity among television executives, however, as to how to win larger audiences. Some turned to Hollywood for assistance in gaining larger audience shares. Others sought to apply some of the new technologies to television. Still others cashed in their investments in broadcasting and turned to what they believed to be potentially more productive pastures.

Knight-Ridder, long a power in publishing and in recent years the owner of numerous television stations, was among those deciding that television was not as attractive an investment as earlier had been the case. After spending $353 million to purchase Dialog Information Services, in 1988, Knight-Ridder disposed of the bulk of its television holdings the following year. Analysts suggested the transactions indicated that "the bloom is off network affiliates because network audiences have been steadily declining." Knight-Ridder, however, apparently was equally convinced of the future of computer information services despite earlier disappointments in Dade County, Florida.

While Knight-Ridder was getting out of television, CBS was attempting to restore some semblance of earlier grandeur, and newcomers were designing innovative strategies in efforts to capture what they perceived to be the potential profits of television. CBS efforts toward profitability focused on persuading Hollywood producers to invest time and talent in creating more marketable products for traditional television audiences. As publisher Knight-Ridder moved into the electronic information industry, electronic giant Mead Data Central was proceeding in the opposite direction, into publishing. Mead invested more than $225 million in Michie Company, a legal publishing firm acquired from Macmillan. The company's objective was diversification, although legal publishing was a logical expansion area for the owner of Lexis, one of the nation's preeminent legal databases.

At the same time, Interactive Game Network of Menlo Park, California, was preparing an aggressive marketing campaign on behalf of interactive television. Interactive in 1990 was scheduled to begin selling a $350 device to enable viewers to "talk back" to their television sets, to obtain Coca-Cola coupons by responding to advertising or, perhaps, by submitting contest entries to the National Football League during ball games.

The Gannett newspapers at about the same time were expanding into the coupon business. Gannett's Four-Color Newspaper Network, which acts as national advertising representative for the chain's newspapers, started soliciting national manufacturers for coupon inserts. Gannett, with a combined circulation of twenty-six million, was entering a market dominated by three other firms with combined circulations of more than forty million each. Gannett also offers a "Flex Plan" under which advertisers can share four-color pages, each of them receiving a coupon and a color illustration of products involved.

CHANGING AUDIENCES

Whether new technology or improved programming can re-engage the attention of television viewers remains to be seen. Available data on grazers and zappers suggest broadcasters are fighting an uphill battle. Grazers, as indicated earlier, are those who move rapidly from one channel to another. Zappers use remote control devices to eliminate commercials.

New technologies applied to audience measurement suggest that the two breeds together are costly to advertisers. A new rating system developed by R. D. Percy and Company and consisting of computers, heat sensors, and hand-held "people meters" indicates that levels of grazing vary with viewer characteristics as well as types of programming. The wealthy tend to graze more rapidly than the poor, and the same tendency arises among those with more sophisticated equipment. Numbers of viewers seeing commercials varies with the nature of adjacent programming and with the nature of the commercials.

Grazers with annual incomes under $15,000 change channels every 6.25 minutes, while those with incomes in excess of $75,000 change every 2.7 minutes. Viewers without cable change channels every 5.86 minutes, while those with cable change every 3.0 minutes. Those without remote control devices change every 5.25 minutes, while those with remote devices change every 3.43 minutes.

Channel changing can eliminate noncommercial programming, but commercial content influences the volume of channel changing activities. In the Grammy music awards show in 1988, for example, Pepsi-Cola commercials featuring singer Michael Jackson lost as little as 1 percent of their audiences while other commercials lost as much as 15 percent.

Relative positioning of commercials in newscasts also influences the extent to which they are seen. Percy data collected during the CBS Evening News in New York City between 7:00 and 7:30 P.M. showed, for example, that the audience increased slightly in size as the program progressed. The audience almost doubled in size, however, during the last seven minutes of the program, leading up to the start of Wheel of Fortune.

Grazers or flippers—those who change channels merely to see what else is on—are a greater threat to commercials than zappers, according to J. Walter Thompson chairman Bertram Metter. Remote control devices have made flippers of yesterday's passive viewers, he contends. As many as fifty-eight million at any given time may be wandering around the dial.

CHANGING ADVERTISING

Advertiser efforts to stop wanderers in their tracks are taking several forms. Advertising content is changing to attract the attention of jaded audiences. Spoofs and parodies have come into style, and some advertisers are investing in localized commercials. Perhaps more significant, the nature of advertising research is being modified to focus more precisely on those audiences.

Other changes are occurring in the ways in which the advertising business is conducted. Negotiated compensation levels are supplanting fixed commission rates. In many cases, these are accompanied by bonus plans of one sort or another. Even production costs are being closely scrutinized and negotiated downward. Advertisers often are hiring independent cost containment consultants to monitor and control expenses attendant to advertising production.

In the management area, the buying and selling of agencies continues, but other trends also are developing. Consultants now train agency executives in prospecting, sales, and other activities long assumed to be adequately handled by any relatively skilled manager, and that trend shows no sign of abating. Aggressive practice development strategies instead can be expected to increase as advertising agencies feel mounting pressure from sales promotion and other areas.

By 1990, competition had changed the once-genteel culture of advertising. Agencies were spending hundreds of thousands of dollars to woo the smallest of new accounts and pressures on the bottom line were building. The competition was being driven in part by public ownership of larger agencies. Two decades earlier, the prestigious J. Walter Thompson agency seldom would consider developing a proposal for an account billing less than several million dollars. Market and stockholder pressures today would bring proposals from not one but many leading agencies for accounts billing as little as $500,000.

The growth of sales promotion, presumably at the expense of advertising, also threatens agency bottom lines. This trend is demonstrated in a growing tendency on the part of advertisers to appoint two "agencies of record," one in advertising and one in sales promotion. Rather than being compensated on a project or hourly basis, more sales promotion agencies also are being compensated on retainer bases. Numbers of clients paying on retainer bases in some firms reportedly have more than doubled in recent years. Even more significant from the advertising perspective, sales promotion expenditures have been growing far more rapidly than has been the case in advertising.

Content Changes

Changes in advertising content are most noticeable to nonmembers of the advertising community, but such changes also can signal durable trends in the industry. Among the more attention-getting, although perhaps short-lived, commercial styles of the late 1980s were spoofs and parodies. Lever Brothers helped launch the spate of parodies by depicting the heartbreak of dingy laundry and water spots on crystal. *TV Guide* advertising parodied the computer gobbledygook used in Wang Laboratories' commercials. And Wendy's

International parodied taste tests by having characters express a preference for cold, dry hamburgers.

A major beer producer took a different and costly approach by producing a set of commercials—one a month for a year—to be broadcast in one state, Texas. Industry experts estimated that the commercials cost $200,000 to $300,000 each to produce and that the series ultimately will cost some $3 million, as much as a national campaign. The jury is still out as to whether the experiment—some label it a gamble—will work. Whether or not it is productive, the effort suggests a willingness to experiment that would not exist were traditional advertising programs adequately productive.

Economic pressures on agencies and their clients in 1989 also were fueling a battle over use of advertising to promote the sales of prescription drugs—ethical drugs, as they're called. Hair loss, smoking and related problems were being brought to the television screen with messages calling on viewers to see their physicians. The American Medical Association and American Pharmaceutical Association protested to the United States Food and Drug Administration (FDA), but that agency did not appear prepared to intervene.

New Research Approaches

Changes of the same magnitude were occurring in advertising agency research departments. Many such departments are pale imitations of those that once specialized in extensive and demanding quantitative research. Their emphasis today is on qualitative rather than quantitative, in two forms. One is single source research, involving in-depth studies of individuals. The other focuses on an elusive element known in Madison Avenue circles as bonding.

Somewhat amorphously defined as "the placement of the product in the consumer's life," the bonding process require identifying "product bonds" and often involves using account planners in campaign development. Account planners are a breed of researchers who spend their time looking for insights or potential bonds that can be incorporated into campaigns.

Single-source research is more precise and more intense. The process involves close up monitoring of message recipients to identify (a) ads to which individuals are exposed and (b) mechanisms through which those ads influence behaviors. In an analysis conducted in one merchandise sector, sales of only seven of twenty advertised brands were found to have been in any way influenced by levels of television advertising.

Fortunately or unfortunately, single source research remains far short of universal application. The process is demanding; the cost is high. Computer programs necessary to analyze mountains of resulting data, in addition, do not exist. Experts expect these problems to be solved by the mid-1990s, enabling advertisers to more precisely design programs and produce enhanced results without additional cost.

Will bonding enhance advertising efficiency? Is qualitative research better than quantitative? Will single source research prove practical and sufficiently productive to justify the costs involved? While awaiting answers to these and related questions, advertisers and agencies are casting about for any communication channel that might be pressed into productive service.

Additional Media

Productive service means the ability to successfully deliver messages to prospective consumers of products or services. Successful delivery means getting messages through with sufficient effectiveness to induce the desired result; in other words, to make the cash register ring. Making the cash register ring requires that advertisers meet several criteria. Messages must be delivered to prospective consumers who can afford the product or service involved.

These conditions are being met, albeit for different consumer groups, through a host of what might be called alternative media. Consider the following, for example:

"Product placements" in motion pictures or television shows.

Video "brochures," in the form of videotaped presentations in cassette form about new computer software programs that are being *sold* in computer stores.

"Diskazines" or "magazettes," which are nothing more than magazines on floppy disks.

Advertising in hardbound books.

Commercials placed in the lead-ins of home videos offered for rent.

Commercially sponsored television shows beamed into public schools.

Product and service brochures on floppy disks and videotapes.

Advertising placards on the inside of stall doors in public restrooms.

Audiovisual presentations shown on screens placed in supermarket shopping cards and activated by transmitters in merchandise displays as carts approach.

All of these devices exist today. Some will succeed. Others will fail. But more will always be waiting in the wings. In most cases, the communication channels involved are more rationally founded then first appears to be the case. Consider, for example, the matter of advertising on floppy disks. The medium obviously might be advantageous to those attempting to reach computer users. Individuals who use computers presumably would constitute a preferred demographic group as well. But think about the other advantages:

There are more than 40 million computer users today. Research demonstrates that information is better retained where recipients participate in presentations, where they are able to interact with message sources, as in the case of computers. Computer users are more than happy to put free diskettes into their computers, and they do not throw away diskettes. If they do not keep the diskettes, they pass them along to others. Computer users prefer disk-based information and, perhaps most important, people tend to believe information that appears on computer screens.

Those in the computer industry were early adopters of floppy disk advertising, but others soon followed. Followers have included most of the major auto manufacturers as well as a number of financial services organizations, especially banks and brokerage houses. Buick in 1987 ran magazine ads encouraging readers to write in for sales brochures—on floppy disks. The strategy was to get the message across effectively and create a high-tech image to boot. The message included animated drawings, data comparing

Buick with competitors, and payment calculation systems. Chase Manhattan, in like manner, provided a spreadsheet for recipient use in estimating the benefits of electronic funds transfer—Chase Manhattan's, of course. The same technique was used by the Illinois Institute of Technology in communicating with prospective students.

The extent to which floppy disks will develop as an advertising medium remains to be determined, but preliminary indications are favorable. Among the indications are a number of "diskazines" or "magazettes," computer magazines on floppy disks. Most consist primarily of computer software, but others, such as *PC Life*, offer more diverse content and circulate around the world. In the process, they acclimate increasing numbers of computer users to assimilating noncomputer information from diskettes.

COMMUNICATION PROFESSIONALS

Amidst all of this activity in the advertising sector, those in marketing, sales promotion, and public relations have remained relatively aloof. Although perhaps for different reasons, members of each group apparently perceived little need to become involved in the competition for the hearts and minds of information consumers.

There may, indeed, be some logic in this approach. Marketers long have selected from among available advertising and public relations techniques to accomplish their objectives. Only rarely have marketers been innovators in the true sense of that word. Public relations practitioners, other than where dealing with organizations' internal audiences, also have depended upon their ability to select from available media. They have been innovators from a technological standpoint only in adapting technologies for use in employee and shareholder relations programs. Sales promotion specialists have been faced with conditions similar to those in public relations. They have been dependent on traditional channels for coupon promotions but have been able to apply some of the new technologies for in-store use. How members of each of these disciplines will react as the newer technologies continue to develop remains to be seen.

IN SUMMARY

Developmental patterns among traditional mass media remain uncertain as society moves into the age of information. Newspaper publishers especially appear ambivalent—perhaps even uncertain—in the face of mounting pressure from existing media, as well as the implied or implicit threats developing in the electronic sector. The electronic media have been and continue to be more responsive to external developments and to changes within their own specialized areas. The extent to which any of the existing media will achieve their objectives over the next several years remains to be seen. Changes large and small are occurring on an almost daily basis among audiences and advertisers as well as media. Only the communication professions themselves seem somewhat at a loss as to how to cope with changing external circumstances.

Newspapers' efforts toward greater profitability in large part have been designed to achieve success by capturing other publications' audiences, through acquisition or otherwise. Only rarely have daily newspaper publishers followed the sort of advice proffered by John Diebold, who urged that they manage technology to their own advantage rather than permitting it to result in weakened economic circumstances. Most have contented themselves with defensive strategies, attempting to discourage the incursions of weekly newspapers on the one hand and the implied threats of electronic classified advertising systems on the other.

Magazines have been somewhat more responsive. Most have been amenable to three-dimensional advertising, to unusual placement of advertising on pages, and to similar techniques designed to enhance advertiser memorability. Magazine publishers also have been closely attuned to any demographic or other change that might signal the development of a new niche of sufficient size to house a profitable publication.

Book publishers long have tended to remain relatively traditional in their business approaches but several developments indicate that they are becoming more innovative and competitive. Product placements in books and advertising in books are among the newer approaches to commercial communication through this medium and more are to be expected as competition for consumer attention intensifies.

The same principle holds true in the electronic sector, where publishing entrepreneur Chris Whittle and television's Ted Turner are on a collision course in terms of in-school programming. Whittle got there first with equipment as well as programming but Turner countered with programs that would be accessible through preexisting delivery systems.

Turner also was among those who joined in a proliferation of networks to provide a broader range of programming for television. Turner was building on the success of Cable News Network with Turner Network Television and other endeavors, including a regional sports network. Rupert Murdoch's Fox was on the way to becoming a fourth major network by the end of the 1980s, while NBC entered the increasingly competitive cable sector with CNBC, a channel oriented to consumer economics.

Skirmishes over audience share among the established electronic media soon broke into open warfare, even as organizations such as new interactive systems were coming into being. The interactive ranged from the Sears-IBM computer-based system to new community systems using fiber optic cable that had been installed for the Los Angeles Olympic Games.

While the media were jockeying for audience and advertising, advertising agencies and the clients also were beset by waves of change. Creative and production rates were becoming more flexible under advertiser pressure, and agencies themselves were being bought and sold with growing frequency. Advertising content also was changing in an unending quest for enhanced attention, while innovative media seemed to be proliferating at an ever-increasing pace.

Only the long-term developmental strategies of communications professionals remained obscure. Advertising seemed too preoccupied with contemporary battles on other fronts to seriously contemplate its own future. Marketing, public relations, and sales promotion appeared unwilling to accept the fact that the problems of the advertising fraternity could be visited on them as well.

ADDITIONAL READING

Alsop, Ronald. "Ads That Make Fun of Ads Are In, As Firms Face a More Jaded Buyer." *Wall Street Journal*, Feb. 22, 1988.
_____. "Advertisers See Big Gains in Odd Layouts." *Wall Street Journal*, June 29, 1988.

_____. "Movie Videos Are Increasingly Offering Viewers More to Watch—Commercials." *Wall Street Journal*, Mar. 29, 1988.

_____. "Soft Selling: Advertisers Make Their Pitches on Floppy Disks." *Wall Street Journal*, Jan. 8, 1987.

Belkin, Lisa. "A Texas-Size Bet in Advertising." *New York Times*, Jan. 8, 1989.

Carnevale, Mary Lu. "Broadcasters Seek Cable Reregulation in New Legislation." *Wall Street Journal*, Apr. 12, 1989.

Carter, Bill. "NBC Walks into a Cable Minefield." *New York Times*, Apr. 10, 1989.

Cowan, Alison L. "Ad Clutter: Even in Restrooms Now." *New York Times*, Feb. 18, 1988.

Cox, Meg. "Cable Television Gets Better Grades in Viewers Survey." *Wall Street Journal*, Mar. 30, 1989.

_____. "Rival Tabloid-TV Shows Stoop Low to Get Scoops." *Wall Street Journal*, Feb. 21, 1989.

Deutsch, Claudia H. "The Brouhaha Over Drug Ads." *New York Times*, May 14, 1989.

Dougherty, Philip H. "Gannett Aims for Coupon Business." *New York Times*, Sept. 19, 1988.

_____. "New Peril: The TV Flipper." *New York Times*, Sept. 30, 1986.

Fabrikant, Geraldine. "Fox Broadcasting's Successful Gambles." *New York Times*, Apr. 3, 1989.

Gerard, Jeremy. "Three Networks Forming Trade Alliance." *New York Times*, Feb. 13, 1989.

Grover, Ronald, and David Lieberman. "Fox Elbows into the Networks' Big Picture." *Business Week*, Feb. 20, 1989.

Kleinfield, N. R., "In Search of the Next Medium." *New York Times*, Mar. 19, 1989.

Kneale, Dennis. "CBS Frantically Woos Hollywood to Help It Win Back Viewers." *Wall Street Journal*, Feb. 9, 1989.

_____. "'Zapping' of TV Ads Appears Pervasive." *Wall Street Journal*, Apr. 25, 1988.

Landro, Laura. "NBC Cable Venture Unites Natural Foes." *Wall Street Journal*, Feb. 8, 1989.

_____. "TV News Show Could Open School Doors to Advertisers." *Wall Street Journal*, Jan. 16, 1989.

Lewis, Peter H. "And Now, A Word from the Sponsor." *New York Times*, Mar. 19, 1989.

Lieberman, David. "Time-Warner Is Wired for Cable Wars." *Business Week*, Apr. 17, 1989.

Lipman, Joanne. "Single-Source Ad Research Heralds Detailed Look at Household Habits." *Wall Street Journal*, Feb. 16, 1988.

_____. "Time-Warner Deal May Yield One-Stop Shopping Possibility." *Wall Street Journal*, Mar. 7, 1989.

_____. "Financial Pressures Transform Industry." *Wall Street Journal*, May 15, 1989.

McDowell, Edwin. "First Novelists with Six-Figure Contracts." *New York Times*, Apr. 10, 1989.

_____. "U.S. Houses Look Abroad at Last." *New York Times*, Nov. 14, 1988.

_____. "Whittle's Publishing Experiment." *New York Times*, Apr. 18, 1988.

Mallory, Maria. "Mead Tries a New-Fangled Medium: Print." *Business Week*, Apr. 10, 1989.

Rasky, Susan. "Tabloid on Capitol Hill Finds Keys to Success." *New York Times*, Apr. 11, 1989.

Reilly, Patrick. "New Whittle Shocker." *Advertising Age*, Jan. 16, 1989.

Robins, J. Max. "Windsong Was on His Mind." *New York Times*, Apr. 2, 1989.

Rothenberg, Randall. "Ad Research Shifts from Products to People." *New York Times*, Apr. 6, 1989.

_____. "Bigger Roles for Sales Promoters." *York Times*, Jan. 24, 1989.

_____. "Network vs. Cable: Battle Heating Up." *The New York Times*, March 21, 1989.

_____. "Translating Environment into Ads." *New York Times*, Nov. 4, 1988.

_____. "A Young Elite's Power Over Ads." *New York Times*, Feb. 1, 1981.

Rothman, Andrea. "Critics of Racy Television Shows Vent Their Anger at Advertisers." *Wall Street Journal*, Feb. 17, 1989.

Schwadel, Francine. "Catalog Overload Turns Off Consumers." *Wall Street Journal*, Oct. 28, 1988.

Sharkey, Joe. "Ingersoll Plans a New Daily Paper for St. Louis in '89." *Wall Street Journal*, Mar. 29, 1989.

_____. "Weekly Newspapers Are Challenging Daily Cousins for Advertising Dollars." *Wall Street Journal*, Apr. 13, 1989.

Starr, Mark. "Today, Class, We'll Learn about Soap." *Newsweek*, Mar. 20, 1989.

Verhovek, Sam Howe. "New York State Bans TV News with Ads from Public Schools." *New York Times*, June 17, 1989.

Waldman, Fred. "Knight-Ridder Has Agreements to Sell Five TV Stations." *Wall Street Journal*, Feb. 21, 1989.

Waters, Harry F., and Janet Huck. "The Future of Television." *Newsweek*, Oct. 17, 1988.

Winkler, Connie. "Diskazines Go To Press." *PC/Computing*, Apr. 1989.

12 Other Disciplines

The advertising industry's intensive and extensive efforts to cope with change in the media world are prompted by two factors. First, the futures of the mass media and their customers are at stake. The search for new media and methodologies, in other words, is driven by self-interest among media, advertisers, and agencies. Second, the results of advertising expenditures can be analyzed in terms of change in sales volumes. Outcomes by which advertising and agency performance can be weighed, as a result, are more readily measured.

Sales promotion, involving coupons, merchandise offers, and the like, is similarly measurable. Ability to measure results in an era of media and audience uncertainty, in fact, may be the primary factor influencing more advertisers to formally appoint sales promotion agencies (see chapter 11). These conditions exert less influence in marketing and public relations, however, to the detriment of practitioners in both areas.

Marketers, to their credit, long have been measurement oriented. The practice of marketing has been the more pragmatic and methodological of the two disciplines. Marketers are charged with identifying needs and assisting clients or employers in designing and delivering products or services that meet those needs. Marketers are at risk in contemporary circumstances, but for reasons different from those that apply in other disciplines. Risk for marketers arises out of declining ability to cope with growing volumes of statistical and other data available from more and more sources. All available data historically have been used in marketing to enhance potential for success, but marketers are limited in their ability to meet contemporary conditions. They are experiencing the first signs of what has been called information overload.

Different circumstances arise in public relations, where practitioners historically have avoided efforts to measure results, and often continue to resist a trend toward accountability. Public relations traditionally has been oriented toward mass media publicity. Media exposure was assumed to be productive, and this, indeed, was once the case. The United States is not far removed from an era in which notoriety was sufficient to political success. "I don't care what they say about me," one politico was reputed to have said, "as long as they spell my name right." While none would seek success through notoriety today, too many in public relations continue to equate media exposure with programmatic success.

Collectively, the communication disciplines are ill prepared for the twenty-first century. Only advertising is attempting to cope with the demands of a changing environment. Sales promotion is enjoying what probably will be transient popularity and is neglecting long-term problems. Marketers apply traditional statistical analyses with increasing difficulty to mounting volumes of data. And public relations focuses on media exposure rather than behavioral results. Each discipline faces a set of challenges—long term and short—that ultimately will establish their levels of social value and, as a result, their potential for survival through the twenty-first century.

Each discipline will prosper or suffer in proportion to its relevance to a society apt to be quite different from that which exists today. Three major attributes of that society will govern the relevance of each of the communication disciplines. One will be the nature of information-gathering patterns. Will individuals continue to be substantially influenced by contemporary mass media or will the media be supplanted in whole or part by new information delivery systems? Another will be the credibility of organizations. Will traditionally exploitative business and industrial practices yield to the demands of more competitive marketplaces? Third, and most important, will be the ability of the communication disciplines themselves to accommodate to change. To what extent will they parade lemming like off the cliffs of traditional practice methodologies?

These questions require careful consideration by all who attempt to forecast the future of mass communication. No one or two answers can provide adequate guidance for communicators or their organizations. All must be evaluated in determining how best to configure the communication organization for success in the twenty-first century.

INFORMATION GATHERING

Like many in the communication disciplines, and especially those in marketing, consumers must be assumed to be approaching information overload. Overload occurs where needed or wanted information exceeds information handling capacity. The circumstances are similar to those with which microcomputer users have been coping for years. They also occur when incoming information exceeds the capacity of the microcomputer's hard drive.

As the hard drive nears capacity, a sort of operational hardening of the arteries sets in. Computer operations start to slow down. The slowing process continues to a full stop if information input continues. The problem can be solved in one of only three ways: by adding a second hard drive or replacing the existing drive with one of greater capacity, by stopping information input, or by deleting information already on the hard drive to make space for more.

Human Reactions

Human beings confronted with larger information flows than they can accommodate must react in similar fashion whether or not the information is needed or wanted. Only three alternatives are open to them: expand capacity, accept no more information than already is arriving, or eliminate some currently arriving information to make room for more. Capacity can be increased only by allocating more time to information-gathering, which usually is an unacceptable option. Arbitrary rejection of all additional information without regard for its potential importance tends to be equally unacceptable.

Most individuals first attempt to cope with overload by controlling incoming information flows. One of two local daily newspapers may be eliminated in favor of a national newspaper. One or two of the three national news magazines may be replaced with business or trade publications. A few network television shows can be dropped in favor of Cable News Network or PBS informational programming.

More Radical Efforts

When control of incoming information flows fails to provide adequate relief, more radical efforts may be necessary. Some can be implemented by computer. Periodic searches of business or professionally oriented computer databases, for example, can replace hours spent with professional journals. The process is not without risk. The best of search strategies is less efficient although faster than manual scanning. Where information is being generated at an accelerating pace, however, computer techniques offer significant benefits. Information obtained from data bases in electronic form is more easily stored, retrieved, and manipulated than otherwise is the case. Two new types of computer software are responsible. One variety, including Apple's Hypercard and Lotus' Agenda, enables users to readily organize large volumes of information. The other, such as Howard Benner's TAPCIS, is designed to automate on-line activities and reduce database usage charges.

Even with state-of-the-art software, however, alternative information-gathering and assimilating processes produce an almost inevitable result: decline in the volume of time individuals dedicate to traditional media. Those who are receiving and manipulating information through their computers are unlikely to spend as much time as earlier was the case with traditional mass media. As other interactive systems come into common use, the tendency to replace old media with new will increase, at least for a part of the population.

Those whose information-gathering patterns will be most changed, for better or worse, are those who use the most information. These individuals also are apt to be the best educated and most highly compensated in any society. As a result, they also constitute those groups most coveted as audiences by all communicators. They are the affluent audiences to whom advertisers address their messages. They are the market makers whose desires are closely monitored by marketers. And they are the opinion leaders who are so important in public relations practice. In the overall, then, information overload should be a major source of concern to communicators of every stripe.

Research by Jacob Jacoby and others on information overload strongly supports the latter points. Consumers can be overloaded with information, Jacoby found, but seldom will be overloaded. They will not attempt to assimilate more information than they can manipulate. Professionals and others who find it necessary to maintain state-of-the-art knowledge and skill, on the other hand, will tend to experience the sort of conditions described above.

ORGANIZATIONAL CREDIBILITY

Successful communication involves more than message design and delivery, although these traditionally have been the primary functions of advertising, sales promotion, public relations, and, to a lesser extent, marketing. Success requires that messages be received, assimilated, and acted upon. Communication can be said to have succeeded, in other words, only where message recipients have responded as senders intended. These events transpire only where senders are credible. Credibility, in turn, requires greater consistency in communication than traditionally has been the case, especially among those presumably attempting to persuade rather than merely inform.

Advertising, marketing, public relations, and sales promotion traditionally have been viewed as persuasive disciplines. Some have suggested that the practices involved essentially are manipulative, which need not be the case. The semantic difficulties involved arise from imprecision in defining persuasion. The word means to prevail on an individual to behave in a specified manner through urging or advising. To induce, on the other hand, implies exercising influence rather than logic to produce desired results.

Influence once was a major element in all communication disciplines. Efforts to exercise influence, usually in the form of exaggerated promises or threats, more recently has been relatively common in advertising, sales promotion, and, to a lesser extent, in marketing. Public relations practitioners have gravitated toward less aggressive strategies. None of the disciplines, however, has come to grips with the consequences of what might be called information overproduction rather than information overload.

Communicators are generating more messages than ever before. Individuals tune out as many as necessary to prevent information overload. The difference between receipt and rejection often is governed by sender credibility. Credibility in most individuals is a function of experience, experience with organizations and their messages and with the extent to which messages and experiences are consistent with one another.

Pragmatically, experiences communicate. More precisely, organizations communicate through the experiences they create for individuals. A strong argument could be made, in fact, that many messages are experienced rather than merely received. This certainly is the intent and, indeed, one of the advantages of messages conveyed through television. While some may challenge the thesis that messages are experienced, few would argue that experiences deliver messages. Most probably would agree that experiences are the most convincing components of learning. While few adults recall the precise details, each learned the meaning of the word *hot* through experience. Heat must be experienced to be understood.

These conditions suggest that individuals' experiences with organizations—with organizational personnel and with the environments that organizations create—are unique message generators. The nature of the communication processes involved, in addition, suggests that experiential messages will be more convincing than the mediated variety. Research has demonstrated the existence of a hierarchy of effectiveness in the four basic forms of communication. Ranked in order from most to least effective, the four communication forms are interpersonal, small group, large group, and mediated.

Individuals' communicative experiences with organizations also can be sorted into one of four categories. Ranked from most to least effective, the four communication categories are environmental, behavioral, interpersonal, and mediated. Organizations communicate, in other words, through the environments they create, through the behaviors they sponsor or condone, through the words of their personnel, and through messages disseminated through various media.

Historically, although seldom viewed in this context, mediated communication probably has been the most expensive and least productive of the four varieties. Expenditures in advertising, marketing, sales promotion, and public relations almost invariably exceed the sums committed to training personnel and to maintaining facilities and/or premises. In fact, while organizational environments are almost grudgingly maintained, and while little or no attention is paid to the interpersonal skills of employees, mediated communication has become a full-blown industry.

Logic suggests these conditions are unlikely to persist as the age of information takes shape. Two factors will militate toward change. One is the continuing fragmentation of the audiences once commanded by the mass media. The other is persistent improvement in the relative efficiency of alternative forms of communication. The audience fragmentation process inevitably will continue as interactive media come into day-to-day use. Mediated communication will become increasingly more difficult and more costly. Organizations, as a result, inevitably will grow attentive to other forms of communication.

The inevitability of the change will be reinforced by national demographics patterns. Rather than the explosive population growth of the late twentieth century, organizations will be dealing with the relative stability of the twenty-first. Neither consumers nor workers, in these circumstances, can be dealt with capriciously. Both will have to be wooed and won in competitive environments. Those environments, and the workers who populate them, will become ever more important to the success of every organization.

Organizational expenditures in worker training and development and in facilities design and maintenance for these reasons will grow rapidly, perhaps with funding reallocated from communication budgets. It remains to be seen, however, whether the functions involved will be performed by organizational staff or by consultants and whether the communication disciplines will suffer or benefit as a result of the changes involved.

PROFIT OR LOSS

Potential for gains and losses exist in each of the communication disciplines as organizations change their communication emphases. Numbers of dollars expended are unlikely to diminish. Budgets are more apt to grow larger because competition for customers and workers will be more intense. The same sort of competition will develop among the communication disciplines, however, and none will be able to relax their competitive vigilance for the foreseeable future.

Competition for personnel and clients will be as intense in the communication disciplines as elsewhere. While personnel problems probably will remain at subcritical levels through the early 1990s, competition for clients already has grown more intense as a result of the merger mania of the 1980s among communication firms and their clients—existing and prospective.

Combinations of problems and opportunities thus await each of the communication disciplines. No two disciplines will find their circumstances alike, and no two are apt to benefit or suffer equally when the transition to the age of information has been completed. The most innovative in each group, and across groups, inevitably will be the most successful.

Advertising's Challenge

Advertising professionals have been aggressive in attacking problems confronting clients and employers. While aggressively pursuing greater efficiency and effectiveness, however, most in advertising have been content to confine their activities to these more traditional arenas. Few have been willing, for example, to link advertising with environments to enhance merchandising effectiveness (see chapter 11). As a result, they may find the transition to the age of information more traumatic than is the case in the other communication disciplines.

Advertising's potential areas of advantage in the age of information probably will be strongly design related. Matching boutique designs to magazine advertisements might add to the effectiveness of some media. Applications of the technique are limited, however, and the concept quickly could be overdone.

Advertising also might benefit from the onset of interactive technologies. Design of on-screen displays, for example, could become an area of advertising expertise. Most computers—some more than others—also have limited "musical" capabilities. There appears no practical reason why sound and graphics could not be productively joined in advertising displayed with services such as Sears, Roebuck's Prodigy. Logically, in fact, the expertise of the advertising profession might be wedded to that of computer technology to create more useful interfaces than now usually exist between databases and their users. Data base operators have the mainframe computer capacity to install virtually any access system. There is every reason to believe that data bases ultimately will compete aggressively for clients. The competition well might focus in part on interface design, components of which could subsequently be incorporated into print as well as electronic advertising.

While interactive media may offer opportunities for advertising, the profession's greatest challenge also is apt to be linked to interactive media and the audience fragmentation they encourage. The challenge will arise in identifying media most appropriate to delivery of messages to specific audiences. Audiences are likely to become more elusive than now is the case, and advertisers probably will be forced to pay a premium to those most capable of delivering specific audience groups. These circumstances suggest that advertising agency personnel and their corporate counterparts should spend time educating themselves in the new technologies. Membership lists of pertinent special interest groups sponsored by utilities such as CompuServe and The Source indicate, however, that few are moving in this direction.

Computer utilities and other interactive media will not develop overnight into major players in the media arena. They should not be overlooked, however, by those who intend to make their livings in advertising or any other communication discipline in the twenty-first century, now less than a decade away.

Problems in Marketing

Advertising's problems will be reflected, to a greater degree than elsewhere, in the marketing community. The research component critical to advertising and marketing may be especially difficult to manage. Research linked to individuals' media usage patterns could become especially complex as more emerging communication channels become significant components of the marketing mix.

More important from the marketing viewpoint, however, is the path the profession will follow in the years ahead. Will marketers focus on what traditionally has been their primary functions? Or will marketing attempt to gain dominance in areas long the functional preserves of others? Substantial evidence has developed in recent years to suggest that major conflicts may arise.

Marketing traditionally has been a research-based discipline. Members have devoted the bulk of their energies to two primary functions: identifying consumer needs and desires and designing products and/or services to meet those needs. Given the products or services in question, marketers traditionally have turned to advertising, public relations, and sales promotion to communicate with target audiences.

Marketing's traditional pattern has not held in recent years, perhaps in part due to increasing competitive pressures. The health care sector, for example, has been a major interdisciplinary battleground. Public relations was first among communication disciplines in most hospitals and in other components of the health care industry. Advertising also was present, but as a minor player, used seldom and then primarily in institutional format. Marketing was introduced in hospitals as federal and state financing formulas made the health care industry more competitive.

Marketers long have been more disposed toward advertising than public relations in communicating with prospective users of the products or services they design. The statistical orientation of marketing probably predisposes members of the discipline more toward the extensive statistics generated by advertising than toward the "softer" information used in public relations. As marketers introduced stronger emphases on advertising into hospitals, interdisciplinary strife developed that persists to this day.

Public Relations Issues

Conflict with marketing, unfortunately, is not the only problem that faces public relations. Public relations as a discipline is relatively young and remains in many respects immature. Only in recent years, for example, have some of public relations' stronger practitioners yielded to client and employer demands that they accept responsibility for producing measurable results. So slow has the transition become that measurable results, even among the relatively enlightened, often are defined in terms of media exposure rather than in levels of behavioral response among audience groups.

Public relations, in other words, remains preoccupied with mass media exposure in an era in which mass media audiences are deteriorating at an unprecedented rate. There are, of course, occasions when mass media exposure is critical, as in the case of Johnson and Johnson's Tylenol problem. Any examination of a cross section of public relations practices, however, shows that the typical public relations problem is neither national in scope nor general in interest. Typical problems, to which typical practitioners devote most of their time, involve smaller groups concerned with more narrowly-defined issues.

Public relations practitioners are interested primarily in the employees, customers, vendors, and stockholders of their clients or employers. Issues that engage the interests of clients or employers on the one hand, and one or more of those "stakeholder groups" on the other, are the day-to-day concerns of public relations. Practitioners' primary objectives are not mass media exposure but predetermined behavioral response among stakeholder groups—responses generated by client or employer behavior as well as communication.

Public relations, in other words, is becoming a process through which organizations achieve accommodation with those groups with which they are interdependent. The practice of public relations thus necessarily deals as much with organizational policy and behavior as with the process of communication. Public relations practitioners are—or should be—engaged in behavioral and environmental communication, as will be discussed below, as well as in mediated communication.

Sales Promotion

Pragmatically, public relations also has come to involve a significant sales promotion component—at least in the sense that product promotion increasingly is a part of public relations practice. Product or sales promotion equally has become part of advertising and marketing, but the growth of the discipline in recent years cannot be taken as an assurance of a problem-free future.

Sales promotion of late has focused in large part on coupons delivered in any of a number of forms in merchandise giveaways and in merchandising displays. These techniques will remain in vogue for the near future, although sales promotion also may have to adjust to market changes as the interactive media develop. The day may not be far away, for example, when coupons are requested through interactive media rather than delivered by newspaper or mail.

The transition from traditional to interactive media in a sense may be a blessing for sales promotion, which long has been caught up in guerrilla warfare between newspapers and mailers. The skirmish lines ebb and flow with changes in postal rates, newspaper and magazine circulation, and other factors important in coupon delivery. Neither side has managed to achieve dominance, although the mailers appear to be gaining ground.

While the coupon wars go on, potential for innovation is virtually limitless in the marketplace—literally, in the stores in which merchandise is offered for sale. A growing body of research suggests that the bulk of buying decisions in many merchandise categories are made after shoppers arrive in stores rather than on being exposed to advertising. More and more in-store communication, in the form of conventional signs and innovative electronic devices, inevitably will develop as a result. Getting the customer into the store or the buyer into the showroom or any consumer to any decision point will be another matter. In this arena, the battles between and among advertising, marketing, and public relations will persist.

TOMORROW'S BATTLE GROUND

The scope of the battles remain to be determined. Battle lines have yet to be drawn. Only the fields of battle can be identified. They are those types of communication long neglected by disciplines oriented primarily, if not exclusively, to the mass media. The mass media have delivered small but significant portions of the messages received by members of postindustrial societies. For better or worse, however, these messages are being delivered at progressively lower levels of efficiency.

Efficiency here refers to the extent to which communicators can successfully reach predetermined audiences through mass media. As the efficiency of mass media deteriorates, communicators will be forced to turn to other channels of communication, especially to those long recognized for effectiveness but seldom acknowledged for prospective efficiency. Communicators long have been aware of the four-part typology of communication: interpersonal, small group, large group and mediated. They often have overlooked the fact, however, that mediated messages are only part of what might be called a typology of nonintimate communication.

Mediated messages are least effective in a hierarchy that also includes, in ascending order, verbal, behavioral, and environmental communication. The verbal component is the equivalent of the interpersonal approach referred to above. Behavioral communication, in contrast, refers to the actions rather than the words of those with whom messages originate—organizations as well as individuals. Environmental communication refers to the implicit messages delivered by those who create environments for workers, customers, and others.

Verbal, behavioral, and environmental communication necessarily will become more important to organizations as the efficiency of mediated communication declines. The verbal form of communication already has been incorporated in part into formal communication programs. The behavioral and environmental usually have been neglected. These will be professional communicators' new frontiers for the twenty-first century. They also may prove to be the killing fields of interdisciplinary warfare.

Verbal Communication

While few professionals have addressed the potential productivity in behavioral and environmental communication, the reverse is true in the interpersonal sector. The influence of interpersonal communication long has been recognized by most professionals. Those in marketing have been especially involved in terms of sales programs. In recent years, however, interpersonal communication has become an integral part of many public relations efforts.

Where used in contemporary public relations practices, interpersonal communication skills are cultivated through training programs for executive officers and other organizational spokespersons. These programs are considered especially important where the nature of organizations or their problems is such that spokespersons may be called upon to make public appearances, especially before the news media.

Television, in any one of several forms, has become pervasive in postindustrial society. The relative strength or weakness of spokespersons in television or in forums in which their comments may be televised can influence public perceptions of the organizations they represent. Stage presence, elocution, and other skills helpful in dealing with the medium are helpful, in fact, even where those involved never appear "in public." Business television (see chapter 9) potentially has become an effective organizational communication tool. The potential involved is best realized where organizational leaders are effective spokespersons.

The word spokesperson, in fact, is readily extended in organizational communication to encompass every manager and supervisor in the organization. The rationale is increasingly important to senior managers: ability to recruit and retain personnel in an era of declining human resources is influenced by the skills of managers and supervisors in communicating with workers. Interest in interpersonal communication training in organizations is growing as a result.

Demand for enhanced interpersonal skills, exercised through electronic media or in person, will continue to increase in all organizations. How and where these skills will be developed is another matter. A number of alternatives exist, and some have been acted upon, albeit somewhat tentatively, in some organizations.

Anecdotal evidence suggests that personnel or human resources departments, since they usually are charged with finding prospective employees who can meet predetermined knowledge and skill criteria, are becoming home to organizational training or professional development programs, as they are sometimes called. The logic of the trend is unquestionable, since as human resources managers inevitably cope with the consequences of interpersonal communication failures on the part of managers and supervisors. Whether human resources departments are logical locales for all interpersonal skills training is another matter.

Groups usually most in need of training in interpersonal skills often are those least likely to participate. They are the clerks, telephone operators, and service personnel with whom clients and customers first come in contact. To customers and clients, at least temporarily, these individuals do more than represent the organization. They *are* the organization. Their interpersonal successes and failures in dealing with consumers govern organizational success or failure.

Need for interpersonal communication skills for these reasons is becoming an area of substantial expansion potential for the communication disciplines. Public relations practitioners arguably are best equipped to move into interpersonal communication, by experience if not by training. Many public relations firms in recent years have expanded into spokesperson training for their clients. Spokesperson training also has become a part of many organizational communication departments. These are the organizational entities responsible for employee communication as opposed to external or public communication. Expanding spokesperson training programs to encompass all managers and supervisors in most cases would be a relatively small step. Adding training for those on the organizational front lines, who deal daily with customers or clients, would not require considerably more effort.

Behavioral Communication

Potential for enhanced organizational productivity through communication is even greater where organizational behavior is concerned. While interpersonal communication is more effective than the mediated variety, what organizations do is still more persuasive from the perspectives of outsiders. The effectiveness of the friendliest personnel, in other words, is too easily undermined by policies and procedures that prevent or complicate solutions to human problems.

Every organizational action or inaction, and perceptions of those actions or inactions among stakeholder groups, can add to or detract from organizational stature. Consider, for example, the disastrous Exxon Valdez oil spill in the spring of 1989. Early inactivity on the company's part was perceived by critics as an uncaring attitude. So severe was the public judgment that even the business-oriented *Wall Street Journal* published a front-page article about the environmental and ecological impact of the spill.

While the Exxon problem dominated the news media for months, other difficulties collectively can be equally damaging to organizations. Policies that prevent consumer complaints from being quickly resolved, for example, almost inevitably are more costly in loss of customers than they are productive in preventing "rip-offs." Work force reductions produced by organizational economy drives that result in long lines at checkout stands can be equally damaging. Consumers take these conditions as indicators of organizational concern—or lack of concern—over their patronage.

The same principles apply in all stakeholder groups. Employees, stockholders, vendors, distributors, and others are equally amenable to being influenced, favorably or unfavorably, by organizational behaviors. The behaviors and the policies, or lack of policies, that produce them both require periodic review. Prompt revision must follow where necessary.

Potential for improved organizational performance through improved behavioral communication is considerable. The logical identity of those who should handle this form of communication is less readily specified. Behavioral communication could become the province of virtually any of the communication disciplines. The potential impact of organizational behavior, for better or worse, is or should be well understood among all communication disciplines. One or several of them inevitably will attempt to claim this area for their own.

Environmental Communication

The same conditions apply, with one minor difference, in environmental communication. The term refers to the environments that organizations create for customers or clients, for employees, and for any others. Like organizational behaviors, environments speak loudly as to organizations' concern or lack of concern for those with whom they come in contact.

The impact of organizational environments varies with the nature of groups and businesses involved. Environments are critical for retail businesses. They are less important among manufacturing and distributing firms. The differences are a matter of exposure. Customers are quick to depart relatively inhospitable or unattractive retail environments. They may be wholly unaware, however, of the conditions in which the products they obtain are produced.

Consider, for example, the typical restaurant. Customers see only the dining room and lounge and, perhaps, the restrooms. Conditions in the kitchen—good or bad—are unknown. Customers will quickly abandon a restaurant where the dining room is less than immaculate but pay no heed to unsanitary kitchen conditions.

Entire organizations are judged by those parts of the organization with which customers or clients come in contact. Professional firms' waiting rooms may be taken as evidence of practitioner quality. Hospital lobbies help shape opinion as to the cleanliness of surgical suites. Neatness and a host of other factors enter into the success of retail establishments.

The range of variables that can influence retail customers, whether they are shopping for clothing or automobiles, is almost endless. Comfort probably is most important to a majority although price and selection of merchandise may be an almost equally strong determinant. Customers also display an affinity for premises that are not overly crowded, for adequate numbers of personnel to meet their needs, for efficient lighting and heating/cooling systems, for adequate parking, for effective security systems, and so forth.

None expect perfection. Weaknesses in one or more of these areas, especially transient weaknesses caused by, for example, the crowds of the Christmas shopping season, are tolerable. Persistent weaknesses are another matter. Consumers are fickle and will not long tolerate what they consider to be vendor inadequacies. They are especially intolerant where they perceive that retailer weaknesses attest to a disregard for customers' feelings. Consider, for example, this overheard exchange between a man and woman in a department store.

She: That's a nice tie. Why don't you buy it.

He (turning toward the cashier's stand): I think I will.

She: (as he starts putting the tie back in the rack): What's the matter?

He: The line's too long.

She: You don't understand; you have to stand in line.

He: You may have to stand in line; I won't. When they advertise a sale, it's their responsibility to have enough cashiers to handle the crowd.

While the problem may be readily identified, responsibility for the solution is not as easily assigned. Unlike behavioral communication, environmental communication has no logical home within the organization. Virtually any of the communication disciplines could step in to claim this small but important bit of turf. Marketing and/or sales departments might be logical homes for the control of environmental communication, especially in retail organizations. Public relations conceivably would be a more appropriate site in manufacturing or distribution firms where worker environments are important.

As the relative efficiency and effectiveness of other forms of communication deteriorate, however, it is most important that responsibility for environmental, behavioral, and interpersonal communication be assigned. Historically, what is everyone's concern in organizational settings is no one's high priority—this is, literally, a formula for communication disaster.

IN SUMMARY

Problems that the advertising industry has been experiencing for several years are but a preview of things to come for the communication disciplines. Even those in advertising will be forced to rethink the basic premises of their businesses as audience fragmentation renders target audiences more and more elusive.

The heart of the problem is information overload. More and more messages aimed at more and more groups are creating a level of background noise so great that more and more are simply being tuned out by resistant prospective recipients. While alternative techniques often are applied by those who deal regularly in the information industries, typical consumer patterns produce the kinds of responses reported by the Jacoby teams in their studies of print and electronic communication. Miscomprehension, they found, is a common result of communication.

Comprehension and, more important, receiver response thus require something more than design and delivery of messages through traditional communication channels. Messages must be received, assimilated, and acted upon, events that are unlikely to occur in the absence of sender credibility.

Credibility requires consistency in messages. Those distributed through the media must be congruent with all others, with those delivered in person or conveyed in behavior or through environments. Individuals' total experiences with organizations rather than any specific messages are apt to govern their behaviors as consumers of ideas, services, or products, and these conditions will become more demanding as the age of information develops.

The same conditions also will create circumstances that can generate profit or loss for each of the communication disciplines. Change in communication emphases to cope with changing external conditions will create opportunities for those prepared for the age of information. Communication budgets will be no smaller and probably will be larger than those that now exist. Competition for personnel and clients will be at least as intense as it is today.

Advertising especially will be forced toward innovative tactics in order to retain market share. Declining efficiency and effectiveness among traditional media can be offset to some extent through greater creativity, but more will be necessary. Greater use of nontraditional media, at a minimum, will be essential to success. Interactive media will be doubly important as higher socioeconomic groups gravitate toward the interactive sector.

Marketing's problems will be no less pressing and perhaps more difficult to resolve. The discipline's traditional orientation toward statistics will conflict with the growing research efforts that conditions can be expected to stimulate in the advertising sector, creating greater competitive stress. Internecine warfare between marketing and public relations also is apt to escalate as each discipline seeks to maintain its economic positions.

Public relations practitioners will confront equally difficult conditions. Practitioners will be forced to set aside their mass media predispositions and look toward other message sources to produce behavioral responses among audiences. Potentially, environmental, behavioral, and interpersonal communication offer considerable growth potential for public relations practitioners. It remains to be seen whether they will take advantage of the opportunities involved.

Sales promotion promises to be the most stable of the persuasive communication disciplines. In-store and coupon promotions have proven their cost effectiveness during a period in which other approaches to the consumer have proven less than wholly rewarding. Sales promotion's risks will occur primarily in the form of incursions on the part of the other disciplines.

The primary battlefields for all disciplines probably will shift from mediated to nonmediated. Mass media communication almost certainly will be de-emphasized as its relative efficiency continues to decline. At the same time, interpersonal, behavioral, and environmental communication will become more important to every organization. Verbal communication already has a foothold in spokesperson training, and that foothold inevitably will expand as senior managers better perceive an already pressing need to enhance the training of managers and supervisors. Behavioral and environmental communication ultimately will achieve equivalent stature as organizations fight for marketplace dominance for their ideas, services, and products.

ADDITIONAL READING

Andrews, Patricia H., and John E. Baird, Jr. *Communication for Business and the Professions*. 3rd ed. Dubuque, IA: Wm. C. Brown, 1986.

Desatnick, Robert L. *Managing to Keep the Customer: How to Achieve and Maintain Superior Customer Services Throughout the Organization*. San Francisco: Jossey-Bass, 1987.

Doyle, Robert J. *Gainsharing and Productivity*. New York: AMACOM, 1983.

Hennessey, Bernard. *Public Opinion*. 5th ed. Monterey, Calif.: Brooks/Cole, 1985.

Jamieson, Kathleen H., and Karlyn K. Campbell. *The Interplay of Influence*. 2nd ed. New York: Wadsworth, 1988.

Kilmann, Ralph H., Teresa J. Covin, and associates. *Corporate Transformation: Revitalizing Organizations for a Competitive World*. San Francisco: Jossey-Bass, 1988.

Schein, Edgar H. *Organizational Culture and Leadership*. San Francisco: Jossey-Bass, 1985.

13   Communication Tomorrow

The age of information is supplanting the industrial age in the United States and other industrialized nations. Necessary hardware exists and links are being forged among communication systems to create an all-encompassing integrated electronic grid. Communicators' concerns, however, are more focused on the nature than on the timing of the postindustrial society's development. Neither the nature of the transition to the age of information and the wired society nor the potential impact can be precisely calculated. Astute observers, however, will be able to detect change in time to develop appropriate responses.

Relatively complete and current information is necessary to accurately assess prospective changes in society and mass communication. The evolution of the computer and the development of the integrated grid, for example, are critical to the age of information. The speed with which they evolve will determine how rapidly the nation and the world make the transition from the industrial age to the age of information. The primary characteristics of information societies also must be considered. These characteristics determine the future of emerging and existing channels of communication. Finally, anticipated changes must be viewed in their historical context. Much of what is about to transpire has occurred before, although perhaps in less radical form and at slower speeds.

HISTORICAL PATTERNS

History provides insights into developments apt to occur as the age of information begins. Contemporary circumstances provide further hints as to the future. In combination, these elements go far toward painting a clear picture of what lies ahead, toward defining the shape of postindustrial information technologies and the changes that will occur in mass communication.

Viewed concurrently, current conditions and historical trends can generate projections that should enable communicators to avoid pitfalls and capitalize on opportunities as the age of information takes shape. Projections at best are tentative. They nevertheless can help planners avoid misconceptions and missteps that otherwise might occur.

Communication Phases

Human communication has progressed through four distinct phases. A fifth now is beginning. Each phase is associated with a specific form of communication. During the first four phases, or stages, humanity proceeded from speaking to writing and then to printing and telecommunication. In the fifth phase, which now is taking shape, the emphasis will be on interactive communication systems.

The era of verbal communication began with the development of language. Language, which probably came into use about 35,000 B.C. in the Cro-Magnon period, enabled humans to more readily communicate with one another. Enhanced communication produced greater efficiency in food gathering and facilitated the development of complex tribal societies.

Five thousand years later, the era of writing began. Sumerian writings on clay tablets dating from 4000 B.C. mark the start of the period. Writing became humanity's dominant communication technology for most of the ensuing six centuries.

The printing era began with Gutenberg and his Bible in 1456. Printing remained the most sophisticated of communication techniques until 1844, when Samuel Morse invented the telegraph. The age of telecommunication began with Morse's telegraph and was perpetuated by Marconi's wireless. Telecommunication predominated among forms of communication until the advent of the computer in 1946.

The impact of each of these developments was greater than many now consider to have been the case. The development of writing, for example, led to ability to maintain historical records and develop libraries. Generations were freed from having to relearn that which had been learned before and could dedicate themselves to adding to the knowledge of humankind. The printing press and the other technological developments were no less momentous. Printing destroyed the clerical monopoly on the bible and led to growing literacy, which in turn enhanced ability to learn. The telephone and telegraph were no less significant and history probably will proclaim the computer as the preeminent scientific advance of the twentieth century.

The University of Pennsylvania's ENIAC, which used eighteen thousand vacuum tubes, marked the beginning of the computer era. ENIAC's offspring spawned interactive communication, which now is developing in six primary forms: microcomputers, teleconferencing, teletext, videotext, interactive cable television, and satellite communication.

Most individuals knowingly have come in contact with no more than one or two of the six forms. The word *knowingly* is necessary in that most of today's mass media are dependent in large part on satellite communication. Television is most dependent, but newspapers and radio stations also are extensive users of satellite signals.

Other than unknowingly in the form of satellite-transmitted information, relatively small percentages of the United States population have had occasion to use a computer or to come in contact with one of the early teletext, videotext, or interactive cable systems. These circumstances cannot be taken, however, as meaning that little progress is being made toward the age of information. A close look at the process of assimilation suggests, in fact, that the information age is closer than many believe.

Assimilating Technology

The impact of interactive communication on contemporary society and on the mass communication disciplines will be a function of the speed with which the technologies involved are assimilated into society. Assimilation follows a well-established path described by J. R. Bright as a "process of technological innovation." Bright's eight steps are scientific suggestion, theory or design concept, laboratory verification of theory or design, laboratory demonstration or application, full scale or field trial, commercial introduction, widespread adoption, and proliferation.

Interactive communication channels already have made considerable progress along this continuum. All have proceeded through field trial to commercial introduction. Some trials, as in the case of the Qube system in Columbus, Ohio and Knight-Ridder's experience in Dade County, Florida, have been less than successful. Their successors, in the process of installation in the late 1980s remain to be proved, but widespread adoption and eventual proliferation appear inevitable.

The microcomputer has made greater progress and probably stands between Bright's widespread adoption and proliferation stages in the assimilation process. Diffusion processes tend to progress more rapidly than most perceive to be the case, as the microcomputer has demonstrated. A 1980 study suggested computers were in about 5 percent of the 80 million United States households and that penetration would increase to more than 25 percent by 1990. Four years later, the estimates already had proved inadequate. Multiple 1984 studies showed that 15 to 16 percent of households then had computers and that the total might reach 40 to 50 percent by 1990.

Household penetration, however, cannot safely be equated with computer use. More than a few computers will be underutilized, although the reasons doubtless will differ from those that prevailed during the 1970s. Early microcomputers lacked the capacity to perform functions claimed for them in much of the advertising of the day. Disappointed buyers often relegated the machines to attics or closets rather than buy more equipment.

Underutilization during the 1990s is more likely to be a product of relatively steep learning curves. Learning problems often are encountered in complex applications software even where user friendly operating systems are used.

A companion issue to underutilization arises out of variety in application. Computers are as readily used for recreational or avocational purposes as for acquiring of information. Computer utilities such as CompuServe probably are as often used for one purpose as the other, although published data on this point are lacking. Lack of information in areas such as these, and the complexity of the interactive media, will render efforts to assess the extent to which the information age has arrived rather difficult.

THE INTEGRATED GRID

While microcomputers are proliferating, technology's largest strides toward the age of information have occurred with little fanfare and beyond the eyes of casual observers. As the 1980s drew to a close, the United States stood at the brink of completing what has been called the integrated grid, a network through which the nation's communication systems would be brought together into a cohesive whole. The grid in 1989 consisted of telephone, cable television, electronic mail, and voice mail systems, all soon to be linked directly or indirectly to satellites, data banks, and to one another.

The major breakthroughs of the 1980s occurred late in the decade in two forms: unification of electronic mail systems and development of bridging mechanisms to permit movement of information across system boundaries. The unification process was a sort of "shotgun wedding" arranged by the Aerospace Industries Association (AIA), whose members send almost a million electronic mail messages annually. AIA's message to the seven sisters of electronic mail (EasyLink, Telemail, Dialcom, MCI Mail and AT&T Mail) was this: develop a uniform system or we will take our business elsewhere.

Within months, because a technological standard had been established in 1984, the uniform system was installed and operating. The technological standard earlier had been permitted to languish only because each of the players apparently felt that adoption might cost more subscribers than it produced.

The electronic mail systems' change to the uniform standard was the latter-day equivalent of the linking of the nation's independent telephone companies. The more recent change was especially momentous, moreover, in that bridges already existed between electronic mail and computer systems. CompuServe Information Service (CIS), a computer utility, already had linked up to MCI Mail and also was offering facsimile services to its customers. South Central Bell concurrently was installing its T.U.G. gateway system, which offered direct access to CompuServe. Only cable television systems were still to be tied in, and telephone companies were moving in that direction as rapidly as legislative and regulatory constraints permitted.

Information Bridges

All that will remain to be accomplished with completion of the network is comparable development in systemic content, which appears to be occurring as well. The value of the grid to users will be limited only by the quality and quantity of accessible information. The information exists in two basic types. One type, already reduced to electronic form, is readily entered into the system. Information in print or on tape is another matter.

Evolving technology already addresses the growing volume of information existing in electronic form and soon will also be able to handle the bulk of printed and taped information. Information in electronic form is contained in the nation's data bases. In 1980, some three hundred data bases existed and communication scholars were predicting they would more than double in number by the end of the century. In 1989, less than ten years later, more than three thousand data bases existed, and the total by the year 2000 was expected to be at double or triple that figure.

Many of the new data bases will contain information that once existed only in mechanical form, information once believed to be beyond reach of economical data entry techniques. Three technological devices in 1989 appeared to evolving to a point at which this obstacle would soon be overcome. One was the optical scanner; the second was a growing collection of software capable of translating documents from one language to another. The third was the voice-activated computer.

Optical Scanners. Optical scanning systems appeared in relatively crude form in the mid-1980s. Like many computer-related technologies, they consisted of three parts: a mechanical scanner, an accompanying software package, and a microcomputer. Early scanners accepted images only in "bit mapped" form. Alphanumeric characters could be loaded into computers via scanners, but only as graphic images. Resulting computer files could not be edited, because characters were handled by computers as drawings. Content of printed or typed pages could not be converted to conventional computer file form for handling as, for example, word processing or data files.

The "bit-mapped barrier," as it might be called, was overcome for most users by 1990 as optical character recognition (OCR) software started to appear in ever more sophisticated and progressively less costly form. OCR software packages enabled scanners to produce conventional computer files suitable for further manipulation in word processor or data base programs. Accuracy rates in reproduction were in excess of 99 percent. Accuracy rate refers to numbers of errors typically appearing in scanned computer files. No more than one character in one hundred, in a file that is 99 percent accurate, would not conform to the original document.

Accuracy rates of 99 percent were acceptable in most applications because resulting word processing files then could be manually or automatically edited. Computer spelling and grammar checkers both could be used to eliminate misspellings. The latter processes were imperfect in that programs could not differentiate between, for example, *farm* and *form* because both are valid words. Resulting documents nevertheless were sufficient to most information users' needs.

Scanners Applied. Scanners equipped with relatively accurate optical recognition software represented a major breakthrough in information management. The technologies involved enabled computer users to easily and rapidly load masses of information that had not been created in electronic form, thus completing state-of-the-art banks of information.

Scanner loading ultimately can be expected to be used, for example, in creating comprehensive professional libraries for organizations such as the Public Relations Society of America (PRSA). The society in 1987 set out to document and bring together in a single repository the body of knowledge underlying the practice of public relations. The first step was a year-long effort by a team of academic researchers and practitioners to specify books and documents to be made part of the collection. The following year was dedicated to abstracting the material involved, creating brief summary statements that could be entered into a computer.

Abstracting work carried out on multiple university campuses was done on computers. Resulting documents thus were readily gathered and indexed in a central location. PRSA had no immediate plans to load the underlying documents. Legal complexities would make this a time-consuming process. Availability of optical character recognition software made the process practical, however, and many in the profession anticipate that the task soon will be undertaken.

The only substantive barrier to creating the sort of comprehensive data library that would result for PRSA is economic. Data loading would be labor intensive even with legal obstacles removed. Costs involved could be justified only if PRSA or an alternative sponsoring organization could establish the data base on a self-sustaining basis.

Self-funding would require a volume of user revenues adequate to cover data base maintenance costs and recapture all initial expenses. A cash flow of that magnitude, in turn, would require a larger user base than immediately was in prospect. Best available estimates in 1990 indicated that fewer than two thousand public relations practitioners were using on-line data bases. The user base was growing, but near-term growth rate did not appear adequate to justify the investment required.

Translation Programs. A further quantum increase in user potential was possible, however, with the advent of computer programs that could translate from one language to another. Program developers by 1989 had met one of the most difficult translation challenges: a program would translate Japanese to English and vice versa. Such a program requires computer recognition and translation to and from symbols as well as alphanumeric characters. Programs to translate virtually every other major language were expected to quickly follow the Japanese-English program.

While superficially a minor step forward, translation programs imply a quantum increase in data base usage. Depending on program size, translators could be stored in either mainframes housing data bases or in personal computers. Data base users could instruct mainframes to translate before downloading or could download and then translate. Benefits to the academic world and resultant increases in database usage in that sector would be unprecedented. Computers, data banks, and translation programs will have reduced by years or decades the time that otherwise would elapse before papers published in obscure academic journals in Japan could be read in the English-speaking world.

While most in the academic world are computer users and comfortable with the technology, lay persons are another problem. Computer phobia is a common although curable ailment in contemporary society. Cures occur as users learn that (a) they are dealing with dumb machines that require specific directions and that (b) no error on the part of the user can harm the machine. At worst, the process involved must be abandoned and restarted.

Voice Activation. Unfortunately, cures historically have been unlikely where prospective users manage to avoid physical contact with computers. Physical contact soon may be unnecessary, however, as more and more computers are equipped with voice activation systems. If computer phobia is the last major barrier to universal computer usage, voice-activated systems may prove to be the ultimate antidote.

Computers that respond to the human voice rather than to keyboards became available in simple form during the late 1980s and promised to quickly come into common usage. While a novelty when first introduced, voice activation offered considerable promise for equipment vendors as well as users. Potential for manufacturers and vendors in the form of increased attractiveness in the marketplace and, consequently, greater sales suggested that voice-activated equipment might proliferate at an unprecedented rate.

The first generally available commercial development in voice-activated computers was a simple translation device designed for use by English-speaking international travelers. Users simply turn on the machine and speak clearly into a self-contained microphone. The machine plays back the phrase or sentence in the designated language.

While prospective users of the translation device were few in number, 1989 also saw the introduction of another voice-reading device aimed at a broader market: a voice-activated telephone that could be programmed to dial the numbers of any of fifty individuals or firms after receiving appropriate verbal commands.

Neither of the voice activation systems was highly sophisticated. Developers of the translation device experienced difficulties in coping with differences in users' voices and inflections. The telephones were programmed to respond to their owners' voices and did not perform as reliably for other household members. There appeared little doubt, however, that voice activated equipment would be quickly refined and more generally applied. As this trend develops and the technology is applied to databases, their use can be expected to increase.

Integrated Systems

Collectively, technologies of the types described above will permit development of highly integrated systems that will accept and deliver information in any form. The basic language probably will be computer code, but "translators" quickly will bridge gaps between systems.

Optical character readers and voice recognition equipment will be the primary bridges. The optical character readers will translate written or printed material into computer language, while voice recognition equipment will do the same for humans or their transcribed messages. Where appropriate, scanners and electronic "cameras" also will be tied to the combined telephone—voice mail–cable television–electronic mail systems to transmit drawings and photos.

The flexibility of these systems will produce massive growth in informational resources. Complexity of systems used in information retrieval also will increase, however, contributing to the complexity of the interactive media.

FUTURE SHOCK?

So complex, pervasive, and potentially rewarding can these systems become that efforts to assess their potential impact are especially difficult. Close examination of a number of factors nevertheless may suggest how future trends may develop and, by implication, the responses that may be necessary on the part of professional communicators.

Perhaps the strongest governor of speed and scope of change will be the relative complexity of the interactive media. Although necessary to handle the volume of information that soon will be available for public use, systemic complexity can discourage use. The responses of individuals and organizations—especially media organizations—to the arrival of the interactive systems also require consideration.

The nature of information societies also will play a role in acceptance of interactive media. Computer literacy already is required in most schools and is fast becoming necessary in most occupations. These conditions may pave the way, at least in part, for the arrival of interactive media. Some insights into potential public response also may be gleaned from earlier experiences with television, although television, it must be remembered, was and remains primarily an entertainment rather than an informational medium.

Media Complexity

Interactivity, most researchers agree, is the primary characteristic of the new media. Definitions of interactivity are difficult to come by, however, and no two come close to full agreement as to the meaning of the term. Most definitions incorporate a half dozen variables present in most interactive media. The variables, according to Michigan State University's Carrie Heeter, are the following:

1. Complexity of choices available to users
2. Level of effort required of users

3. Media responsiveness to users
4. Extent to which media monitor users
5. Extent to which users can add information to sources
6. Extent to which interpersonal communication is supported

Heeter's list is not all-inclusive. It does, however, provide multiple bases for comparing interactive media.

User Choices. The extent to which interactive media enable users to be selective is important in that audiences tend to fragment as selectivity levels increase. In television, for example, individual channel audiences shrink as numbers of channels increase. Addition of interactive channels will produce further audience fragmentation.

This phenomenon will be of special interest in that the content of some new channels may be wholly informational, as in the case of Cable News Network, while others may consist entirely of entertainment, as with HBO or Cinemax. Entertainment channel audiences, to the extent that their members avoid information, will become a challenge to communicators.

Effort Required. Ease of access also has always been a factor in the extent to which mass media are used. Newspaper circulation, for example, tends to be better where home delivery is available than elsewhere. Magazine circulation levels climb where publications are available on newsstands as well as by mail.

Accessibility of information varies to a greater extent among the new media. Cabletext systems, for example, need only be turned on. Preprogrammed material scrolls up the screen automatically, requiring no effort on the part of the viewer. Electronic data bases such as CompuServe and The Source provide access to more information but require much greater user involvement in retrieval.

Responsiveness. Higher levels of effort seem to be better tolerated where systems are highly responsive. A number of researchers have defined system responsiveness as the extent to which interactive media function in human fashion. In phone mail, for example, systems give callers exhaustive sets of options (buttons to push) as they obtain information or organizational responses. Phone mail, in the late 1980s, probably came closest to this definition of responsiveness in that computer responses were delivered in "human" voices.

Interactivity, then, in part is measured by the extent to which media can react responsively to users. The key word here is *responsively*. The ultimate is reached in this dimension of interactivity when the medium's second, third, and subsequent responses are functions of earlier human input.

User Monitoring. Where interactivity exists, user monitoring also is usually present. While included by most scholars as a dimension of interactive media, user monitoring alone is a marginal attribute. Telephone companies for years have been able to monitor the extent to which their services are used. Origin, destination, time of placement, and elapsed time of telephone calls long have been recorded for billing purposes.

User monitoring of interactive media differs from telephone company practices only as to (*a*) level of user privacy and (*b*) application of resulting data. Telephone companies historically have been protective of customers' privacy. Whether media will be equally protective is open to question, especially since collected data conceivably could be both sold to advertisers and used to fine tune content for maximum commercial value.

Interpersonal Communication. Privacy also can be an issue where interpersonal communication exists. The degree to which systems facilitate interpersonal communication is a major variable among media. Traditional media offer no potential for interpersonal exchanges. Computer-based systems, in contrast, offer conferencing capabilities similar to those of television and telephone-based systems. CompuServe, The Source, and other computer utilities also offer electronic mail, bulletin board, and, in some cases, facsimile services. Bulletin boards are open systems, but user privacy is protected in electronic mail and facsimile systems.

Collectively, Heeter suggests, the six attributes of interactivity create a broader range of user options than ever existed before. The existence of these options, she said, suggest four propositions concerning popular concepts of mediated communication:

1. Information is always sought or selected rather than merely disseminated.
2. Media systems require different levels of user activity.
3. Activity varies with users as well as media.
4. Person-machine interaction is a unique form of communication.

The first and last of these propositions are especially important to communicators, although the others are noteworthy as well. There appears to be little doubt that the information that individuals assimilate in the age of information will consist primarily of that which has been sought or selected. So great will the total amount of available information have become that individuals will have little choice but to establish formal or informal screening mechanisms. These may include more frequent changing of television channels, limiting numbers of magazine and newspaper subscriptions, or even using computer-based information gathering services to select information on specific topics.

Person-machine interaction inevitably will be necessary in the latter circumstances, and more and more of this type of communication is to be expected. The trend is apt to be stimulated by growth in available information in the context of more demanding occupational circumstances. To this extent, at least, variation in types of users will produce variation in information use and in level of communication activity.

The Television Experience

What can communicators anticipate with the onset of the age of information, or as the interactive media become part of individuals' daily lives? Individuals' information-gathering patterns inevitably will change. Those who can apply the interactive media in ways that will make their lives easier, more enjoyable, or more productive inevitably will do so. Just how their usage patterns will develop, however, is open to conjecture.

Some sense of direction might be gained by examining changes in media use patterns that developed in the wake of the introduction of television. A 1955 study published by the United States Department of Health, Education, and Welfare showed massive shifts in individual use of time subsequent to acquisition of television sets. The study of twenty-five hundred homes showed the following results:

- Magazine use declined 41 percent.
- Newspaper use declined 18 percent.
- Radio use declined 57 percent.
- Television use increased 1441 percent.

The increase in television use was based on the amount of time respondents previously had spent viewing television away from home (an average of 12 minutes daily) compared with time they subsequently spent with television at home (267 minutes daily). More important in the overall, however, was the fact that the average individual increased by 41 percent the amount of time spent with *all media*.

Where did the additional time come from? Research by J. P. Robinson indicates that the public appetite for television was satisfied by sacrificing the following activities:

- 13 minutes of sleeping
- 12 minutes of social time away from home
- 8 minutes of radio time
- 6 minutes of reading listening
- 7 minutes of housework
- 5 minutes of travel
- 5 minutes of conversation

Television induced users, in other words, to sleep less, stay home more, spend less time with other media, and converse less than they had before. Other than in the case of radio, media usage patterns showed little immediate change. Change that did occur, moreover, apparently involved the entertainment rather than the informational component of the new medium.

The broad impact of television cannot, however, be assumed to have created uniform results. An analysis of sources of voter information during the 1984 elections and earlier, for example, showed that television progressively became more popular as a source of national political news. Voters continued to depend on other sources, however, for information on state and local issues.

The Information Society

To what extent will the television experience be repeated with the onset of the age of information? The question is difficult if not impossible to answer at this juncture. The age of information, according to Rutgers University's Jorge R. Schement, can be identified generally through the presence of six characteristics:

1. Information exchanged as a commodity
2. A large information work force
3. Interconnectedness among individuals and institutions
4. The special status of scientific knowledge
5. A social environment with many messages and channels
6. Widely diffused information technology

All of these elements, to a greater or lesser extent, exist today. The issue of magnitude then becomes paramount in determining whether the age of information has indeed arrived. The best answer probably can be structured in keeping with the extent to which the interactive media have become pervasive in the society. What is pervasive? Some suggest that telephones, television, and automobiles, for example, are pervasive in our society. Pervasiveness, they contend, implies that the element in question would be missed were it absent. The telephone, for, example, is pervasive in that it would be quickly missed were it suddenly to disappear.

By the pervasiveness standard, microcomputers remain in their juvenile years. While proliferating at rates greater than anticipated by many early forecasters, they have yet to appear in half of the nation's households. The mechanics of the information age, however, are quietly putting the finishing touches on a system that will leapfrog the microcomputer into the lives of every individual. That system is the integrated electronic grid, an amalgamation of telephone, electronic mail, and computer systems that soon will reach into virtually every household in the nation and much of the industrial and postindustrial world.

The electronic grid readily could provide all the convenience of a computer at negligible cost by enabling individuals to access and use mainframes by telephone or cable systems. Futurists' dreams of computers in every home thus may remain far away while at the same time standing much closer to realization than many believe. With the electronic grid, homeowners will require nothing more than keyboards attached to their television sets to access mainframe computers. Microcomputers, in many of their applications, may become unnecessary in home applications.

INFORMATION FOR PROFIT

All of these changes will take place in an essentially capitalist society populated by media organizations that have no intention of yielding the dominant positions. All are engaged in what for years has been a simple and lucrative pursuit: selling information for profit. The sale of information for profit underpins all of the communication disciplines. Advertising, marketing, public relations and sales promotion all add value to information that in the end is disseminated by the mass media. All of the costs ultimately are paid by consumers.

Neither the businesses nor the disciplines involved, from the largest of publishing or broadcasting organizations to the single-professional advertising consultancy, necessarily want to change the ways in which they have been generating profits for years. Neither corporate nor personal preferences, unfortunately, will exert any real influence in the marketplace. Change inevitably will reshape all media and all communication disciplines.

Preparedness Lacking

While the media have been preparing for change, and while those involved in advertising have been on the front lines in preliminary economic skirmishes, most communicators have yet to feel the cutting edge of the information age. Advertising, marketing, public relations, and sales promotion all have evolved in concert with change in society and technology. Recent experiences among members of the communication disciplines leave them ill prepared, however, for changes yet to come.

Members of the communication disciplines—advertising, marketing, public relations, sales promotion, and related fields—experienced little difficulty in adjusting to contemporary circumstances. Many, perhaps most, practitioners readily adapted to using computers, videotape, facsimile systems, and electronic mail. Too many have concluded that, in adjusting to these technologies, they have mastered the ability to manage change. They tend to assume, as a result, that the 1990s and the 2000s will be similar to the 1980s. Those assumptions are tenuous at best, dangerous at worst.

The United States and other developed nations have been caught up in what Peter Drucker described as an age of discontinuity, a turbulent era of transition from industrial to postindustrial society. The 1980s saw the traumatic weaning of the economy from dependence on the nation's industrial base. The 1990s will see the equally difficult onset of the postindustrial age of information. Problems that accompanied the decline of industry during the 1980s were met with relative ease among the communication disciplines. Clienteles and their needs changed, but few practitioners or counseling firms found themselves in dire straits as a result. The 1990s and 2000s promise to be less comfortable. Communicators will be called on to cope with basic structural change occurring at an accelerating pace. The change involved, moreover, will be fundamental to the communication disciplines rather than to the organizations communicators serve.

The latter distinction is important. Counseling or otherwise assisting organizations caught up in discontinuity is a relatively easy task. Professional detachment permits dispassionate problem analysis and prescription of logical and rational remedies. Coping with changes that threaten personal economic survival requires identical procedures in emotion-laden environments more conducive to panic than logic.

Developmental Alternatives

The behaviors of the mass media offer guidance to members of the communication disciplines as to how to prepare for the future. While remaining active in their primary business, all of the mass media have broadened or diversified or both to ensure continuing profitability in a fast-changing media marketplace.

Knight-Ridder has purchased a major computer information utility. *USA Today* has ventured into television. So have *The New York Times* and a number of other publishers. NBC has moved into cable television with CNBC. As a result of these and a host of other similar activities, the media organization that today continues to concentrate its resources in a single medium is rare indeed.

Advertising, marketing, public relations, and sales promotion organizations—as components of larger organizations and as independent businesses—have been less entrepreneurial. A few moved toward vertical integration, acquiring or establishing ventures in such areas as design, printing, and typography. Others have sought to expand horizontally, primarily with advertising firms acquiring organizations in public relations and sales promotion.

Seldom have any attempted to move beyond traditional boundaries to the areas described in chapter 12—interpersonal, behavioral and environmental communication. Expansion into the interpersonal area has been most prevalent, especially in the form of spokesperson training in public relations and several of its subspecialties, especially public affairs and employee relations. Only rarely, however, have any communication specialists sought to expand their practices into behavioral or environmental communication.

Behavioral and environmental communication will increase in importance as the productivity of mediated communication deteriorates. Organizations, especially those in service rather than in manufacturing or distribution, recognize the extent to which the environments they create and the behaviors of their personnel influence stakeholder groups. Many already have installed training programs for personnel and periodically conduct facilities assessments. Since the communication attributes of the behaviors and environments involved are primary organizational concerns, responsibility logically could be placed in any of the communication disciplines.

If the future does, indeed, belong to those who prepare for it, the primary remaining question must deal with preparedness. More specifically, which of the communication disciplines and which organizations within the specific disciplines, will be most prepared? Will the young and hungry be more prone to innovate than the old and better established? In some cases, as almost inevitably occurs, this will be the case. In others, perceptive leaderships will steer large communication organizations successfully into the age of information. Leaders of transnational organizations, especially in advertising and public relations, believe that the future of their disciplines is in international practice. Their perspectives may be valid as to the few mega-firms in their disciplines. There is no reason to believe, however, that the needs of prospective employers and clients will diminish at local, state, regional and national levels.

Only one conclusion can be safely drawn. The 1990s will be an era of unprecedented change in mass communication and in the disciplines that have grown up around the mass media. Those years, and the new century, will belong to those best prepared to manage the many changes—internal and external to their organizations and the organizations they serve—that inevitably will occur.

IN SUMMARY

The age of information, otherwise known as the postindustrial age, is supplanting the smokestack era in the United States and in many other industrialized nations. History suggests that the technological transitions involved will be as far-reaching as the advent of human speech, the printing press, the telephone, and the telegraph. The computer rapidly is approaching pervasiveness in domestic society. The integrated grid already is in place and requires but a few information bridges to make it a complete and all-pervasive system.

With the completion of these transitions, virtually every building in the United States will be linked to a system of interactive media unprecedented in human history. The complexity of the new media inevitably will influence the rate at which they are adopted, but the benefits they promise may be more than sufficient to encourage prospective users to attack the steep learning curves involved. As learning proceeds, users will become involved in media in which information delivered is always sought or selected by users rather than being provided automatically by the media.

If the onset of the interactive media produces responses on the scale that the United States experienced with the advent of television, society may never be the same. Television produced a massive shift in personal time allocations that extended far beyond the mass media. Magazine, newspaper, and radio usage declined by 18 to 57 percent, but television also drew people away from virtually every other discretionary activity.

The extent to which this experience will be duplicated with the onset of the age of information is impossible to predict with any degree of accuracy. The primary characteristics of the age of information already are evident in domestic society. Information is exchanged as a commodity. The information work force encompasses a large percentage of the population, interconnectedness is growing while messages and channels are proliferating, and the diffusion of information technology continues.

Communication professionals, unfortunately, are not responding to changing conditions to the same extent as the mass media. Media organizations are attempting to reallocate resources in order to perpetuate their economic power in the information age. Professionals in advertising, marketing, public relations, and sales promotion appear to be little concerned with what is going on around them or with what may occur tomorrow. If the future belongs to those who prepare for it, the destiny of these disciplines remains in doubt.

ADDITIONAL READING

Bright, J. R. "The Process of Technological Innovation—an Aid to Understanding Technological Forecasting." In *Guide to Practical*

Technological Forecasting, edited by J. R. Bright and M. E. F. Shoeman. Englewood Cliffs, N.J.: Prentice-Hall, 1973.

Dutton, William H., Jay G. Blumler, and Kenneth L. Kraemer, eds. *Wired Cities: Shaping the Future of Communications*. Boston: Hall, 1986.

Ettema, James S. "Interactive Electronic Text in the United States: Can Videotex Ever Go Home Again?" In *Media Use in the Information Age*, edited by Jerry L. Salvaggio and Jennings Bryant. Hillsdale, N.J.: Erlbaum, 1989.

Gardner, James H., ed. *Technology and the Future of United States Industry in World Competition*. Indianapolis: White River Press, 1985.

Heeter, Carrie. "Implications of New Interactive Technologies for Conceptualizing Communication." In *Media Use in the Information Age*, edited by Jerry L. Salvaggio and Jennings Bryant. Hillsdale, N.J.: Erlbaum, 1989.

Klopfenstein, Bruce. "Problems and Potential in Forecasting the Adoption of New Media." In *Media Use in the Information Age*, edited by Jerry L. Salvaggio and Jennings Bryant. Hillsdale, N.J.: Erlbaum, 1989

Robinson, J. P. "TV's Impact on Everyday Life." In *Television and Social Behavior, Technical Report of the Surgeon General's Scientific Advisory Committee*, edited by E. J. Rubenstein et al. Washington: United States Department of Health, Education and Welfare, 1973.

Rothfeder, Jeffrey, John J. Keller, and Susan Gelfond. "Neither Rain, Nor Sleet, Nor Computer Glitches . . ." *Business Week*, May 8, 1989.

Schement, Jorge R. "The Origins of the Information Society in the United States: Competing Visions." In *The Information Society*, edited by Jerry L. Salvaggio. Hillsdale, N.J.: Erlbaum, 1989.

Schramm, Wilbur, and William E. Porter. *Men, Women, Messages and Media: Understanding Human Communication*. 2nd ed. New York: Harper and Row, 1973.

Sterling, C. J., and T. R. Haight. *The Mass Media: Aspen Institute Guide to Communication Industry Trends*. New York: Praeger, 1978.

Turow, Joseph. *Media Industries: The Production of News and Entertainment*. New York: Longman, 1984.

Webster, James. G. "Television Audience Behaviors: Patterns of Exposure in the New Media Environment." In *Media Use in the*

Information Age, edited by Jerry L. Salvaggio and Jennings Bryant. Hillsdale, N.J.: Erlbaum, 1989.

Williams, Frederick, ed. *Measuring the Information Society*. Beverly Hills, Calif.: Sage, 1988.

Selected Bibliography

Agee, Warren K., Phillip H. Ault and Edwin Emery. *Introduction to Mass Communication*. 9th ed. New York: Harper and Row, 1988.

Alten, Stanley R. *Audio in Media*. 2nd ed. Belmont, Calif.: Wadsworth, 1986.

American Newspaper Publishers Association. *Facts About Newspapers, '88*. Washington, D.C.: 1988.

——. *Facts About Newspapers, '83*. Washington, D.C.: 1983.

——. *Facts About Newspapers, '78*. Washington, D.C.: 1978.

Bates, Benjamin J. "Evolving to an Information Society: Issues and Problems." In *The Information Society: Economic, Social and Structural Issues*, edited by Jerry L. Salvaggio. Hillsdale, N.J.: Erlbaum, 1989.

Bell, Daniel. *The Coming of Post-Industrial Society*. New York: Basic Books, 1976.

Beniger, James R. *The Control Revolution: Technological and Economic Origins of the Information Society*. Cambridge: Harvard University Press, 1986.

Berger, A. A., ed. *Television in Society*, New Brunswick, N.J.: Transaction Books, 1987.

Berko, Roy M., Andrew D. Wolvin and Ray Curtis. *This Business of Communication*. 3rd. ed. Dubuque, IA: Wm. C. Brown, 1986.

Berlo, David K., *The Process of Communication: An Introduction to Theory and Practice*. New York: Holt, Rinehart and Winston, 1960

Bogart, Leo. *Press and Public: Who Reads What, When, Where and Why in American Newspapers*. Hillsdale, N.J.: Erlbaum, 1981.

Bright, J. R. "The Process of Technological Innovation—An Aid to Understanding Technological Forecasting." In *Guide to Practical Technological Forecasting*, editied by J. R. Bright and M. E. F. Shoeman. Englewood Cliffs, N.J.: Prentice-Hall, 1973.

Brock, Gerald. *The Telecommunications Industry*. Cambridge: Harvard University Press, 1981.

Burnett, John J. *Promotion Management: A Strategic Approach*. 2nd ed. St. Paul, Minn: West, 1988.

Caddy, Douglas. *Exploring America's Future*. College Station, Texas: Texas A&M University Press, 1987.

Campbell, Jeremy. *Grammatical Man: Information, Entropy, Language and Life*. New York: Simon and Schuster, 1982.

Carey, James T. *Sociology and Public Affairs: The Chicago School*. Beverly Hills, CA: Sage, 1975.

Castells, Manuel, ed. *High Technology, Space and Society*. Beverly Hills, Calif.: Sage, 1985.

Congressional Office of Technology Assessment. *Technology and the American Economic Transition: Choices for the Future*. Washington, D.C.: U.S. Government Printing Office, 1988.

Czitrom, Daniel J. *Media and the American Mind: From Morse to McLuhan*, Chapel Hill: University of North Carolina Press, 1982.

DeFleur, Melvin L., and Sandra Ball-Rokeach. *Theories of Mass Communication*. 3rd ed. New York: David McKay, 1975.

Degan, Clara, ed. *Understanding and Using Video*. New York: Longman, 1985.

Deutsch, Karl W. *The Nerves of Government: Models of Political Communication and Control*. New York: Free Press, 1963.

Devtouzis, Michael, and Joel Moses, eds. *The Computer Age: A Twenty-Year View*. Cambridge: MIT Press, 1980.

Didsbury, Howard F., Jr. *Communications and the Future: Prospects, Promises and Problems*. Washington, D.C.: World Future Society, 1982.

Dizard, Wilson P. *The Coming Information Age*. New York: Longman, 1982.

Dominick, Joseph R., *The Dynamics of Mass Communication*. Reading, Mass.: Addison-Wesley, 1983.

Drucker, Peter. *The Age of Discontinuity*. New York: Harper and Row, 1969.

Dutton, William H., Jay G. Blumler, and Kenneth L. Kraemer, eds., *Wired Cities: Shaping the Future of Communications.* Boston: Hall, 1986.

Edelstein, Alex, John E. Bowes and Sheldon Harsel. *Information Societies: Comparing the Japanese and American Experiences.* Seattle, Wash.: University of Washington, 1978.

Eisenstein, Elizabeth L. *The Printing Press as an Agent of Change.* New York: Cambridge University Press, 1979.

Ellul, Jacques. *The Technological Society.* New York: Knopf, 1964.

Emery, Edwin, and Michael Emery. *The Press and America: An Interpretive History of the Mass Media.* 5th ed. Englewood Cliffs, NJ: Prentice-Hall, 1984.

Estabrook, Leigh. *Libraries in Post-Industrial Society.* Phoenix: Oryx Press, 1977.

Ettema, James S. "Videotext for Market Information: A Survey of Prototype Users." In *Evaluating the New Information Technologies*, edited by Jerome Johnston. San Francisco: Jossey-Bass, 1984.

Evans, Christopher. *The Micro Millennium.* New York: Viking Press, 1979.

Fendrock, John J. *Managing in Times of Radical Change.* New York: American Management Association, 1971.

Ferkiss, Victor C. *Technological Man: The Myth and the Reality.* New York: Braziller, 1969.

Fisher, Glen. *American Communication in a Global Society.* Norwood, N.J.: Ablex, 1979.

Forester, Tom, ed. *The Microelectronics Revolution.* Cambridge: MIT Press, 1981.

Gardner, Howard. *Frames of Mind.* New York: Basic Books, 1983.

Gardner, James H., ed. *Technology and the Future of U.S. Industry in World Competition.* Indianapolis: White River Press, 1985.

Goldhaber, Gerald. *Organizational Communication.* 4th ed. Dubuque, Iowa: Wm. C. Brown, 1986.

Gumpert, Gary, and Robert Cathcart, eds. *Intermedia: Interpersonal Communication in a Media World.* 3rd ed. New York: Oxford, 1986.

Gunter, Barrie. *Poor Reception: Misunderstanding and Forgetting Broadcast News.* Hillsdale, N.J.: Erlbaum, 1987.

Hammelink, Coes. *Cultural Autonomy in Global Communications.* New York: Longman, 1983.

Hanan, Mack. *Life-Styled Marketing: How to Position Products for Premium Profits*. 2nd ed. New York: AMACOM, 1980.

Howard, V. A., and J. H. Barton. *Thinking on Paper*. New York: Morrow, 1986.

Howitt, Dennis. *The Mass Media and Social Problems*. 4th ed. New York: Pergamon, 1986.

Hudson, Heather E., and Louis Leung. "The Growth of the Information Sector." In *Measuring the Information Society*, edited by Frederick Williams. Newbury Park, Calif.: Sage, 1988.

Husni, Samir. *Samir Husni's Guide to New Magazines*. University, Miss.: University of Mississippi Department of Journalism, 1988.

Innis, Harold A. *Empire and Communications*. Toronto: University of Toronto Press, 1972.

Jacoby, Jacob, and Wayne D. Hoyer. *The Comprehension and Miscomprehension of Print Communications: An Investigation of Mass Media Magazines*. New York: Advertising Educational Foundation, 1987.

Jamieson, Kathleen H., and Karlyn K. Campbell. *The Interplay of Influence: Mass Media and Their Publics in News, Advertising, Politics*. 2nd ed. New York: Wadsworth, 1988.

Johnson, Eugene M., Eberhard E. Scheuing and Kathleen A. Gaida. *Profitable Service Marketing*. Homewood, Ill.: Dow Jones-Irwin, 1986.

Kaatz, Ronald B. *Cable: An Advertiser's Guide to the New Electronic Media*. Chicago: Crain, 1982.

Klapper, Joseph T. *The Effects of Mass Communication*. New York: Free Press, 1960.

Klopfenstein, Bruce. "Problems and Potential in Forecasting the Adoption of New Media." In *Media Use in the Information Age*, edited by Jerry L. Salvaggio. Hillsdale, N.J.: Erlbaum, 1989

Kuhn, Thomas S. *The Structure of Scientific Revolutions*. Chicago: University of Chicago Press, 1970.

Kuhns, William. *The Post-Industrial Prophets*. New York: Harper and Row, 1971.

Laux, James M., and Patrick Fridenson. *The Automobile Revolution: The Impact of an Industry*. Chapel Hill, N.C.: University of North Carolina Press, 1982.

Lazar, Ellan A., ed. *The Video Age: Television Technology and Applications in the 1980s*. White Plains, NY: Knowledge Industry Publications, 1982.

Lodziak, Conrad. *The Power of Television: A Critical Appraisal.* New York: St. Martin's Press, 1986.

Luther, William M. *The Marketing Plan: How to Prepare and Implement It.* New York: AMACOM, 1982.

Lynd, Robert S. *Knowledge for What?* Princeton, N.J.: Princeton University Press, 1939.

McCarthy, E. Jerome, and William D. Perreault, Jr. *Basic Marketing.* 9th ed. Homewood, IL: Irwin, 1987.

McCombs, Maxwell. *Newspaper Readership and Circulation.* ANPA News Research Report 3, 1977.

Machlup, Fritz. *The Production and Distribution of Knowledge in the United States.* Princeton, N.J.: Princeton University Press, 1962.

MacKuen, Michael B., and Steven L. Coombs. *More Than News: Media Power in Pubic Affairs.* Beverly Hills, Calif.: Sage, 1981.

McLuhan, Marshall. *Understanding Media: The Extensions of Man.* New York: McGraw-Hill, 1965.

Martin, James. *The Wired Society.* Englewood, N.J.: Prentice-Hall, 1978.

Masuda, Yoneji. *The Information Society as Post-Industrial Society.* Tokyo: Institute for the Information Society, 1981.

Mohr, Lawrence B. *Explaining Organizational Behavior: The Limits and Possibilities of Theory and Research.* San Francisco: Jossey-Bass, 1982.

More, E. A. and R. K. Laird. *Organisations in the Communications Age: An Introduction to Organisational Communications Technology for Management.* Australia: Pergamon, 1985.

Mumford, Lewis. *The Pentagon of Power.* New York: Harcourt Brace Jovanovich, 1970.

Oliver, John W. *History of American Technology.* New York: Ronald Press, 1956.

Pattison, Robert. *On Literacy.* New York: Oxford University Press, 1982.

Petty, Richard E., and John T. Cacioppo. *Communication and Persuasion: Central and Peripheral Routes to Attitude Change.* New York: Springer-Verlag, 1986.

Phelan, John M. *Mediaworld.* New York: Seabury Press, 1977.

Pool, Ithiel de Sola, ed. *The Social Impact of the Telephone.* Cambridge: MIT Press, 1977.

—. *Technologies of Freedom.* Cambridge: MIT Press, 1983.

Porat, Marc. *The Information Economy: Definition and Measurement*. Special Publication 77-12, U.S. Department of C o m - merce, Office of Telecommunications. Washington, D.C.: U.S. Government Printing Office, 1977.

Ray, Michael L. *Advertising and Communication Management*. New York: Prentice-Hall, 1982.

Read, William H. *America's Mass Media Merchants*. Baltimore: Johns Hopkins University Press, 1983.

Rice, Ronald E. "Evaluating New Media Systems." In *Evaluating the New Media Technologies*, edited by Jerome Johnson. San Francisco: Jossey-Bass, 1984.

Rogers, Everett M. *Communication Technology: The New Media in Society*. New York: Free Press, 1986.

—. *Diffusion of Innovations*. New York: Free Press, 1983.

Rogers, Everett M., and Francis Balle, eds. *The Media Revolution in America and Western Europe*. Norwood, N.J.: Ablex, 1985.

Rogers, Everett M., and D. Lawrence Kincaid. *Communication Networks: Toward a New Paradigm for Research*. New York: Free Press, 1981.

Rogers, Everett M., and Judith K. Larsen. *Silicon Valley Fever: Growth of High-Technology Culture*. New York: Basic Books, 1984.

Robinson, J.P., "TV's Impact on Everyday Life," In *Television and Social Behavior, Technical Report of the Surgeon General's Scientific Advisory Committee*, edited by E. J. Rubenstein et al. Washington: U.S. Department of Health, Education, and Welfare, 1973.

Rothfeder, Jeffrey, John J. Keller, and Susan Gelfond. "Neither Rain, Nor Sleet, Nor Computer Glitches . . ." *Business Week*, May 8, 1989.

Schement, Jorge R., "The Origins of the Information Society in the United States: Competing Visions." In *The Information Society*, edited by Jerry L. Salvaggio. Hillsdale, N.J.: Erlbaum, 1989.

Schiller, Dan. *Telematics and Government*. Norwood, N.J.: Ablex, 1982.

Schiller, Herbert I. *Communication and Cultural Domination*. White Plains, N.Y.: International Arts and Sciences Press, 1976.

—. *The Mind Managers*. Boston: Beacon Press, 1973.

—. *Information and the Crisis Economy*. New York: Oxford, 1986.

——. "Information for What Kind of Society." In *The Information Society: Economic, Social and Structural Issues*, edited by Jerry L Salvaggio. Hillsdale, N.J.: Erlbaum, 1989.

Schramm, Wilbur. *Mass Communications*. Urbana: University of Illinois Press, 1949.

——. *Mass Media and National Development: The Role of Information in the Developing Nations*. Stanford, Calif.: Stanford University Press, 1964.

——. *The Process and Effects of Communication*. Urbana: University of Illinois Press, 1954.

Schramm, Wilbur, and William E. Porter. *Men, Women, Messages and Media: Understanding Human Communication*. 2nd ed. New York: Harper and Row, 1973.

Selnow, Gary W., and William D. Crano. *Planning, Implementing and Evaluating Targeted Communication Programs: A Manual for Business Communicators*. New York: Quorum, 1987.

Shannon, Claude E., and Warren Weaver. *The Mathematical Theory of Communication*. Urbana: University of Illinois Press, 1949.

Singleton, Loy. *Telecommunications in the Information Age: A Nontechnical Primer on the New Technology*. Cambridge: Ballinger, 1983.

Slack, Jennifer D. *Communication Technology and Society: Conceptions of Causality and the Politics of Technological Intervention*. Norwood, N.J.: Albex, 1984.

Smith, Anthony. *The Geopolitics of Information*. London: Faber and Faber, 1980.

——. Smith, Anthony. *Goodbye Gutenberg*. New York: Oxford University Press, 1980.

Steinfield, Charles W. *Communicating via Electronic Mail: Patterns and Predictors of Use in Organizations*. Ph.D. diss. University of Southern California, Los Angeles, 1983.

Sterling, C. J., and T. R. Haight. *The Mass Media: Aspen Institute Guide to Communication Industry Trends*. New York: Praeger, 1978.

Strassmann, Paul A. *Information Payoff: The Transformation of Work in the Electronic Age*. New York: Free Press, 1985.

Turow, Joseph. *Media Industries: The Production of News and Entertainment*. New York: Longman, 1984.

Valaskakis, Kimon, "Leapfrog Strategy in the Information Age." In *Communication and the Future: Prospects, Promises and*

Problems, edited by Howard F. Didsbury. Bethesda, Md.: World Future Society, 1982.

Webster, James. G. "Television Audience behaviors: Patterns of Exposure in the New Media Environment." In *Media Use in the Information Age*, edited by Jerry L. Salvaggio. Hillsdale, N.J.: Erlbaum, 1989.

Williams, Frederick. *The Communications Revolution*. Beverly Hills, Calif.: Sage, 1982.

——. *Technology and Communication Behavior*. Belmont, Calif.: Wadsworth, 1987.

——, ed. *Measuring the Information Society*, Beverly Hills, Calif.: Sage, 1988.

Index

About the Author

E.W. Brody teaches public relations in Memphis State University's Department of Journalism in Tennessee and maintains a public relations counseling practice in Memphis.

Communication Tomorrow is his eighth book. The others, all published by Praeger, include *Public Relations Research* (with Gerald C. Stone, 1989), *Professional Practice Development: Coping in a Competitive Environment* (1989), *Public Relations Programming and Production* (1988), *Communicating for Survival: Coping with Diminishing Human Resources* (1987) and *The Business of Public Relations* (1987).

Dr. Brody's articles on public relations have appeared in *Public Relations Journal*, *Public Relations Review*, *Journalism Quarterly*, *Legal Economics*, *Health Care Management Review*, *Journal of the Medical Group Management Association*, *Modern Healthcare*, *Hospital Public Relations*, and *Public Relations Quarterly*.

Dr. Brody holds degrees from Eastern Illinois University, California State University and Memphis State University. He is accredited by the Public Relations Society of America and the International Association of Business Communicators.